CHICKEN SOUP FOR THE SOUL® UNLOCKING THE SECRETS TO LIVING YOUR DREAMS

Chicken Soup for the Soul: Unlocking the Secrets to Living Your Dreams
Inspirational Stories, Powerful Principles and Practical Techniques to Help You Make Your Dreams Come True
Jack Canfield, Mark Victor Hansen

Published by Backlist, LLC,
a unit of Chicken Soup for the Soul Publishing, LLC. www.chickensoup.com

Front cover design by Larissa Hise Henoch
Originally published in 2003 by Health Communications, Inc.

Back cover and spine redesign by Pneuma Books, LLC

Distributed to the booktrade by Simon & Schuster. SAN: 200-2442

Publisher's Cataloging-in-Publication Data
(Prepared by The Donohue Group)

Chicken soup for the soul : unlocking the secrets to living your dreams : inspirational stories, powerful principles and practical techniques to help you make your dreams come true / [compiled by] Jack Canfield [and] Mark Victor Hansen.

   p. : ill. ; cm.

   Originally published: Deerfield Beach, FL : Health Communications, c2003.
   ISBN: 978-1-62361-120-0

   1. Self-realization--Literary collections. 2. Self-realization--Anecdotes. 3. Conduct of life--Literary collections. 4. Conduct of life--Anecdotes. 5. Anecdotes. I. Canfield, Jack, 1944- II. Hansen, Mark Victor. III. Title: Unlocking the secrets to living your dreams

PN6071.S412 C43 2012
810.8/02/0353   2012945889

PRINTED IN THE UNITED STATES OF AMERICA
on acid free paper

21 20 19 18 17 16 15 14 13 12   01 02 03 04 05 06 07 08 09 10

CHICKEN SOUP FOR THE SOUL® UNLOCKING THE SECRETS TO LIVING YOUR DREAMS

Inspirational Stories, Powerful Principles and Practical Techniques to Help You Make Your Dreams Come True

Jack Canfield
Mark Victor Hansen

Backlist, LLC, a unit of
Chicken Soup for the Soul Publishing, LLC
Cos Cob, CT
www.chickensoup.com

Contents

4 ♥ It's Never Too Late

5 ♥ The Power of Support: You Can't Do It Alone

9 ♥ Never Give Up

Introduction

Congratulations. You've just picked up a book that could significantly change your life forever. You hold in your hands a blueprint for creating any success and achieving any dream you want—a better lifestyle, more interesting work, greater abundance, financial freedom, more meaningful and fulfilling relationships, a healthier body, and more frequent and enjoyable leisure activities.

Living your dream is always the result of information, inspiration and perspiration. This unique book contains the first two; you will have to supply the third. We will teach you a ten-step blueprint for making any dream you have come true. It doesn't matter if that dream is in the arena of wealth, health, sports, relationships, spiritual growth, education, travel, politics or social change. The same principles and techniques for making a dream come true apply at home, school, work, church and in the larger community.

You will also find *Chicken Soup* stories that will inspire you to believe that anything is possible—and you'll be motivated to turn your heartfelt dreams into your daily reality.

We believe that living your dreams is as simple as completing one of those connect-the-dots puzzles you find in the Sunday newspaper. If you just start at number one and keep connecting the dots, eventually you solve the puzzle. Dreams are like that, too. It's simply a matter of moving from point to point until you achieve your dream.

You Can Have the Life You Dream About

We have spent over thirty years studying America's most successful people—including those who are considered the world's greatest experts on success. We've applied what we have learned to our own lives. And the result is that we live the kind of magical lives most people would think are attainable only by the few. But we know that anyone who ardently desires to succeed, and is willing to apply themselves, can attain these same levels of success. How do we know with such certainty? Because we have taught these principles and techniques to hundreds of thousands of people just like you in our seminars and workshops, and we have watched them become star athletes, start and grow phenomenal businesses, become leaders in their fields, achieve millions of dollars in net worth, create dream relationships with their spouses and children, heal life threatening diseases, solve seemingly intractable social problems and achieve a happy balance between work and family.

It doesn't matter where you live, how old you are, what your level of education, or how much money you currently have. As you'll see in the inspirational stories that follow this first chapter, none of that matters. All that matters is that you are willing to decide what you want, believe you can have it, learn the principles of success, apply them to your life, persevere through the tough times, and never give up. You can literally have the life you dream of—if you are willing to pay the price of learning, assimilating and applying a few basic principles and developing a few powerful disciplines over time.

Read the Book Twice

We suggest that you read this book twice—once for a general overview and for the inspiration and insights you will get from the stories. Then read this first chapter a second time and begin to write down your goals, write out your affirmations, make time to visualize your ideal life, create or join a Dream Team, and utilize all the other techniques that we teach you.

This book contains a success system that never fails—if you put it into practice. All it requires to work is for you to work it. We are excited about the new possibilities that this will open up for you. And we are eager to hear from you once you start living your dream. Please write to us and share your successes. We look forward to hearing from you.

Have a great adventure, and remember to enjoy the ride as well as the destination.

Love to you!

—*Jack Canfield and Mark Victor Hansen*

How to Live Your Dream

The human spirit cannot be paralyzed.
If you are breathing, you can dream.

—Mike Brown

How to

In our dreams we all aspire to be, do and have great things. Yet most of us simply aren't creating the results we want. We don't have enough money, romance, success or joy in our lives. What we need to understand is that greatness exists in all of us, but it is up to us to pull it out of ourselves. It is true that we all have genius. We just need to learn how to apply our genius.

This book is divided into ten sections that parallel the ten strategies that you will need to employ to successfully live your dreams. Each one is an important piece of the overall system that will take you from where you are to where you want to be. Let's get started.

Step 1. Decide What You Want

The indispensable first step
to getting things you want out of life
is this: Decide what you want.

—Ben Stein, actor and author

In order to *get* what you want, you must first *decide* what you want. Most people get stuck at this crucial first step because they simply can't see how it's possible to get what

they want—so they don't even let themselves want it. Don't
sabotage yourself that way! What we now know about how the
brain works is that you must first decide WHAT you want,
before your brain can figure out HOW to get it.

Be willing to dream big dreams

*Always dream and shoot higher than you
know you can do. Don't bother just to be
better than your contemporaries or
predecessors. Try to be better than yourself.*
—William Faulkner

When the two of us decided to write *Chicken Soup for the
Soul,* we had a big dream. We wanted to create a book that
would change millions of lives. Our dream was to sell 150,000
copies the first year and a million copies by the end of the following year. We were thinking number one on the bestseller
lists from the very beginning. We wanted to touch as many
lives as possible—to make a big difference in the world. Our
corporate mission statement is to inspire and empower people
to live their highest vision in a context of love and joy. Through
the *Chicken Soup for the Soul* books we wanted to heal and
change the world one story at a time. It was a big dream.

We have learned that as soon as you commit to a big dream
and really go after it, not only will your creative mind come up
with big ideas to make it happen, you will also start attracting the people you need into your life to make your dream
come true. Big dreams inspire you and others to want to play
all out. So let your dreams be as big as you want them to be.

Set Goals That Will Stretch You

Another value in giving yourself permission to go after the big dreams is that big dreams require you to grow in order to achieve them. In fact, in the long run, that is the greatest benefit you will receive from pursuing your dreams: mastery over your life. It is not just about the material benefits you receive (the car, the house, the money), but who you become in the process. As we all have seen many times over, the outer symbols of success can be easily lost. Houses burn down, companies go bankrupt, relationships end in divorce, cars get old, clothes go out of style, bodies age and fame wanes, but who you are, what you have learned and the new skills you have developed never go away. These are the true prizes of achieving success. Our friend Jim Rohn advises: You want to set a big enough goal so that in the process of achieving it, you become someone worth becoming.

In the process of building what has become the *Chicken Soup* phenomenon, we had to stretch and expand in many areas. We had to learn about publishing, marketing, PR, radio and television. As our staff grew from four to sixteen people, we had to learn new business and management skills. As our opportunities and projects grew, we had to learn how to better balance our work life and family lives. We had to hire consultants, take courses, attend conventions, read books, listen to tapes and ask for advice from many quarters. Through all of that, we gained valuable skills, learned many lessons and gained a lot of wisdom. We are better and stronger for it.

Don't Compromise When You Write Down Your Goals

Remember that your life is a story. Why not write your own ending—and then make it happen!

To begin, ask yourself this question: What would I do with my life if I knew I were not going to fail? Put yourself into the mindset of an imaginative child; they will ask for anything and everything—without the fear of rejection.

Here are a few suggestions to get you started:

1. I am earning $_____ this year.
2. I will earn $_____ next year.
3. I will earn $_____ in the next five years.
4. I am maintaining my ideal weight of _____ pounds.
5. A new habit I have developed is _____.
6. The bad habits I have let go of are _____.
7. A new personality trait I have developed is _____.
8. My dream home has _____ square feet, _____ bedrooms, and _____ bathrooms, and is located in _____.
9. The cars I own include _____ _____.
10. My next home improvement is _____.
11. My next vacation is _____.
12. I am improving my family communication by _____ _____.
13. I am improving my work communication by _____ _____.
14. My right livelihood (vocation with a purpose) is _____ _____.

15. My new hobbies include _____

_____.

16. To become fit I am _____

_____.

17. The new skills I am learning for work include _____

_____.

18. The new skills I am learning for me include _____

_____.

19. My ideal soul mate is _____

_____.

20. To reduce my life stress I am _____

_____.

21. Additional education I want to get is _____

_____.

22. Each month I will save $_____.

23. Each month I will contribute $_____.

24. Each month I will invest $_____.

25. The new financial habit I will acquire is _____

_____.

26. To become debt free I will _____

_____.

27. The debts I will pay off are _____

_____.

28. I will serve my community by _____

_____.

29. I would like others to describe me as _____

_____.

30. The people I want to meet are _____

_____.

31. My spiritual growth will include _____

32. I can support my spouse/partner, parents and family better by_____

_____.

33. I can support my friends better by _____

_____.

34. Other dreams I have are _____

_____

_____.

The Genie in the Lamp

Another way to get clear about your dreams and desires is to imagine that a genie pops out of a magic lamp and grants you three wishes in each of the following areas of your life. There are no limitations on what those wishes would be. Decide what you would choose and write them down now:

Business and career
Financial security
Family and friends
Health and fitness
House or apartment
Recreation and free time
Skills and abilities
Contribution, legacy, service to the world

When You Achieve Your Goals

When you achieve your goals, don't just cross them off your list. Write VICTORY across them! Crossing off signifies that it is just a shopping list that has been easily handled. But writing VICTORY signals the subconscious mind that it's a true achievement.

Keep your lists, and when you may be feeling a little down and discouraged, look back over your lists of achievements. All the victories will re-inspire and motivate you toward new, greater and even more exciting successes.

Your Ideal Vision

A deeper method for defining your dreams is to set aside a longer period of time—say thirty minutes to an hour—to reflect in depth on what your ideal life would look like in each of the eight areas listed on the previous page. We recommend sitting in a comfortable chair, putting on some relaxing instrumental music, closing your eyes and focusing on each area for several minutes. Let the part of you that knows your true heart's desires create your ideal vision in each area.

When you are through, take an equal amount of time and write down everything you thought of—in as much detail as you can. We also suggest that you share this vision with someone you love and trust. The more you write about it and talk about it, the more clear and believable it will become.

Write Down Your Dream List

In our longer seminars we ask participants to make a list of 101 goals that they want to achieve in their lifetime. Let yourself dream without any limitations at all. List everything you would like to do, be or have sometime in your life.

Then, take the time to imagine that you have all the resources that you will ever need to achieve these goals—unlimited money, time, talent and connections. Just writing them down will set into motion an amazing process of bringing these things into your life. One of our students wrote such a list, put it in a drawer and forgot about it. A year later when he was moving, he found the list. He had already achieved thirty-six things on his list in just one year!

Turn Your Dreams into Goals and Objectives

Once you are clear about what you want, you must turn every aspect of your dream list into a measurable objective. By measurable, we mean measurable in space and time—how much and by when. For instance, if you were to tell us that you wanted more money, we might pull out a dollar and give it to you, but you would probably protest, "No, I meant a lot more money—like $20,000!" Well, how are we supposed to know unless you tell us? Similarly, your boss, your friends, your spouse, your brain, God, can't figure out what you want unless you tell them exactly what you want and when you want it by.

To help you see what we mean by "be specific," consider the difference between the following "vague wants" and "clear objectives."

VAGUE WANT	CLEAR OBJECTIVE
I would like to own a nice home.	I will own a 4,000-square-foot house on Pacific Coast Highway by April 30, 2004, at noon.
I want to lose weight.	I will weigh 185 pounds by September 1, 2004, at 5 P.M.
We need to reduce staff turnover.	We will have a staff turnover of 5 percent or less during calendar year 2004.
I need to treat my employees better.	I will acknowledge a minimum of six employees for their contribution to the department by Friday at 5 P.M.

You must take each and every part of your vision and turn it into an objective. Make a comprehensive list. Once you have done this, you are ready to go on to the next step of making your dreams come true.

Start by Eliminating All the Little Things That Annoy You

If you are serious about living your dreams, you need to start by eliminating all the little things that annoy you, all the little things that you put up with. These can range from something as petty as a rip in your jeans that needs repairing to something as big as a filing system that doesn't work. There may also be things on the interpersonal level that you are tolerating—your husband's snoring, your son leaving his athletic equipment on the kitchen table, or your best friend's constant complaining about her boss. Everything that you "put up with" saps your energy, makes you edgy and slowly wears you down. Research has shown that the average person tolerates anywhere from sixty to one hundred things.

Yet you will find it very difficult to create the life of your dreams if you are in the habit of tolerating these little irritations. You simply need to get rid of them.

Make a List

Get a pad of paper and go through your home, office, garage and car. Look in all of your closets and drawers. If you live in a house, walk around the yard. Jot down what bothers you. Make note of everything you would like to be different. Notice everything that irritates you in any way—that wall that needs painting, the plant that is dying, the drawer that sticks, the disorganized medicine cabinet, the shoes that need resoled, the disorganized music collection, the light in the garage that needs replacing, the mess in the drawer next to the telephone, the remote control that doesn't work— everything. Next, move on to your relationships. Take time to reflect on what you are tolerating. Write it down.

Then enroll another family member or friend who also wants to clean up his or her life so he or she can pursue his or her dreams with greater energy and focus. Schedule a weekend to work on cleaning up those irritating items on your list. You may just want to support each other over the phone as you work on your lists separately, or you may want to team up and spend one day working on your list and one day working on theirs. Reward yourself at the end of the day with a night out, a hot bath, massage, dinner or a movie.

Some things, like cleaning out your garage or creating a whole new filing system, may take more than just a day to clean up. Schedule time for these things over the next several months. In order to tackle the big dreams of financial independence, career goals and social change, you need to clear the decks. Spend time every week clearing up the little irritations until it becomes a habit to handle them the moment they arise.

Step 2. Believe in Yourself: Use Positive Self-Talk

If you keep believing what you've been believing, you'll keep achieving what you've been achieving.

—Source Unknown

The second strategy that you must employ to achieve your dreams is to develop an unshakable belief in your worthiness to have what you desire—and in your ability to achieve what you set out to accomplish.

Ultimately you must eliminate any negative and limiting beliefs, learn to control your self-talk, and maintain a constant state of positive expectations.

Control Your Self-Talk

*You are either the captive
or the captain of your thoughts.*
—Denis Waitley

Researchers have found that the average person thinks as many as 50,000 thoughts a day. Sadly, many of those thoughts are negative: "I'm not management material. ... I'll never lose weight. ... It doesn't matter what I do, nothing ever works out for me." This is what psychologists call victim language. Victim language actually keeps you in a victim state of mind. It is a form of self-hypnosis that lulls you into a belief that you are unlovable and incompetent.

In order to live your dreams you need to give up this victim language and start talking to yourself like a winner: "I can do it. ... I know there is a solution. ... I am smart enough and strong enough to figure this out. ... Everything I eat helps me maintain my perfect body weight."

You Are Always Programming Your Subconscious Mind

Your subconscious mind is like the crew of a ship. You are its captain. It is your job to give the crew orders. When you do this, the crew takes everything you say literally. The crew (your subconscious) has no sense of humor. It just blindly follows orders. When you say, "Everything I eat goes straight to my hips," the crew hears that as an order: "Take everything she eats, turn it into fat and put it on her hips." On the other hand, if you say, "Everything I eat helps me maintain my perfect body weight," the crew will begin to bring that into reality by helping you make better food choices, exercise more often and maintain the right metabolism rate for your body.

This power of your subconscious mind is the reason you must become very vigilant and pay careful attention to your spoken and internal statements. Unfortunately, most people don't realize they are committing negative self-talk, which is why it is best to enlist another person—your Dream Team partner—to help you monitor your speaking (see Step 4). You can have a signal for interrupting each other when you use victim language. Some of our students are so committed to cleaning up their language that they wear a rubber band on their left wrist, and every time they say something that is negative and self-defeating like "I can't . . . ," they snap the rubber band as a little negative reinforcement to heighten their awareness.

Several years ago, we implemented a plan in our offices to fine everyone a dollar every time they used victim language ("We'll never get this book finished on time."). At the end of the month we would donate the collected money to charity, or use it to buy lunch for the staff. The goal was awareness, not punishment. And it worked. After several months, we were able to stop, because everyone had pretty much eliminated all negative self-talk.

Cancel, Cancel

When you find yourself saying something negative and self-defeating to yourself, just stop and say "Cancel, cancel!" That sends a message to your subconscious that you are rescinding the order you just sent down. Then replace what you said with the positive alternative. Here's an example:

"I just can't seem to lose that last
twenty pounds." (Oops!)
"Cancel—cancel! I can find a way to
lose that last twenty pounds."

No Matter What You Say or Do to Me, I'm Still a Worthwhile Person

Sometimes the negative and defeating words are coming from someone else—a parent, spouse, friend, classmate or boss. It is important to understand that what other people say is not what makes you feel bad. It is what you say to yourself *after* they stop talking that determines how you feel.

Think about it. If someone says something critical or mean to you, instead of agreeing with them, just say internally to yourself, *No matter what you say or do to me, I am still a worthwhile person.* This will cancel out the negative effect of what they have said, and allow you to maintain your self-esteem and self-confidence.

Use Affirmations to Build Self-Confidence

One of the most powerful tools for building worthiness and self-confidence is the repetition of positive statements until they become a natural part of the way you think. These "affirmations" act to crowd out and replace the negative orders you have been sending your subconscious all these years. We suggest that you create a list of ten to twenty statements that affirm your belief in your worthiness and your ability to create the life of your dreams. Here are some examples of affirmations:

I am worthy of love, joy and success.
I am smart enough to get everything I want.
I am loveable and capable.
I create joy wherever I go.
I am able to solve any problem that comes my way.
I enjoy total success in all I do.
I handle conflict with grace and ease.
I find it easy to express myself.
I have all the energy I need to do everything I want to do.
I think prosperous thoughts and become ever more prosperous.
My prosperity makes everyone better off and no one worse off.
I am attracting all the right people into my life.

Step 3. Build on Your Core Genius

Everyone is born with a unique set of talents and abilities—what we refer to as your areas of brilliance or your core genius. There are certain things you do that are easy for you, that you love to do, and from which you gain feedback that people receive value from them. In fact, some of you do these things so easily and so well, you feel almost embarrassed or guilty about taking money for them.

For the two of us, our core genius lies in the area of teaching and motivating. We love to do it, we do it well, and people report that they get great value from us when we do it. Another area of brilliance is compiling and writing books. Between the two of us we have written, coauthored, compiled and edited over eighty-five books.

Take time to determine what your core genius is and begin to focus more of your time on it. Begin to delegate the tasks that are not your core genius to those people who love to do those tasks. We believe that you can trade, barter, pay for and find volunteer help to do almost everything you don't want to do, leaving *you* to do what you are best at—and which will ultimately make you the most money and bring you the most happiness.

We recently met a woman who loves to travel. She comes alive when she is discovering new places, and she loves to teach people about her discoveries. She has made a business out of putting together and leading tours to spiritual places such as Italy, Israel, Egypt, India, Machu Picchu, Sedona and Hawaii.

When we were working on *Chicken Soup for the NASCAR Soul,* we met hundreds of people whose passion is working on cars, making them safer, making them go faster, making them stay on the track longer. Some were obsessed with figuring out how to orchestrate faster and shorter pit stops during races. That was their core genius.

No matter what your love, believe that you can find a way to turn your passion into your livelihood. Rosie O'Donnell loved to watch television. Many thought she was wasting her time. Her fascination with Hollywood and its celebrities eventually led to her own career as a comedienne and talk show host. Jay Leno was the class clown all through high school. He has used his core genius to become America's premier late-night entertainer.

Step 4. Build an Awesome Dream Team Alliance

One of the most critical elements of living your dreams is being part of a Dream Team Alliance. It is a powerful way to support your dreams and bring unlimited resources to your business and personal life.

What Is a Dream Team Alliance?

A Dream Team Alliance is two or more individuals who voluntarily come together to creatively put their energy behind a definite purpose—increase their income, build a business, raise their kids better or solve a social problem. Within the Dream Team Alliance, you benefit from the other members who empower you and draw out your full talents, resources and abilities. They trigger you, stimulate and motivate you to become all you are capable of being. As part of a Dream Team, you use blended mind-power in action to obtain your desired result.

You cannot be totally successful alone. You need other people to support you, encourage you and empower you to fulfill your greater purpose. For several years, we were on the faculty of The Million Dollar Forum and Income Builders International, two incredible Dream Team Alliances that were dedicated to empowering people to make their entrepreneurial dreams come true. Even though we were on the faculty, we got as much out of every program as the students did, just by spending a week six times a year in an amazing space of "anything is possible." We would always leave with our own visions expanded and our support network widened by another hundred or so people. It was during this time that we envisioned *Chicken Soup for the Soul* being what it has become today, even though the publishing world had not yet caught the vision.

Creating Your Dream Team

In forming your Dream Team (sometimes also referred to as a Mastermind Alliance), start by carefully enrolling another friendly, on-purpose, like-minded individual. Start by meeting together and then adding other selected, unanimously agreed upon individuals who will work in total harmony for the good of each other and for the good of the group.

Our friend and coach, Dan Sullivan, suggests asking potential members this question: "If we were to sit down together three years from today, what would have to have happened to make you feel happy, successful and fulfilled?" (By the way, this is a great question to ask anybody you are thinking of doing business or having a relationship with. It cuts right to the core of what people are about.)

Dream Team Guidelines

1. Your Dream Team should consist of four to eight people. Most people find that six is the ideal number.
2. Meet weekly, if possible, for an hour to an hour and a half. This meeting must be held sacred as a life-enhancing priority. The meetings should be upbeat, enriching, encouraging and beneficial to each individual and the group's purposes. We

always start our meetings with a prayer or an invocation. You could also start with an inspiring story.

3. Each member must agree to play all out—to openly share ideas, support, contacts, information, feedback and anything else that will help advance the individual and group goals.

4. After the invocation, start by having each member share something positive and good that happened since the last meeting.

5. Next have each member share an opportunity or problem they have experienced since the last meeting and ask for whatever support they would like. Appoint a timekeeper to make sure that everyone gets the same amount of time. This is important if you want your Dream Team to last. Everyone must get value at each meeting.

6. End by sharing appreciations and acknowledgments.

Dream Team Training and Coaching Programs That Can Accelerate Your Success

Income Builders International offers a seven-day business training and forum with many forms of follow-up support to help you define and manifest your dreams in the business world. Contact them for a brochure at IBI Global Free Enterprise Forum, Inc., 200 Lime Quarry Road, Madison, Alabama 35758, or call 256-774-5444, or visit their Web site at *www.ibiglobal.org.*

The Enlightened Millionaire Program and Training (started by Mark Victor Hansen and Robert Allen, coauthors of *The One Minute Millionaire*) is designed to help you learn and discover how to become financially successful. Contact them at *www.oneminutemillionaire.com.*

The Strategic Coach Program with Dan Sullivan. Offers an ongoing coaching program for business and sales professionals in the U.S. and Canada. In the U.S. call: 800-387-3206. In Canada: 416-531-7399. Their Web site is *www.strategiccoach.com.*

Achievers Coaching Program with Les Hewitt (coauthor with us of *The Power of Focus: How to Hit Your Business, Personal and Financial Targets with Absolute Certainty*) provides coaching, seminars and workshops in Canada, Europe and the United States. In Canada call: 403-295-0500. In the U.S.: 408-357-0616. In the U.K.: 0846-667227. Their Web site is *www.achievers.com.*

Step 5. Visualize and Affirm Your Desired Outcomes

You have within you an awesome power that most of us have never been taught to use. Elite athletes use it. The super rich use it. And peak performers in all fields are now starting to use it. That power is called visualization. The daily practice of visualizing your dreams as already complete can rapidly accelerate your achievement of those dreams. Visualization of your goals and desires accomplishes four very important things:

1. Visualization activates your creative subconscious, which will start generating creative ideas to help you achieve your goal.
2. Visualization programs your brain to more readily

perceive and recognize the resources you will need to achieve your dreams.

3. Visualization activates the law of attraction, thereby drawing into your life the people, resources and circumstances you will need to achieve your goals.

4. Visualization builds your internal motivation to take the necessary actions needed to accomplish your dreams.

Visualization is really quite simple. You sit in a comfortable position, close your eyes and imagine—in as vivid detail as you can—what you would be looking at if the dreams and goals you have were already realized. Imagine being inside of yourself, looking out through your eyes at the ideal result.

If your dream is to travel to China, then close your eyes and imagine being in China. See the wide expanse as you climb the Great Wall, imagine looking down on the terra cotta soldiers in Xian, experience the thrill of walking across a crowded Tianemen Square, and delight in the image of feasting on the best Chinese food in the finest restaurants in Beijing and Shanghai.

If your dream is to win the national ice-skating competition, imagine every detail from the moment you enter the arena complex, your warm-up skate, and then staying centered and relaxed while waiting your turn to complete. Visualize every detail of the competition from the moment you step onto the ice, the first strains of music, every exhilarating jump and perfect landing, the final spins and your ending, and then the crowd leaping to their feet as they give you a thunderous standing ovation. See the judges' scores of 9.9s and 10s, the announcement of you as the winner, the medal ceremony, bending down to receive the medal, the flowers, the music, the ovations—every single detail, exactly as you want it.

Mental Rehearsal

I never hit a shot, not even in practice,
without having a very sharp,
in focus picture of it in my head.
—Jack Nicklaus, professional golfer

I visualized every step of the 400-meter race
until I saw every stride I would take.
—Lee Evans, Olympic gold medallist

Athletes call this visualization process "mental rehearsal," and they have been using it since the 1960s when we first learned it from the Russians. A research study recently conducted at Ohio State University divided basketball players with equal foul-shooting records into three groups. Group A practiced shooting foul shots for thirty minutes every day for a month. Group B did not touch a basketball, but instead visualized in their mind successfully shooting foul shots for thirty minutes every day. Group C did neither. At the end of thirty days, Group A had improved their ability by 24 percent. Group B, which had not touched a ball in thirty days, had improved an amazing 23 percent. And Group C showed no improvement.

Since its introduction into the realm of sports, visualization has been used in schools to accelerate reading levels by as much as one-and-a-half years in just one month, to reduce drop-out rates in inner-city schools from 80 percent to 20 percent over a four-year period, and to reduce school violence. It has been used in business to increase sales, reduce turnover and improve management skills. And now *you* can use visualization to improve an existing skill, develop a personal quality like patience or compassion, or rehearse a speech or performance.

All you have to do is set aside a few minutes a day. The best times are when you first wake up, after meditation or prayer, and right before you go to bed. Do the following three steps with your eyes closed:

1. Imagine sitting in a movie theater, the lights dim and then the movie starts. It is a movie of you doing perfectly whatever it is that you want to do better. See as much detail as you can create, including your clothing, the expression on your face, small body movements, the environment and any other people that might be around. Add in any sounds you would be hearing: traffic, music, other people talking, cheering. And finally, recreate in your body any feelings you would be experiencing as you engage in this activity.

2. Get out of your chair, walk up to the screen, open a door in the screen and enter into the movie. Now experience the whole thing again from inside of yourself, looking out through your eyes. It will deepen the impact of the experience. Again, see everything in vivid detail, hear the sounds you would hear, and feel the feelings you would feel.

3. Finally, walk back out of the screen that is still showing the picture of you performing perfectly, return to your seat in the theater, reach out and grab the screen and shrink it down to the size of a cracker. Then, bring this

miniature screen up to your mouth, chew it up and swallow it. Imagine that each tiny piece—just like a hologram—contains the full picture of you performing well. Imagine all these little screens traveling down into your stomach and out through your bloodstream into every cell of your body. Then imagine that every cell of your body is lit up with a movie of you performing perfectly. It's like one of those appliance store windows where fifty television sets are all tuned to the same channel.

When you have finished this process—it should take less than five minutes—you can open your eyes and go about your business. If you make this part of your daily routine, you will be amazed at how much improvement you will see in your life.

See Yourself at Your Ideal Weight

You can use this same technique to achieve your ideal body weight. Twice a day, close your eyes and visualize yourself with the body you want. If you have trouble imagining yourself at your ideal weight, you can take a picture of a person you admire from a magazine, cut a picture of your head from a photo, and glue it down over the other head in the picture. Then put this doctored photograph where you will see it every day. Two good places are on the door of the refrigerator and on your bathroom mirror.

Every time you look at the picture it will register in your subconscious mind. Eventually you will notice you are eating healthier foods, eating smaller amounts, drinking more water and exercising more. You will notice articles in newspapers and magazines that will support your new healthier body. You will draw into your life people and resources that will help you realize your ideal weight. One of us did this recently and lost thirty-three pounds in less than two months. Our friend John Gray, the author of *Men Are from Mars, Women Are from Venus,* called and raved about a new nutritional product he had discovered that had led to dramatic weight loss. We checked it out and had the same results. (Note: You can visit Jack's Web site at *www.jackcanfield.com/GetHealthy/* if you would like more information about this revolutionary new weight loss technology.) As soon as you align your subconscious with internal and external images of what you want, miracles like this will begin to occur.

Create Goal Pictures

Another powerful technique is to create a photograph or picture of yourself as if your goal were already completed. If one of your goals is to own a new car, take your camera down to your local auto dealer and have a picture taken of yourself sitting behind the wheel of your dream car. If your goal is to visit Paris, find a picture or poster of the Eiffel Tower and cut out a picture of yourself and place it into the picture. With today's technology, you could probably make an even more convincing image using your computer.

Diana von Welanetz Wentworth, the coauthor of our *Chicken Soup for the Soul Cookbook,* keeps a leather journal into which she pastes pictures of everything she wants to achieve, acquire and experience—dream vacations, places to visit, projects to complete, jewelry, clothing, furniture, art, cars

. . . even people she wants to meet. It is a beautiful goal/wish book that she reviews regularly. We also just learned that her husband Ted will often look through the book when he is looking for ideas for a birthday or anniversary gift to buy her. Smart idea! But as a result of her dream book, Diana has achieved and met almost all of her goals.

Take the time to create a goal/wish book for yourself. It is an incredibly energizing experience. Why not schedule an evening and make it a family affair? It is very powerful when everyone in the family supports everyone else in achieving their dreams.

Create a Visual Picture and an Affirmation for Each Goal

We recommend that you find or create a picture to represent every aspect of living your dream. Create a picture or a visual representation for every goal you have—financial, career, recreational, new skills and abilities, things you want to purchase, and so on. When we were writing the very first *Chicken Soup for the Soul* book, we took a copy of the *New York Times* bestseller list, scanned it into our computer and, using the same font as the newspaper, typed *Chicken Soup for the Soul* into the number-one position in the *Paperback Advice, How-To and Miscellaneous* category. We printed several copies and hung them up around the office. Less than two years later, our book was the number one book in that category and stayed there for over a year!

One of our students created a three-ring binder with a full-page collage for each of her goals. She placed each collage in a page protector, placed a label with the goal and its completion date on it, and placed it into the binder. She reviews the entire binder—page by page—every day. As a result, she is one of the most successful people we know.

Index Cards

We practice a similar discipline every day. We each have a list of about thirty to forty goals we are currently working on. We write each goal on a three-by-five inch index card and keep those cards near our bed and take them with us when we travel. Each morning and each night we go through the stack of cards, one at a time, read the card, close our eyes, see the completion of that goal in its perfect desired state for about fifteen seconds, open our eyes and repeat the process with the next card.

Use Affirmations to Support Your Visualization

An affirmation is a statement that evokes not only a picture, but the experience of already having what you want. Here's an example of an affirmation:

**"I am proudly driving my new black
BMW (500 Series) down Pacific Coast Highway."**

Repeating an affirmation several times a day keeps you focused on your goal, strengthens your motivation, and programs your subconscious by sending an order to your subconscious crew to do whatever it takes to make that goal happen.

Creating Goal Affirmations That Work

Let's look at how to create an affirmation. There are eight guidelines for creating an affirmation that works.

1. **An affirmation starts with "I am . . ."** "I am" are the two most powerful words in your vocabulary. Whatever words you say after the words "I am," your crew takes as an order. If you say "I am fat," even though you think you are just describing a current condition, your subconscious hears that as a command—a request to keep you fat. What you have thought of as only a description is actually a prescription for the future.

2. **An affirmation is stated in the positive.**
    Avoid using the word "not" in an affirmation because the subconscious mind deletes this negative word as it takes in the rest of the command.

    WRONG: "I am not afraid of job interviews."
    RIGHT: "I am calmly answering every question in my job interviews."

    Here's another illustration to help you understand how this works. If we tell you not to think of elephants, you instantly think of elephants. You can't help it. The concept of an elephant overpowers the "not." If we really don't want you to think of elephants, we will tell you to think about roses or ice cream. Likewise, if you want your children to stop slamming the door, say, "Close the door softly," instead of "Don't slam the door." They won't hear the "don't." They'll just hear "slam the door," and sure enough they will. Your subconscious is just like a child.

Tell it what you want rather than what you don't want.

3. **An affirmation is stated in the present tense.**
   Say it as if it is happening now. This creates a mental phenomenon psychologists call "structural tension," which, if you repeat the affirmation often enough, requires the brain to eventually figure out how to make the affirmation come true in order to relieve the tension. Structural tension is the basis of all motivation, and you can purposely create it through the consistent use of visualization and affirmations.

4. **An affirmation is short.**
   Affirmations work best when they are short and easy to remember. The subconscious also loves affirmations that rhyme and that are clever. That's why it is so easy to remember song lyrics. If your ideal weight is 175 pounds, you might say:

   "I am feeling alive at 175!"

5. **An affirmations is specific.**
   WRONG: "I am driving a new car."
   RIGHT: "I am driving a 2004 crystal-white Lexus LS430."

6. **An affirmation includes an action verb ending in -ing.**
   "I am *driving* a 2004 crystal-white Lexus LS430."
   "I am *wearing* my Tae Kwan Do black belt."

7. **An affirmation has a feeling word in it.**
   "I am *happily* driving my new 2004 crystal-white Lexus LS430."
   "I am *proudly* wearing my Tae Kwan Do black belt."

8. **Affirmations are about yourself.**

All of your affirmations should describe your own behavior and achievements, not somebody else's. For example, do not create an affirmation that says, "I am happily watching my teenage son clean up after himself." Instead say, "I am enjoying lounging in my well-cleaned and orderly house."

Some Examples of Effective Goal Affirmations

1. I am calmly and enthusiastically answering all the questions during my job interview.
2. I am easily and happily earning $50,000 a year as an executive assistant at Xerox.
3. I am happily looking at my first month's income of $6,000 from my highly successful house-cleaning service.
4. I am happily hosting my own television talk show on KCET.
5. I am proudly accepting my diploma from St. Ambrose University.
6. I am proudly accepting the gold medal for winning my first six-mile race.
7. I am excitedly opening the doors of my own auto-repair shop.
8. I am joyfully looking at my trim and fit 135-pound body in the mirror.
9. I am happily celebrating my 500th new patient in my thriving dental practice.
10. I am feeling exhilarated having completed my first day of downhill skiing at Copper Mountain.

Expect Results

Through writing down your goals, using the power of visualization and repeating your affirmations, you can achieve amazing results. Visualization and affirmations allow you to change your beliefs, assumptions and opinions about the most important person in your life—YOU! They allow you to harness the 18 billion brain cells in your brain and get them all working in a singular and purposeful direction.

Your subconscious will become engaged in a process that transforms you forever. The process is invisible and doesn't take a long time. It just happens over time, as long as you put in the time to visualize and affirm, surround yourself with positive people, read uplifting books and listen to audio programs that flood your mind with positive, life-affirming messages.

Repeat your affirmations every morning and night for a month and they will become an automatic part of your thinking—they will become woven into the very fabric of your being.

Step 6. Act to Create It

What we think or what we know, or what
we believe is, in the end, of little consequence.
The only consequence is what we do.
—John Ruskin

The thing that most separates winners from losers in life is that winners take action. If you want to live your dreams, not only must you decide what you want, turn your dream into measurable goals, break those goals down into specific action steps, and visualize and affirm your desired outcomes—you must start taking action.

We recommend making the commitment to do something every day in at least three different areas of your life that moves you in the direction of your dreams. If one of your goals is physical fitness, make a commitment to do some sort of exercise—aerobics, weight training, stretching—four to five times a week for a minimum of twenty minutes. We read recently that if you simply go for a thirty-minute walk four times a week, that would put you in the top 1 percent of those people getting physical exercise! If your goal is financial independence, start saving and investing a portion of your income every month with no exceptions. If your goal is to write a book, write for a minimum of one hour every day.

Our Australian friend Bryce Courtenay decided he wanted to write a novel. While holding down a full-time job in advertising and spending two hours with his family every evening, he spent four hours a night, from 8 P.M. to midnight, plus eight hours on weekends, writing his first novel. He finished it in one year. *The Power of One* became a bestseller and went on to garner Bryce a one-million dollar fee for the movie rights. Bryce says the secret to writing a book is "bum glue"—gluing your bum (Australian for posterior) to the chair. You write a book by working on it every day. You learn to play the piano by playing the piano. Practice, practice, practice!

The Rule of Five

When the first *Chicken Soup for the Soul* book was released, we decided that we would do five things every day to promote the sale of the book. We would do five interviews, contact five reviewers, send out five books to celebrities who might be able to help us, make five calls to sell the book to network marketing sales organizations—five measurable actions every single day, no matter what. On Sunday we would give sermons at local churches in exchange for their making the books available for purchase after the service. As a result of this commitment, which we maintained for more than two years, *Chicken Soup for the Soul* went on to sell more than eight million copies.

What could you accomplish if you were to do five things every day to further the achievement of your most important goals? You would literally astound yourself.

Satisfaction Comes from Action

If you look up the origin of the word "satisfaction" you will find that it comes from two Latin words—*satis*, which means "enough," and *facere*, which means "to make." *Facere* is also the root of the words *factory* and *manufacture*. So enough making—or enough action—is what produces satisfaction.

Don't Let Fear Stop You

And the trouble is, if you don't risk anything, you risk even more.

—Erica Jong

Most people never get what they want because they let their fears stop them. They are afraid of making a mistake, looking foolish, getting ripped off, being rejected, being hurt, wasting their time and feeling uncomfortable.

Fear is self-created by imagining catastrophic consequences that have yet to happen. It is all in your mind. If the clock strikes midnight and your teenage son or daughter is not yet home, you may begin to imagine them wrapped around a tree, drunk at a party, or being taken advantage of sexually. You can scare yourself by imagining all of these images. Eventually, when your teenager does come home, you are likely to yell, "Don't you ever do that to me again!" But the problem is not that they were doing it to you. You were the one imagining the worst all on your own. Stop the catastrophic thoughts and images, and the fear goes away.

The same holds true in regard to living your dreams. You are going to have to stop imagining failure and take some risks. Visualize the outcomes you *want*, not the outcomes you *don't*.

*E*ven if you're on the right track,
you'll get run over if you just sit there.
—Will Rogers

If You Want to G-E-T, You Have to A-S-K!

Eight years ago, we wrote a book called *The Aladdin Factor: How to Ask for and Get Everything You Want in Life*. What prompted us to write the book was the realization that so many people were afraid to ask, were uncomfortable asking, or didn't know how to ask for what they wanted. Often, all that separates the successful from the unsuccessful is their willingness to ask for what they want and need.

As you pursue your dreams, have the courage to ask for

what you want. If you receive a no, just say "Next!" Keep moving and asking until you eventually get what you want. Somewhere out there is a person or organization that wants to give you what you want and who will be willing to say yes to you. It's simply a matter of asking enough people. Chapter 8 of this book is filled with stories of people who had the courage to take action and ask for support. As you read their stories we hope you will be inspired to ask for what you want.

Rejection Is a Myth

*I have lived a long life
and had many troubles,
most of which never happened.*

—Mark Twain

One of the biggest fears that stops people from asking for support, guidance, advice, money, a date, a job, the sale, or anything else, is the fear of rejection. In fact, it's been known to literally paralyze people. They become tongue-tied and refuse to reach for the phone or walk across the room. They break out in a sweat at the mere thought of asking for what they want.

We have come to realize that the whole concept of rejection is false—that rejection doesn't really exist. Think about it for a moment. If you asked someone to join you for dinner, and they said no, you *could* tell yourself that you had been rejected. But think about it. Did you have anyone to eat dinner with before you asked her? No! Did you have anyone to eat dinner with after you asked her? No! Did your life really get worse? No. It stayed the same!

If you apply to Harvard University and you don't get in, you weren't in Harvard before you applied and you are not in Harvard after you applied. And you've spent your whole life not going to Harvard, so you know how to handle that. It doesn't get worse. If there's something to gain and nothing to really lose, then you should by all means ask!

Act as If

One of the secrets of success is to start acting like a success before you are one. Act as if. If you had already achieved your dream, what kinds of clothes would you be wearing? How would you act? How would you treat others? Would you tithe a portion of your income to your church or favorite charities? Would you have more self-confidence? Would you take more time to spend with your loved ones?

We suggest that you begin to do those things now. When Jack decided that he wanted to be an "international" consultant, he immediately went and applied for a passport, bought an international clock that told what time it was anywhere in the world, printed business cards with the words "Inter - national Self-Esteem and Peak-Performance Consultant," and decided he would like to first go to Australia. He bought a poster of the Sydney Opera House and placed it on his refrigerator. Within one month, he received an invitation to speak in Sydney and Brisbane. Since then, he has spoken and conducted trainings in more than twenty countries.

You may not be able to fill your closets with expensive Italian suits and designer clothing, but why not invest in one or two really great outfits, so that when you do need them, they are there. When you dress like you have already made it, you will look the part, and successful people will naturally be attracted to you and invite you to participate with them.

In our seminars, we often ask participants to imagine they are all successful millionaires. We then ask them to stand up and walk around as if they were at a cocktail party, interacting with the other participants—all the time acting as if they were millionaires. At the end of the fifteen-minute exercise, everyone reports having been more self-confident, more outgoing, more generous of spirit, happier and more enthusiastic. It is a very high-energy exercise. Then we remind everyone that, in fact, they are not yet millionaires—unless, of course, a few of them actually are—but that by acting as if they were rich they created an entirely different experience for themselves and everyone else.

Start acting as if you already have everything you want. Most people think that if they have a lot of money, they could do the things they want to do, and they would be much happier. In fact, the reverse is true. If you start by creating a state of happiness and abundance, then do the things you are inspired to do from that state of being, you will end up having all the things you ultimately desire. The Law of Attraction states that you will attract to you those things that match your state of being. If you focus on having gratitude for what you do have, you will feel rich, and you will attract more abundance into your life. If you focus on what you don't have, you will send out a message of lack and you will attract more lack into your life. Remember the old adage about "the rich getting richer and the poor getting poorer?" It isn't just that the rich have more money to invest and earn interest on, it is also the fact that their state of abundance attracts more abundance.

Develop New Habits of Success

Research has shown that about 90 percent of all our behavior is habitual. We have both good habits and bad habits.

One of the worst habits we have is watching too much television. The average American watches six hours of television a day. If you are part of the average, that's one-fourth of your life! That amounts to fifteen years of your life spent watching television by the time you are sixty! Imagine what you could achieve if you spent those fifteen years working on your dreams.

If you cut out just one hour of television a day, that would give you an additional 365 hours a year. That is the equivalent of over nine forty-hour workweeks. That's two-and-a-half months of extra time. Just think what you could accomplish. Just think of how much you could study, learn and produce with an extra two months a year. Turning off the TV takes a lot of discipline, but it is well worth it.

We recommend that you identify four bad habits a year and replace them with new, more productive habits. In five years that will give you twenty new habits to support you in living your dreams. Some of the more recent habits that we have made a part of our lives are regular exercise, drinking ten glasses of water a day, handling a piece of paper only once, reading a book every two days, taking time to appreciate at least ten people a day, answering e-mails within twenty-four hours, taking power naps in the middle of the afternoon, delegating more and stretching every day.

Don't Wait . . . Get Started Today

Take the first step in faith.
You don't have to see the whole staircase.
Just take the first step.

—Martin Luther King Jr.

Step 7. Respond to Feedback

Feedback is the breakfast of champions.
—Ken Blanchard and Spencer Johnson,
The One Minute Manager

As you begin to take action toward the fulfillment of your dreams, you must realize that not every action will be perfect. Not every action will produce the desired result. Not every action will work. Making mistakes, getting it almost right, and experimenting to see what happens are all part of the process of eventually getting it right.

Thomas Edison is reported to have tried more than two thousand different experiments that failed before he finally got the light bulb to work. He once told a reporter that from his perspective he had never failed at all; inventing the light-bulb was just a two thousand-step process. Whether it is looking for the perfect fitness and weight management program, attempting to create the ideal balance between work and family life, or introducing a new product into the marketplace, everything is an experiment. If you can adopt that attitude, then you can be free to take an action, notice what result you get, and then adjust your next actions based on the feedback you get.

Ready, Fire, Aim!

Don't be afraid to just jump in and get started moving toward your goals. As long as you pay attention to the feedback you receive, you will make progress. In fact, life is kind of like a game of darts. You need to approach it with the same attitude. In the game of darts you simply take a dart and throw it, as best you can, toward the bull's-eye. Invariably the dart misses the intended bull's-eye—let's say it's off to the right and too low. So on the next throw you correct for that and throw it higher and a little more to the left. Invariably you over-compensate and now it is too high and too far to the left. But with each shot you keep correcting until eventually you hit the target. Everything in life works like that. Getting into the game and firing allows you to correct and refine your aim.

When we wrote this book, we wrote many drafts before we got it to where we wanted it. You just have to start writing, put the manuscript aside for a few days and then come back to it and edit it to make it better. Each time you do that, it gets better and better.

Ask Others for Feedback

When we compile and edit a *Chicken Soup for the Soul* book, we also ask others to read what we have written and tell us how we could improve on it. We have a panel of at least

40 people who volunteer to read the last 160 stories that we are considering for inclusion. They are asked to grade each story on a scale of 1 to 10. Then we enter all those scores into an Excel spreadsheet and calculate the average score. Only the top 101 stories make it into the book. The average score for a story in a *Chicken Soup for the Soul* book is usually 9.5 or higher. And that's after reviewing more than 2,000 stories for each title (more than 20,000 for one of our *Chicken Soup for the Teenage Soul* books!).

We also ask people to help us edit the stories to make them better. In the first *Chicken Soup for the Soul* book we edited almost every story six times. It's a lot of work, but it results in an incredibly good book.

On a Scale of 1 to 10

One of the most valuable questions we have ever learned for soliciting valuable feedback is this:

"On a scale of 1 to 10, how would you rate the quality of our relationship during the past week?"

Here are a number of variations on the same question that have served us well over the years.

On a scale of 1 to 10, how would you rate:

   our service?
   our product?
   this meeting?
   our performance?
   my coaching/managing?

my parenting/babysitting?

my teaching?

this class/seminar/workshop?

our date/vacation?

this meal?

this book/recording/show?

Any answer less than a 10 always gets this follow-up question:

"What would it take to make it a 10?"

This is where the valuable information comes from. Knowing that a person is dissatisfied is not enough. Knowing in detail what will satisfy them gives you the information you need to do whatever it takes to create a winning product, service or relationship.

Ask Yourself for Feedback

In addition to asking others for feedback, you need to ask yourself for feedback, too. More than any other source of feedback, your body will tell you whether or not you are living your dream. When you are relaxed and happy, your body is telling you that you are on track. When you are constantly exhausted, tense, in pain, unhappy and angry, you are off track.

Take time to listen to what your body is saying to you. Take time to listen to your physical sensations and your feelings. They are sending you important messages. Are you listening?

If you are not happy, start doing those things that make you happy. Follow your bliss.

Ask Your Higher Self for Feedback

One of the most powerful ways to stay on track as you create the life of your dreams is to ask your inner wisdom for guidance and feedback. You can do that by taking a moment to close your eyes and imagining your inner wisdom as a wise being. You might imagine Jesus, Mohammed, Moses, Buddha, Gandhi, Martin Luther King Jr., Mother Teresa, your grandmother, Merlin or an owl. Ask the wise inner being any question you have regarding how to better live your dream in any area of your life. Then simply listen for the answer.

Some people find that the answer comes quickly and easily. Others have to wait for a few moments. If you don't understand what you are told, just ask as many follow-up questions as you would like. Always end by thanking this wise person for their wisdom.

When you open your eyes, be sure to write down the answers right away. It is important to capture them on paper before they are forgotten.

Step 8. Never Give Up:
The Power of Determination

Press on. Nothing in the world can take the place of persistence. Talent will not; nothing is more common than unsuccessful men with talent. Genius will not; unrewarded genius is almost a proverb. Education alone will not; the world is full of educated derelicts.

*Persistence and determination
alone are omnipotent.*
—Calvin Coolidge,
thirtieth president of the United States

After taking action, the most important quality you will need to develop in order to live your dreams is persistence. You must be persistent in your disciplines and habits; perseverant in the face of adversity, hardship and challenge; and determined to achieve your dreams no matter what.

There will be many times when you will want to quit, give up, and just go back to doing something else, but the one quality that will guarantee you success is the willingness to stick with it, to see it through to the end, to refuse to settle for anything less than your dream.

In chapters 7 and 9 of this book you will read stories of people who triumphed over amazing odds to pull off their dreams. History is filled with stories of people who have overcome debilitating diseases, paralysis, disfigurement, bankruptcy, defeat, public humiliation and more, and still come back to achieve their dreams—all through the power of perseverance. Orison Swett Marden spent one year writing an 800-page book *Peace, Power and Plenty,* only to return from dinner one night to find his boarding house on fire and his manuscript destroyed. Employing his power of persistence, he proceeded to spend the next year rewriting the book. When it was eventually published, it became a runaway bestseller and is now considered a self-help classic. You have that same power of perseverance in you. All you have to do is believe it and draw upon it.

Adversity and Discouragement Are Inevitable

No matter how well you plan and how well you execute your plan, you are bound to meet with disappointments, adversity and failure along the way to your ultimate triumph. Adversity is what gives you the opportunity to develop your inner resources of character and courage. Adversity is a great teacher. It will test you and make you stronger. But you have to hang in there and not give up.

More than four thousand years ago in China, Confucius wrote, "Our greatest glory is not in never falling, but in rising every time we fall."

As long as you know there will be times when you will fail, then you will know that failing is simply part of the process. Just take it in stride and press on—no matter what. As Harriet Beecher Stowe said, "When you think it is never going to change, press on a bit further, and that is when the tide changes."

Remember, *Chicken Soup for the Soul* was rejected by more than 140 publishers. After it was rejected by every major publisher in New York and San Francisco, our agent gave the book back to us and said, "I can't sell it." We took more than a hundred copies of the book proposal to the American Booksellers Association Convention that year and walked from booth to booth for over two days asking publishers, "Would you publish our book? Would you publish our book?" We got one no after another. Finally, toward the end of the second day, Peter Vegso and Gary Seidler at the Health Communications booth said, "We'll read it on the airplane home and get back to you." A week later they agreed to publish the book. The rest is history.

But what if we had given up after the 100th rejection? We hate to think about it.

On our journey to living our dreams we found the following facts very encouraging: The average millionaire in America has gone bankrupt or out of business 3.5 times on his or her way to becoming a millionaire, and there are now over 4.5 million millionaires in America. The Texas Banking Association estimates that one out of every thirty-six American workers is a millionaire. If financial independence is part of your dream, you, too, can fail your way to success if you simply stay the course.

Step 9. Celebrate Your Victories and Give Thanks

If you do stay the course, you will eventually begin to realize all of your goals. Once that happens, you have to do two things: 1) celebrate your successes, and 2) express your gratitude to everyone—including God—who helped you along the way. Let's look at each of these final steps in the ten steps to living your dreams.

Celebrate Your Victories

In order to justify all of the sacrifice and persistence that is required to create the life of your dreams, you have to enroll your family, your friends, your colleagues and co-workers, your employees, your clients and, most importantly, yourself to pay the price. In order to be willing to pay the price there needs to be payoffs along the way. Every time you reach a milestone on the path to ultimate success, and every time you achieve a major goal, you need to celebrate by doing something fun and nurturing.

Every time we finish a *Chicken Soup for the Soul* book we celebrate with a luncheon for our staff, or a champagne-and-strawberries party or an outing to the local bowling alley. Just recently, when we finished editing *Chicken Soup for the Horse Lover's Soul,* our publisher, who coauthored the book with us, flew our entire editorial team from Santa Barbara to Las Vegas just to have dinner. Everyone said it was one of the most enjoyable evenings they had ever spent. As a result of celebratory activities like these, people are willing to put in the long hours when it's necessary to meet a deadline.

Your Inner Child

It is important to reward your inner child as well. Every time you work hard to meet a goal, the part of you that just wants to have fun has to sit still and be good. However, just like any kid, if it knows it will be rewarded later with a treat, it will hang in there with you.

We make a point of always rewarding our inner child with the following kinds of things:

- Taking a twenty-minute walk after an hour or two of concentrated work.
- Going for walks in the morning with our wives.
- Taking twenty minutes to listen to music and daydream.
- Taking most weekends totally off.
- Taking several weeklong vacations throughout the year.

- Getting regular massages.
- Daily meditation, exercise and yoga.
- Taking piano lessons.
- Going to movies, concerts and plays.
- Listening to comedy tapes and watching Comedy Central.
- Listening to uplifting motivational programs when driving.

Have an Attitude of Gratitude

Take the time to thank every one who helped you achieve your goal. Write them a letter, call them, send them an e-mail or send them a present. It can be as simple as a hug and a thank you—to something as elaborate as letting someone use your summer vacation home for a week.

The Power of Acknowledgment

When you take the time to thank someone, they feel acknowledged for their contribution and will be more likely to want to help again. In a famous study, researchers asked people if they would be willing to place a large sign supporting a local potential candidate for election in their front yard. Most people said, "No." They then asked if they could put a small poster in their front window. Most people said, "Yes."

After two weeks, they called all the people back, told them they greatly appreciated them putting the poster in their window and that it was having a positive effect on the campaign. When they called back yet another week later to say the election was really close and asked if the homeowners would be willing to now place a larger sign in their front yard, almost everyone responded with a yes. The power of acknowledgment had turned the tide.

Take a moment to make a list of all the people you need to acknowledge and make it a practice to thank everyone who helps you. It will return huge dividends in your life.

When we were doing research for *Chicken Soup for the Teacher's Soul*, we became painfully aware of how inadequately our teachers are acknowledged. We received many stories by people who, many years after graduation, decided to locate and thank a teacher who had been special in their lives. In almost every case, the teacher broke down crying and said, "You're the first person who has ever come back and thanked me." How sad.

We also received a story about a school district that had almost no staff turnover and no early retirements. The reason turned out to be a group of parents in the district who organized a thank-you letter campaign. At the end of every year, all parents were asked to write a letter to each of their children's teachers detailing all the progress they had seen in their child that year, as well as anything else they were thankful for. Some letters were brief while others were elaborate—some even with pictures. The PTA collected all of the letters, put them in decorated shoe boxes, and presented them to the teachers. The teachers felt so acknowledged and appreciated, they didn't want to work anywhere else.

Thank Your Higher Power

Finally, it is important to thank God, or however you perceive your higher power, for all of the abundance that comes into your life. Start with the little stuff—another day of life, healthy children, good weather, people who love you, family and friends. Be thankful for the flowers, the birds, your pets, the clothes you have and the food you eat.

And be especially thankful for any additional blessings that come into your life. Take time each day to say a prayer of thanks when you first arise, before meals, and again at night before bed. Having an attitude of gratitude opens up the channels for even more abundance to flow into your life. The more grateful you are, the more you will attract to be grateful for.

Step 10. Give Something Back

Tithing always pays the best ROI (Return on Investment).

—John Marks Templeton,
past president, Chief Executives Organization

A great philosopher once said, "Whatever you want more of, give it away." That simple message has been the driving force behind the prosperity of not only individual icons like Carnegie, Ford and Rockefeller, but of lesser fortunes generated by everyday people. Giving, and by that we mean the regular, systematic, faithful giving of 10 percent of your gross income to a church or charity of choice, does not cause you to have less—but in fact, guarantees that ultimately and inevitably you will have more.

The Miracle of Tithing

The best way to ensure an ongoing flow of abundance into your life is to share with others the wealth you receive. We are big believers in tithing—giving away 10 percent of your income to your church and favorite charities. We believe that it does indeed come back multiplied. This has been demonstrated in our lives and the lives of our readers over and over again. We are such great believers in this principle that Mark wrote a book entitled *The Miracle of Tithing,* in which he published scores of personal anecdotes of peoples' experiences with tithing. You can order the book from Mark's Web site, *www.markvictorhansen.com.*

We have been tithing for years and we believe it is one of the major factors of our phenomenal success. Along with Peter Vegso, our publisher at Health Communications, we have given away a portion of the proceeds from the income on every *Chicken Soup for the Soul* book we have ever published to a charity we picked related to the theme of the book. For *Pet Lover's Soul,* nine different charities benefited, including the American Society for the Prevention of Cruelty to Animals and the American Humane Association. For the *Sports Fan's Soul,* it was the Children's Miracle Network and the Larry King Cardiac Foundation.

Together, we have given away millions of dollars to over seventy charities and non-profit organizations. We have also distributed 150,000 copies of *Chicken Soup for the Soul* and *Chicken Soup for the Prisoner's Soul* to inmates in all of America's prisons. One prisoner recently wrote to us saying, "If I had read stories like this when I was a kid, I wouldn't be in prison today." It's very rewarding to know that we continually make a difference in the lives of others.

If you have never tried tithing, give it a three-month trial and see what happens. Remember that when you are giving, like attracts like. The more you give, the more will come back to you. If need be, start with one percent of your income, time, energy or effort and build up to 10 percent.

Tithe Your Time as Well as Your Money

You can tithe your time, as well as your money. If you are uncomfortable tithing ten percent of your income, try tithing ten percent of your time. You can make a huge difference in so many areas of your community by giving of your time. There are numerous schools, churches and other non-profits that are all clamoring for help. When we were collecting stories for *Chicken Soup for the Volunteer's Soul*, we were constantly reminded of a universal message—whether it was from doctors and dentists who had given up their vacation time to go on medical missions to Third World countries or from everyday people who had volunteered to be Big Brothers and Big Sisters in their local communities—everyone reported they felt they had received so much more than they had given. Once again, their service had come back multiplied.

In Summary

The concepts and strategies we have covered in this chapter are the essence of what we know works . . . and what we have seen proven to work time and time again for individuals from all walks of life. Everyone today has the opportunity to create the life of their dreams—but it takes determination, planning resolve and effort . . . the qualities you'll find in the stories that follow.

As you continue reading this book, we hope you will also take the time to write down the details of your dreams—and complete the exercises we have provided to help you develop the framework and the action plan you will need to start living the dreams you desire.

You don't need to wait until you have finished this entire book to get started. Select one or two projects now and take some first steps. This will help you get moving and build up momentum. Make sure to read a couple of these stories every day to keep you motivated and inspired.

We wish you a great journey as you begin to create the life of your dreams.

Dare to Dream
and Set Goals

Nothing happens unless first a dream.

—Carl Sandburg

Together, Achieving Our Olympic Dream

It didn't start out as an Olympic dream. Back in elementary school, we were a pair of overweight, uncoordinated twins. When teams were chosen, it didn't matter if the game was baseball or dodge ball, we were always last to be picked.

It was so bad, our gym teacher said to us one day, "Penny and Vicky, you have been chosen, along with four other kids, to miss music class and go to remedial gym." This was because neither of us could catch or throw a ball. We were totally mortified.

Although this humiliation whittled away at our self-esteem, we continued to try other sports and activities outside of school. At age eight we discovered synchronized swimming. It was as if the sport had chosen us; we found we had a natural talent for it, and we loved it. It was an ideal sport for identical twins: The goal was to swim like mirror images with perfect synchronization. We had an advantage since we were as strong as each other, had identical arm and leg angles and the same sense of timing. We looked so identical that in one photograph even we couldn't tell who was who. At one competition, a little girl said, "Look, Mommy, they're wearing the same face!"

As youngsters, we were inspired to follow in the footsteps of our role models, the National Duet champions—also twins. We passionately loved working with other swimmers and our coaches and we worked incredibly hard. As twins, we were on the same wavelength; we had shared values and implicit trust.

At our first Nationals, we placed 24th out of 28 competitors. There we saw how great the best swimmers were, so we set our sights higher and worked toward one common goal. We rose to 6th place the following year, and then to National Junior Champions the next. Subsequent victories allowed us to travel all over the world, and our dream to participate in the Olympics was born.

We achieved many of our goals, becoming seven-time Canadian Synchronized Swimming Duet champions, world champions in team, and the first duet in the world to ever receive a perfect mark of "10".

But to our great disappointment, the 1980 Olympic Games eluded us when they were boycotted by many countries, including Canada. And then in 1984, we didn't make the team. After fourteen years of training and striving, we had to accept that our Olympic dream would remain out of reach. We retired from swimming to finish our degrees at McGill University.

Then one day five years later, while watching a synchro competition, we both experienced an unexpected sensation. Penny leaned over and whispered: "What if we tried one more time? What do you think about shooting for '92?" My eyes

opened wide as one eyebrow lifted slightly. We suddenly realized our Olympic dream was still alive, and we could no longer
ignore it. On April Fool's Day 1990, we decided to make an
unprecedented comeback and shoot for the 1992 Olympics. We
were afraid to announce our plans in case we didn't make it,
but in the end, we were more afraid of not trying and having
to live with the thought of *What if?*

Everyone said it would be impossible, but our intense desire
provided the energy we needed to persevere. We had only two
years to get back in shape, only two years to become among the
best in the world. No swimmer had ever come back after a
five-year absence, especially not at the age of twenty-seven!

We weren't eligible for any funding, so we both maintained full-time jobs and trained five hours every day after
work. We still had to support ourselves and fund all our
travel to international competitions. For two full years we
maintained that grueling schedule without ever knowing
whether we'd make it.

Thankfully, we had four dedicated coaches who poured
their souls into helping us achieve our dream. Though pushed
to our physical limits during training (we had to make up for
the five years off), we still loved it. Sometimes we laughed so
hard with our head coach, Julie, we ran out of air and ended
up sinking to the bottom of the pool. Julie helped us to continue believing in ourselves.

When the day of the Olympic trials finally came, we were
confident but nervous. We could hardly breathe as we waited
after the finals to hear our marks. When they were
announced, we jumped up and down, hugging each other: We
had won by 0.04!

We could hardly contain our excitement as the '92 Olympic Team gathered in Toronto, en route to Barcelona. During the Opening Ceremonies, we were thrilled to walk into the packed stadium to thunderous applause. Our spirits received another tremendous lift during those last few stressful days of training, thanks to the Olympic Mailbag Program. After practice each day, we would rush to dig through the giant pile of bright yellow postcards sent to the Canadian Team, and pick out those to us, many addressed simply to "Penny and Vicky Vilagos—Barcelona." The messages came from old childhood friends, complete strangers and former athletes. Imagine how we felt when we read, "Dear Penny & Vicky: You are swimming my dream. I used to be able to swim two lengths of the pool in a single breath. I am now disabled, and can no longer swim at all. I am sending you my strength—May the sun shine on you." And the sun did shine on us in Barcelona.

When our big day finally came, and we stepped onto the pool deck and heard "Competitor #9 . . . Canada," our considerable stress turned to *a sunburst of pride*. As the crowd cheered and waved their maple leaf flags, we ignored the temptation of the moment to reflect on the 30,000 hours of training it had taken to get there, and looked at the water in order to fully focus on the job at hand.

Swimming that day was magical. Despite the stress, we enjoyed every moment. As the music ended and the applause began, we looked up at Julie, and her expression told us what we already felt—we had given the performance of our lives!

Finally, we marched around the pool for the medal ceremony. As we stepped on the podium to receive our silver medals, our joy was doubled as we shared the moment together. We hugged each other, as if to say, "Thanks for your commitment, support and encouragement."

We'll remember forever the electric atmosphere as everyone swayed back and forth and joined in singing "Amigos Para Siempre," or "Friends for Life." That's when it began to sink in: After twenty-one years, our Olympic dream had come true!

As one of the many celebrations after we returned from Barcelona, all five Quebec medalists were invited to throw the opening pitch at the Montreal Expos baseball game! Now a lot of things had changed since elementary school, but throwing a ball was not one of them. When we received the invitation, we immediately thought, "Oh, no!" and for an instant we both felt like little kids again, as memories of "I don't want her on my team," came flooding back.

On game day, we drove to the stadium with a sinking feeling. We followed the organizer onto the field, along with the other Olympic medalists—Sylvie Fréchette, Guillaume Leblanc and Nicolas Gill. The baseballs felt unnatural in our hands; our single solace was knowing we would only have to throw them a short distance.

We watched uneasily as the organizer kept on walking . . . and walking . . . all the way to the pitcher's mound! Glancing sideways, we saw fear in each other's eyes . . . and tens of thousands of fans who were cheering loudly and doing the wave. Time for the opening pitch . . . five catchers lined up, ready to catch our five balls. . . . On cue, we wound up and threw. Penny's catcher leaped forward—but neither fast enough, nor nearly far enough. Her ball, falling short, hit the dirt with an embarrassing thud.

For a split second we froze, reliving that awful, elementary school feeling. We prepared ourselves for the laughter, but this time, everything was different. As we heard the roar and the applause, the sinking feeling evaporated and we smiled—at the crowd, at each other, at the memories—and we waved back.

Penny and Vicky Vilagos
Chicken Soup for the Sister's Soul

Follow Your Dream

I have a friend named Monty Roberts who owns a horse ranch in San Ysidro. He has let me use his house to put on fund-raising events to raise money for youth at-risk programs.

The last time I was there he introduced me by saying, "I want to tell you why I let Jack use my house. It all goes back to a story about a young man who was the son of an itinerant horse trainer who would go from stable to stable, race track to race track, farm to farm and ranch to ranch, training horses. As a result, the boy's high school career was continually interrupted. When he was a senior, he was asked to write a paper about what he wanted to be and do when he grew up.

"That night he wrote a seven-page paper describing his goal of someday owning a horse ranch. He wrote about his dream in great detail and he even drew a diagram of a 200-acre ranch, showing the location of all the buildings, the stables and the track. Then he drew a detailed floor plan for a 4,000 square-foot house that would sit on the 200-acre dream ranch.

"He put a great deal of his heart into the project and the next day he handed it in to his teacher. Two days later he received his paper back. On the front page was a large red F with a note that read, 'See me after class.'

"The boy with the dream went to see the teacher after class and asked, 'Why did I receive an F?'

"The teacher said, 'This is an unrealistic dream for a young boy like you. You have no money. You come from an itinerant family. You have no resources. Owning a horse ranch requires a lot of money. You have to buy the land. You have to pay for the original breeding stock and later you'll have to pay large stud fees. There's no way you could ever do it.' Then the teacher added, 'If you will rewrite this paper with a more realistic goal, I will reconsider your grade.'

"The boy went home and thought about it long and hard. He asked his father what he should do. His father said, 'Look, son, you have to make up your own mind on this. However, I think it is a very important decision for you.'

"Finally, after sitting with it for a week, the boy turned in the same paper, making no changes at all. He stated, 'You can keep the F and I'll keep my dream.'"

Monty then turned to the assembled group and said, "I tell you this story because you are sitting in my 4,000-square-foot house in the middle of my 200-acre horse ranch. I still have that school paper framed over the fireplace." He added, "The best part of the story is that two summers ago that same schoolteacher brought 30 kids to camp out on my ranch for a week. When the teacher was leaving, he said, 'Look, Monty, I can tell you this now. When I was your teacher, I was something of a dream-stealer. During those years I stole a lot of kids' dreams. Fortunately you had enough gumption not to give up on yours.'"

Don't let anyone steal your dreams. Follow your heart, no matter what.

Jack Canfield
Chicken Soup for the Soul

CHANGING THE WORLD
ONE STORY AT A TIME

Dear Jack and Mark,

My husband gave me *Chicken Soup for the Soul* as a Christmas gift, on the recommendation of a coworker who had also read it. I have to agree with his friend—it was totally delightful and uplifting, and one of the most enjoyable books I've ever read. It moved me to both laughter and tears, and renewed my optimism in a most refreshing way. Thank you both for such a magnificent book.

The story "Follow Your Dream," about Monty Roberts and his horse ranch, really hit home for me because I had a nearly identical experience. Like Monty, I was exposed to (and totally captivated by) my father's profession—but my dad was a crop-duster pilot. I was in the third grade (in 1959) when my teacher gave us the "What do you want to be when you grow up?" assignment. I let my dreams run wild and said that I wanted to be an airline pilot for a living; but first I wanted to crop-dust, make parachute jumps and seed clouds, something I'd seen on a TV episode of *Sky King*. You guessed it—she flunked my paper, saying it was a "fairy tale." Her reasoning was that none of the occupations I listed were women's jobs.

I always regretted that I didn't save that paper, but as a nine-year-old (who'd never earned less than a "B-"), I was pretty humiliated, and I threw it away. As it turned out, nineteen years later, I did become an airline pilot. In 1978, I was one of the first three female pilots for United Airlines and one of the first fifty in the nation at the time. Along the way, I made parachute jumps (almost 300), did some crop-dusting for a summer and worked as a weather modification (cloud-seeding) pilot through a special program offered only by the college I happened to attend. So, dreams really can come true!

Take care, thanks for all the light you spread, and please always keep up the great inspirational work!

Sincerely,

Jean Harper

P.S. I'm still flying with United as a Boeing 737 captain!

[EDITORS' NOTE: *After receiving this letter, we asked Jean for her full story, which you can read in* Chicken Soup for the Woman's Soul *entitled* "Wing Beneath Her Wings."]

Finding My Wings

*Reach high, for stars lie hidden in
your soul. Dream deep, for every
dream precedes the goal.*

—Pamela Vaull Starr

Like so many other girls, my self-confidence growing
up was almost nonexistent. I doubted my abilities, had
little faith in my potential and questioned my personal worth.
If I achieved good grades, I believed that I was just lucky.
Although I made friends easily, I worried that once they got to
know me, the friendships wouldn't last. And when things
went well, I thought I was just in the right place at the right
time. I even rejected praise and compliments.

The choices I made reflected my self-image. While in my
teens, I attracted a man with the same low self-esteem. In spite
of his violent temper and an extremely rocky dating relationship, I decided to marry him. I still remember my dad whispering to me before walking me down the aisle, "It's not too late,
Sue. You can change your mind." My family knew what a terrible mistake I was making. Within weeks, I knew it, too.

The physical abuse lasted for several years. I survived serious injuries, was covered with bruises much of the time and had to be hospitalized on numerous occasions. Life became a blur of police sirens, doctors' reports and family court appearances. Yet I continued to go back to the relationship, hoping that things would somehow improve.

After we had our two little girls, there were times when all that got me through the night was having those chubby little arms wrapped around my neck, pudgy cheeks pressed up against mine and precious toddler voices saying, "It's all right, Mommy. Everything will be okay." But I knew that it wasn't going to be okay. I had to make changes—if not for myself, to protect my little girls.

Then something gave me the courage to change. Through work, I was able to attend a series of professional development seminars. In one, a presenter talked about turning dreams into realities. That was hard for me—even to dream about a better future. But something in the message made me listen.

She asked us to consider two powerful questions: "If you could be, do, or have anything in the world, and you knew it would be impossible to fail, what would you choose? And if you could create your ideal life, what would you dare to dream?" In that moment, my life began to change. *I began to dream.*

I imagined having the courage to move the children into an apartment of our own and start over. I pictured a better life for the girls and me. I dreamed about being an international motivational speaker so that I could inspire people the way the seminar leader had inspired me. I saw myself writing my story to encourage others.

So I went on to create a clear visual picture of my new success. I envisioned myself wearing a red business suit, carrying a leather briefcase and getting on an airplane. This was quite a stretch for me, since at the time I couldn't even afford a suit.

Yet I knew that if I was going to dream, it was important to fill in the details for my five senses. So I went to the leather store and modeled a briefcase in front of the mirror. How would it look and feel? What does leather smell like? I tried on some red suits and even found a picture of a woman in a red suit, carrying a briefcase and getting on a plane. I hung the picture up where I could see it every day. It helped to keep the dream alive.

And soon the changes began. I moved with the children to a small apartment. On only $98 a week, we ate a lot of peanut butter and drove an old jalopy. But for the first time, we felt free and safe. I worked hard at my sales career, all the time focusing on my "impossible dream."

Then one day I answered the phone, and the voice on the other end asked me to speak at the company's upcoming annual conference. I accepted, and my speech was a success. This led to a series of promotions, eventually to national sales trainer. I went on to develop my own speaking company and have traveled to many countries around the world. My "impossible dream" has become a reality.

I believe that all success begins with spreading your W.I.N.G.S.—believing in your *worth,* trusting your *insight, nurturing* yourself, having a *goal* and devising a personal *strategy*. And then, even impossible dreams become real.

Sue Augustine
Chicken Soup for the Woman's Soul

Reprinted by permission of Randy Glasbergen.

Glenna's Goal Book

In 1977 I was a single mother with three young daughters, a house payment, a car payment and a need to rekindle some dreams.

One evening I attended a seminar and heard a man speak on the I x V = R Principle. (*Imagination mixed with Vividness becomes Reality*.) The speaker pointed out that the mind thinks in pictures, not in words. And as we vividly picture in our mind what we desire, it will become a reality.

This concept struck a chord of creativity in my heart. I knew the Biblical truth that the Lord gives us "the desires of our heart" (Psalms 37:4) and that "as a man thinketh in his heart, so is he" (Proverbs 23:7). I was determined to take my written prayer list and turn it into pictures. I began cutting up old magazines and gathering pictures that depicted the "desires of my heart." I arranged them in an expensive photo album and waited expectantly.

I was very specific with my pictures. They included:

1. A good-looking man
2. A woman in a wedding gown and a man in a tuxedo

3. Bouquets of flowers (I'm a romantic)
4. Beautiful diamond jewelry (I rationalized that God loved David and Solomon and they were two of the richest men who ever lived)
5. An island in the sparkling blue Caribbean
6. A lovely home
7. New furniture
8. A woman who had recently become vice president of a large corporation. (I was working for a company that had no female officers. I wanted to be the first woman vice president in that company.)

About eight weeks later, I was driving down a California freeway, minding my own business at 10:30 in the morning. Suddenly a gorgeous red-and-white Cadillac passed me. I looked at the car because it was a beautiful car. And the driver looked at me and smiled, and I smiled back because I always smile. Now I was in deep trouble. Have you ever done that? I tried to pretend that I hadn't looked. "Who me? I didn't look at you!" He followed me for the next fifteen miles. Scared me to death! I drove a few miles, he drove a few miles. I parked, he parked. . . . and eventually I married him!

On the first day after our first date, Jim sent me a dozen roses. Then I found out that he had a hobby. His hobby was collecting diamonds. Big ones! And he was looking for somebody to decorate. I volunteered! We dated for about two years and every Monday morning I received a long-stemmed red rose and a love note from him.

About three months before we were getting married, Jim said to me, "I have found the perfect place to go on our honeymoon. We will go to St. John's Island down in the Caribbean." I laughingly said, "I never would have thought of that!"

I did not confess the truth about my picture book until Jim and I had been married for almost a year. It was then that we were moving into our gorgeous new home and furnishing it with the elegant furniture that I had pictured. (Jim turned out to be the West Coast wholesale distributor for one of the finest eastern furniture manufacturers.)

By the way, the wedding was in Laguna Beach, California, and included the gown and tuxedo as realities. Eight months after I created my dream book, I became the vice president of human resources in the company where I worked.

In some sense this sounds like a fairy tale, but it is absolutely true. Jim and I have made many "picture books" since we have been married. God has filled our lives with the demonstration of these powerful principles of faith at work.

Decide what it is that you want in every area of your life. Imagine it vividly. Then act on your desires by actually constructing your personal goal book. Convert your ideas into concrete realities through this simple exercise. There are no impossible dreams. And, remember, God has promised to give his children the desires of their heart.

Glenna Salsbury
Chicken Soup for the Soul

The Little Girl
Who Dared to Wish

As Amy Hagadorn rounded the corner across the hall from her classroom, she collided with a tall boy from the fifth grade running in the opposite direction.

"Watch it, squirt," the boy yelled as he dodged around the little third-grader. Then, with a smirk on his face, the boy took hold of his right leg and mimicked the way Amy limped when she walked.

Amy closed her eyes. *Ignore him,* she told herself as she headed for her classroom.

But at the end of the day, Amy was still thinking about the tall boy's mean teasing. It wasn't as if he were the only one. It seemed that ever since Amy started the third grade, someone teased her every single day. Kids teased her about her speech or her limping. Amy was tired of it. Sometimes, even in a classroom full of other students, the teasing made her feel all alone.

Back home at the dinner table that evening, Amy was quiet. Her mother knew that things were not going well at school. That's why Patti Hagadorn was happy to have some exciting news to share with her daughter.

"There's a Christmas wish contest on the radio station," Amy's mom announced. "Write a letter to Santa, and you might win a prize. I think someone at this table with blonde curly hair should enter."

Amy giggled. The contest sounded like fun. She started thinking about what she wanted most for Christmas.

A smile took hold of Amy when the idea first came to her. Out came pencil and paper, and Amy went to work on her letter. "Dear Santa Claus," she began.

While Amy worked away at her best printing, the rest of the family tried to guess what she might ask from Santa. Amy's sister, Jamie, and Amy's mom both thought a three-foot Barbie doll would top Amy's wish list. Amy's dad guessed a picture book. But Amy wasn't ready to reveal her secret Christmas wish just then. Here is Amy's letter to Santa, just as she wrote it that night:

Dear Santa Claus,

My name is Amy. I am nine years old. I have a problem at school. Can you help me, Santa? Kids laugh at me because of the way I walk and run and talk. I have cerebral palsy. I just want one day where no one laughs at me or makes fun of me.
Love,
Amy

At radio station WJLT in Fort Wayne, Indiana, letters poured in for the Christmas wish contest. The workers had fun reading about all the different presents that boys and girls from across the city wanted for Christmas.

When Amy's letter arrived at the radio station, manager Lee Tobin read it carefully. He knew cerebral palsy was a muscle disorder that might confuse the schoolmates of Amy's who didn't understand her disability. He thought it would be good for the people in Fort Wayne to hear about this special third-grader and her unusual wish. Mr. Tobin called up the local newspaper.

The next day, a picture of Amy and her letter to Santa made the front page of the *News Sentinel*. The story spread quickly. All across the country, newspapers and radio and television stations reported the story of the little girl in Fort Wayne, Indiana, who asked for such a simple yet remarkable Christmas gift—just one day without teasing.

Suddenly the postman was a regular at the Hagadorn house. Envelopes of all sizes addressed to Amy arrived daily from children and adults all across the nation. They came filled with holiday greetings and words of encouragement.

During that unforgettable Christmas season, over two thousand people from all over the world sent Amy letters of friendship and support. Amy and her family read every single one. Some of the writers had disabilities; some had been teased as children. Each writer had a special message for Amy. Through the cards and letters from strangers, Amy glimpsed a world full of people who truly cared about each other. She realized that no amount or form of teasing could ever make her feel lonely again.

Many people thanked Amy for being brave enough to speak up. Others encouraged her to ignore teasing and to carry her head high. Lynn, a sixth-grader from Texas, sent this message:

"I would like to be your friend," she wrote, "and if you want to visit me, we could have fun. No one would make fun of us, 'cause if they do, we will not even hear them."

Amy did get her wish of a special day without teasing at South Wayne Elementary School. Additionally, everyone at school got another bonus. Teachers and students talked together about how bad teasing can make others feel.

That year, the Fort Wayne mayor officially proclaimed December 21 as Amy Jo Hagadorn Day throughout the city. The mayor explained that by daring to make such a simple wish, Amy taught a universal lesson.

"Everyone," said the mayor, "wants and deserves to be treated with respect, dignity and warmth."

Alan D. Shultz
Chicken Soup for the Kid's Soul

One Person *Can* Make a Difference

*You pay God a compliment by asking
great things of him.*

—St. Teresa of Avila

It was the first weekend in June 1985, and I was conducting a weekend seminar at Deerhurst Lodge in
Muskoka. Late that Friday afternoon, a tornado swept
through the town of Barrie, killing dozens of people and doing
millions of dollars' worth of damage. On the Sunday night as
I was driving back to Toronto down Highway 400, I stopped
when I got to Barrie. I got out of the car, about where the
Holiday Inn is, to have a good look. The destruction was
incredible—it was an absolute mess. There were cars upside
down, smashed houses, and many buildings torn apart. I'd
never seen anything like it.

Well, the same night, Bob Templeton was driving down the
400 from a fishing trip on the French River. Bob was vice president of Telemedia Communications, which owned a string of
radio stations in Ontario and Québec. While at the fishing
camp, Bob had heard about the tornado. When he got to

Barrie, he also got out of his car, stunned by the devastation. Up on the hill, he saw a house that looked as if a sickle had sliced right through it. The back was totally gone, and in the other half, a picture still hung on the wall. Just a few feet were between total disaster and nothing. Bob only lived about thirty kilometers away in Aurora. Waiting at home for him were his wife and three small children. They were his whole world. *My gosh,* he thought, *that could have been my home.*

On the radio, they were appealing for people to come out and help clean up the mess. The whole thing disturbed Bob enormously. He really wanted to do something to help, but felt that lugging bricks or writing a check was just not enough. *There has to be something we can do for these people with our string of radio stations,* he thought.

The following night, he and another vice president with Telemedia came in and stood at the back of the room to evaluate a seminar I was doing to see if he wanted me to work with his company. During my presentation, Bob got an idea and after the seminar, the three of us went back to his office. He knew if you can visualize something, and really believe it and attach to it emotionally, wonderful things can happen. He was now excited and committed to the idea of doing something for the people of Barrie.

The next day he went to see the president and CEO of Telemedia, a marvelous man with a huge heart. When Bob told him his idea, he was given carte blanche with the company to make it happen. He put together a team, and the following Friday he hosted a meeting. He told them he wanted to use the awesome power they had right across Canada, and create something that could raise a serious amount of money.

Bob took a flip chart, and wrote three "3s" on the top. And then he said to all these executives, "How would you like to raise three million dollars in three hours, three days from now, and give it to the people in Barrie?"

Now they were acutely aware of the situation because their own radio station had been broadcasting it every few minutes. At first, they all said, "Templeton, you're crazy, you couldn't raise three million in three hours in three months from now, let alone in three days from now!" And Bob said, "Now wait a minute, I didn't ask you if we could, or even if we should. I asked 'Would you like to?'"

So he said, "Here's how we're going to do it." Under the three 3s he drew a line, and then he put a line right down the centre of the flip chart. On the left side of this "t" he wrote, "Why We Can't," and on the other side he wrote, "How We Can." Underneath "Why We Can't," he put a big "X". Then he said, "Every time an idea comes of why we can't do it, we're not going to spend any time on it. That's of no value. We're simply going to say, 'Next!' and we're going to spend the next few hours concentrating on how we can do this. And we're not going to leave the room until we have it figured out."

At first he didn't get much cooperation. And then somebody said, "We can have a radiothon right across Canada." So he wrote that down, under "How We Can", and then somebody else said, "We can't do that—we don't have radio stations right across Canada!"

Well, someone in the back of the room quietly said, "Next!" And Bob said, "No, a radiothon is a good idea—that will stand." Once they started buying into the process, it was magical. The creativity that began flowing from these broadcasters was really something to see. At that time, they had the sports rights for the Toronto Maple Leafs and the Blue Jays, and the people from that wing of Telemedia said, "We can get you the celebrities and the hockey players!" Somebody else was in network broadcasting and had contacts all across the country. Once they were locked into it, it was amazing how fast and furiously the ideas kept coming. The project took off like a brush fire!

Then someone said, "We could get Harvey Kirk and Lloyd Robertson, the biggest names in Canadian broadcasting, to anchor the show." Someone else replied, "We'll never get these guys to anchor the show; they're anchors on national television. They're not going to work on radio!"

And then a few of them said all together, "Next!"

So they put the thing together. Radio stations rarely work together; they're extremely competitive, and they're very cutthroat in every market. But somehow they got fifty radio stations across Canada to participate, based on the idea that it didn't matter who got the credit, as long as the people in Barrie got the money. The following Tuesday, they had a radiothon that went right across Canada. And yes, Harvey Kirk and Lloyd Robertson anchored it—on the radio. The dynamic duo had been apart for a number of years, but Bob and his team reunited them. When asked, they both responded "Absolutely, count on me."

Many legendary Canadian performers were asked to participate, and each one said, "I'll be there," "Count on me." If they were in town, they were there. One after the other they showed up at the station, and Lloyd and Harvey would talk with them about the tornado, and about their experiences living in the area. Some were on tour and phoned in from wherever they were. A lot of them were from the Toronto area, and of course, they were all shocked. It was kind of like, "This is something that happens in Kansas, not in our backyard!" It was very emotional.

The radiothon drew a huge audience. Lloyd and Harvey received nothing for their efforts; it was all out of the generosity of their hearts. But they raised the three million in three hours, three days after they began.

Back then, those homes were worth about 100 thousand dollars each. So Bob and his team like to think that instead of each of them writing a check to help out, they built thirty homes! Bob told me how very proud he is of being part of that effort. Obviously, he couldn't have done it alone. But one idea by one person, with the right people buying into it, can have dramatic and magical effects and produce something of greatness!

Bob Proctor
Chicken Soup for the Canadian Soul

Standing Tall on a Surfboard in Midlife

A wave rose behind me, but it was barely a swell. If I had been standing instead of lying on a surfboard, it might have been tall enough to splash my calves.

Still, I stroked the water like a man about to be swallowed by a shark. If the board was moving, I couldn't tell. I started to think this was an awful idea, that maybe this was not meant to be.

Maybe I had waited too long to learn how to surf.

Middle-aged egos can be painful to watch. A man can turn forty, spot a few gray hairs and do all kinds of things to prove he's still younger. Some men have affairs with leggy redheads, others start jogging. I decided to make good on a promise I made to myself when I was twelve.

I was going to learn to surf.

I often told myself it wasn't right to have grown up in Hawaii and not have learned how to surf. All my life, this concept got steady reinforcement. Everywhere, I saw people with surfboards—young people, old people, men, women. Once, I saw a five-year-old "carving wave." Another time, I saw a dog "hang ten." How hard could it be to learn this?

And yet, I didn't do anything about it. Instead, I made excuses about not having enough time and not knowing anyone who would teach me.

Then I saw a yellow flyer for a surf school in Waikiki, and the child in me spoke up, telling me it was time.

That was how I found myself floating off Diamond Head at a surf break called Tonggs. My arms were stroking the water as if my life had no other purpose. The wave scooped me up as my instructor grabbed the back of my surfboard and gave me a quick shove forward.

I was moving, but I wasn't surfing. Before I could persuade myself to react, the ride was over. I'd blown it on my first attempt.

My instructor didn't know what to make of this. Then he shoved my board toward shore so quickly, I thought he was angry. "Paddle, now!" he shouted.

What happened next didn't take long: I stood up. I fell down. The wave passed me by.

Each new wave generated the same result: a wipeout with all the grace of a drunken belly flop.

Another wave rose like a dare. And then it happened. It was over in twenty seconds, but I'll remember it forever. Even if it never happens again.

I'll remember the sky was slightly overcast, and the ocean was an undulating slab of gray-blue, streaked with white breakers. I'll remember the taste of salt water on my lips and the ache between my shoulder blades.

But most of all, I'll remember that I stood up. I surfed.

Mike Gordon
Chicken Soup from the Soul of Hawaii

Believe in Yourself

We cannot rise higher than
our thought of ourselves.
–Orison Swett Marden

You Can't Afford to Doubt Yourself

*The fear of rejection is worse
than rejection itself.*

—Nora Profit

On a spring evening some years ago, while living in New York, I decided to take in an off-Broadway musical where I heard Salome Bey sing for the first time. I was enthralled. I believed I had just discovered the next Sarah Vaughn.

The moment was magical. Even though half the seats were empty, Salome's voice filled the room and brought the theater to life. I had never witnessed anything quite like it. I was so moved by Salome's performance, yet disappointed about the sparse audience, I decided to write an article to help promote her.

Struggling to contain my excitement, the next day I phoned the theater where Salome Bey was appearing and unabashedly acted like a professional writer:

"May I speak with Salome Bey, please?"

"Just one moment, please."

"Hello, this is Salome."

"Miss Bey, this is Nora Profit. I'm writing an article for *Essence* magazine, spotlighting your singing achievements. Is it possible for us to meet so that we might talk about your career?"

Did I say that? Essence *is going to have me arrested,* I thought. *I don't know a thing about her singing achievements.* My inner voice shouted, *You have really done it this time!*

"Why, of course," said Salome. "I'm cutting my fourth album next Tuesday. Why don't you meet me at the studio? And bring along your photographer."

Bring my photographer! I thought, my confidence fading rapidly. *I've really tied myself in a noose this time. I don't even know anyone who owns a camera.*

"While I'm thinking about it," continued Salome, "Galt McDermot, producer of *Hair, Dude* and *Highway Life* will be performing a benefit with me at the Staten Island Church-on-the-Hill. So why don't you plan to come to that, too, and I'll introduce you to him."

"Umm—of course," I said, trying to sound professional. "That will add an extra dimension to the article."

An extra dimension? How would you know? snapped the nagging voice in my head.

"Thank you, Miss Bey," I said, bringing the inquiry to a close. "I'll see you next Tuesday."

When I hung up, I was scared out of my mind. I felt as though I had jumped into a pool of quicksand and was about to be swallowed up with no chance at salvaging my dignity.

The next few days flashed by quickly. I made an emergency run to the library. *Who is this Galt McDermot anyway?* And I frantically searched for anyone with a 35mm camera. A real photographer was out of the question. After all, I had spent all my extra cash on the Broadway theater ticket.

Then I lucked out. I learned my friend Barbara had become quite an accomplished photographer, so after I begged and pleaded, Barbara agreed to accompany me to the interview.

At both the recording session and the church benefit, Barbara clicked away, while I, a bundle of nerves, sat there looking very pensive, taking notes on a yellow pad, asking questions that all began with, "Can you tell me . . . "

Soon it was all over, and once outside the church, I ran frantically down the street, wanting to hail an ambulance because I thought I was going to die from the stress. I hailed a taxi instead.

Safe at home, I calmed down and began writing. But with every word I wrote, a small, stern voice inside me kept scolding: *You lied! You're no writer! You haven't written anything. Why, you've never even written a good grocery list. You'll never pull this off!*

I soon realized that fooling Salome Bey was one thing, but faking a story for *Essence,* a national magazine, was impos - sible. The pressure was almost unbearable.

Putting my heart into it, I struggled for days with draft after draft—rewriting and reediting my manuscript countless times. Finally, I stuffed my neatly typed, double-spaced manuscript into a large envelope, added my SASE (self-addressed stamped envelope), and dropped the package into a mailbox. As the mail-man drove away, I wondered how long it would take before I'd get the *Essence* editor's unqualified "YUCK!" reply.

It didn't take long. Three weeks later there it was, my

manuscript—returned in an envelope with my own handwriting. *What an insult!* I thought. *How could I have ever thought that I could compete in a world of professional writers who make their living writing? How stupid of me!*

Knowing I couldn't face the rejection letter with all the reasons why the editor hated my manuscript, I threw the unopened envelope into the nearest closet and promptly forgot about it, chalking up the whole ordeal as a bad experience.

Five years later, while cleaning out my apartment preparing to move to Sacramento, California, to take a job in sales, I came across an unopened envelope addressed to me in my own handwriting. *Why would I send myself a package?* I thought. To clear up the mystery, I quickly opened the envelope and read the editor's letter in disbelief:

> *Dear Ms. Profit,*
>
> *Your story on Salome Bey is fantastic. We need some additional quotes. Please add those and return the article immediately. We would like to publish your story in the next issue.*

Shocked, it took me a long time to recover. Fear of rejection cost me dearly. I lost at least five hundred dollars and having my article appear in a major magazine—proof I could be a professional writer. More importantly, fear cost me years of enjoyable and productive writing. Today, I am celebrating my sixth year as a full-time freelance writer with more than one hundred articles sold. Looking back on this experience, I learned a very important lesson: You can't afford to doubt yourself.

Nora Profit
Chicken Soup for the Writer's Soul

KUDZU

Discouraged?

As I was driving home from work one day, I stopped to watch a local Little League baseball game that was being played in a park near my home. As I sat down behind the bench on the first-baseline, I asked one of the boys what the score was.

"We're behind fourteen to nothing," he answered with a smile.

"Really," I said. "I have to say you don't look very discouraged."

"Discouraged?" the boy asked with a puzzled look on his face. "Why should we be discouraged? We haven't been up to bat yet."

Jack Canfield
A 2nd Helping of Chicken Soup for the Soul

IN THE BLEACHERS   By Steve Moore

IN THE BLEACHERS. ©1977 Steve Moore. Reprinted with permission of Universal Press Syndicate. All rights reserved.

A Salesman's First Sale

Keep away from people who try to belittle your ambitions. Small people always do that, but the really great make you feel that you, too, can become great.

—Mark Twain

I hurried home one Saturday afternoon in the fall of 1993 to try to get some much-needed yard work done. While raking leaves, my five-year-old son, Nick, came over and pulled on my pants leg. "Dad, I need you to make me a sign," he said.

"Not now, Nick, I'm real busy," was my reply.

"But I need a sign," he persisted.

"What for, Nick?" I asked.

"I'm going to sell some of my rocks," was his answer.

Nick has always been fascinated with rocks and stones. He's collected them from all over, and people bring them to him. There is a basket full of rocks in the garage that he periodically cleans, sorts and restacks. They are his treasures. "I don't have time to mess with it right now, Nick. I have to get these leaves raked," I said. "Go have your mom help you."

A short while later, Nick returned with a sheet of paper. On it, in his five-year-old handwriting, were the words "ON SALE TODAY, $1.00." His mom had helped him make his sign, and he was now in business. He took his sign, a small basket and four of his best rocks and walked to the end of our driveway. There he arranged the rocks in a line, set the basket behind them and sat down. I watched from the distance, amused at his determination.

After half an hour or so, not a single person had passed by. I walked down the drive to see how he was doing. "How's it going, Nick?" I asked.

"Good," he replied.

"What's the basket for?" I asked.

"To put the money in," was his matter-of-fact answer.

"How much are you asking for your rocks?"

"A dollar each," Nick said.

"Nick, nobody will pay you a dollar for a rock."

"Yes, they will!"

"Nick, there isn't enough traffic on our street for people to see your rocks. Why don't you pack these up and go play?"

"Yes, there is, Dad," he countered. "People walk and ride their bikes on our street for exercise, and some people drive their cars to look at the houses. There's enough people."

Having failed to convince Nick of the futility of his efforts, I went back to my yard work. He patiently remained at his post. A short while later, a minivan came driving down the street. I watched as Nick perked up, holding his sign up and pointing it at the van. As it slowly passed, I saw a young couple craning their necks to read his sign. They continued on around the cul-de-sac and as they approached Nick again, the lady rolled down her window. I couldn't hear the conversation, but she turned to the man driving and I could see him reaching for his billfold! He handed her a dollar and she got out of the van and walked over to Nick. After examining the rocks, she picked up one, gave Nick the dollar and then drove off.

I sat in the yard, amazed, as Nick ran up to me. Waving the dollar, he shouted, "I told you I could sell one rock for a dollar—if you believe in yourself, you can do anything!" I went and got my camera and took a picture of Nick and his sign. The little guy had held tough to his belief and delighted in showing what he could do. It was a great lesson in how not to raise children, but we all learned from it and talk about it to this day.

Later that day, my wife, Toni, Nick and I went out to dinner. On the way, Nick asked us if he could have an allowance. His mom explained that an allowance must be earned and we would have to determine what his responsibilities would be. "That's okay," said Nick, "how much will I get?"

"At five years old, how about a dollar a week?" said Toni.

From the backseat came, "A dollar a week—I can make that selling one rock!"

Rob, Toni and Nick Harris
A 2nd Helping of Chicken Soup for the Soul

"Of course you realize there is a
fifteen-year waiting period."

Batgirl

*Go confidently in the direction of your
dreams. Live the life you have imagined.*

—Henry David Thoreau

"So what, Ray? So what if I'm not a boy? I can hit
better than everybody, except maybe Tommy—and
maybe you on a good day. And I'm faster than all of you put
together."

"You can still play with the girls at recess," he said.

I stared him down, eye to eye, both of us sitting cross-legged
on the sidewalk in front of my house. The cement felt warm.
Crabgrass poked through and scratched my thigh.

I won the stare-down.

Ray looked down at the Big Chief tablet on my lap.

"And you sure can't win that contest, Dandi," he mumbled.
"I don't know why you're even entering."

A blue-lined page from his tablet stuck to his knobby
knee. He pushed a shock of brown hair, straight as harvest wheat, out of his eyes. Ray's mom cut both of our
hair. I shoved mine out of my face. Then I pulled out the

coupon I'd torn from the *Kansas City Star* sports page.

"I'm entering," I said, "and I'm winning."

Ray jerked the coupon out of my hand and pointed his finger at the print.

"See!" he said triumphantly. "It says right here: 1959 batboy contest. Write in seventy-five words or less why you want to be batboy for the KC Athletics pro baseball team. Not batgirl." He cackled as if a batgirl was the funniest thing he'd ever heard.

"Well, it's not fair!" I said, half to Ray, half to myself.

I was tired of not getting to do stuff just because I was a girl. Ray played Little League. I could knock him down with a line drive, hitting from my Stan Musiel batting stance. But our small Missouri town didn't have a girls' baseball team.

I was ten, the age when boys stopped caring that you were the only one who could hit an inside-the-park homer or the only one who knew the infield fly rule. They simply wouldn't let you play because you were a girl.

My sister, Maureen, slammed the screen door.

"What's going on out here?" she asked.

Maureen, who was my older sister, couldn't tell a baseball from a football if it hit her in the face.

"Nothing," I answered. I tucked the coupon in my tablet. "We're . . . umm . . . drawing," I lied.

Ray looked confused. "Drawing? I thought we were . . . "

I nudged him into silence.

Maureen tried giving me one of our mother's suspicious looks. The attempt made her look more like Bruno, our hound dog, when he had to go outside.

the end of an hour, I had fourteen paper wads to show.

"I'm done," Ray announced.

"Read it," I demanded.

I crossed my fingers and hoped it would be awful.

Ray swatted at a horsefly, then held up his paper and read aloud. "I want to be a batboy for the Kansas City A's because I really, really, really like baseball and I really, really, really like Kansas City and the Athletics."

He looked wide-eyed at me. "What do you think, Dandi?"

I hadn't hoped it would be *that* awful.

"Why so many *reallys?*" I asked.

He looked wounded. "I need the words! What do you know, anyway? You can't even enter the contest."

Ray left me standing alone on the sidewalk. I took in the sweet scent of the cornfields across the road and thought about what I might write.

The words began to flow as I put pen to paper:

> *My whole life people have told me that I can't. My sister has said that I can't sing. My teacher has said that I can't spell. Mom has said that I can't be a professional baseball player. My best friend has said that I can't win this contest. I'm entering this contest to prove them wrong. I want to be your next Kansas City A's batboy.*

I signed it "Dan Daley." My dad always called me "Dan," short for Dandi. I addressed the envelope and mailed my entry.

As the months passed, filled with sandlot baseball, I played whenever I could force my way into a game. Then late one autumn afternoon, there was a knock at our door. When I opened the door, I was surprised to find two men in suits, carrying briefcases. Surely they were from out of town.

"Hello, little girl," the shorter man said. "We'd like to speak to your brother."

"Don't have a brother," I said.

The taller man wrinkled his forehead and popped open his briefcase. He took out a handful of papers. Both men studied them while I stood in the doorway, guarding my brotherless home.

"Is this 508 Samuel Street?" asked the shorter one.

"I guess," I answered.

Nobody used house numbers in our neighborhood. There were only two houses on our road.

"Isn't this the home of Dan Daley?"

A light went on in my head. Then I got it.

"Mom!" I screamed, without taking my eyes off the strangers. "Come here! Hurry!" Sure enough, I had won the batboy contest. My words had done the trick!

I let Mom explain about my not having a brother. I confessed I'd entered as "Dan." Maureen and Bruno started to congratulate me—but not the strangers.

"What's wrong?" I asked, a familiar feeling of dread creeping up my spine.

"Well," said the taller one, "you're not a boy."

"Well, duh," I answered.

"Contest rules clearly state 'a boy aged eight to twelve,'" said the shorter one.

"But I won!" I protested.

"Little girl," he said, "this was not a batgirl contest."

The men left, taking with them my dream of being a Kansas City A's batboy. Hoping to make up for it, they sent us season tickets, team jackets, autographed baseballs, hats and a hardwood bat. I never did wear that hat. I became a St. Louis Cardinals fan instead. But I did grab that bat the day it came. I marched to our school playground where Ray, Tommy and the guys were in the middle of a pickup game.

"I'm batting," I said, one-arming Ray away from the plate.

The guys groaned, but Ray seemed to know something more was at stake. He nodded to the pitcher. I took the first pitch, high and outside, just the way I liked it. Before the crack of the bat, I knew I'd send that ball over the fence for a home run. I turned my back before the ball hit the street, finally bouncing into a ditch.

Gently, I released my Kansas City Athletics bat and heard it bounce in the dirt. I proudly walked the bases to home plate, leaving that bat where it had fallen.

"Let the batboy get it."

Dandi Daley Mackall
Chicken Soup for the Kid's Soul

There Are No Vans

I remember one Thanksgiving when our family had no
money and no food, and someone came knocking on
our door. A man was standing there with a huge box of food,
a giant turkey and even some pans to cook it in. I couldn't
believe it. My dad demanded, "Who are you? Where are you
from?"

The stranger announced, "I'm here because a friend of yours
knows you're in need and that you wouldn't accept direct help,
so I've brought this for you. Have a great Thanksgiving."

My father said, "No, no, we can't accept this." The stranger
replied "You don't have a choice," closed the door and left.

Obviously that experience had a profound impact on my
life. I promised myself that someday I would do well enough
financially so that I could do the same thing for other people.
By the time I was eighteen I had created my Thanksgiving ritual. I like to do things spontaneously, so I would go out shopping and buy enough food for one or two families. Then I
would dress like a delivery boy, go to the poorest neighborhood
and just knock on a door. I always included a note that
explained my Thanksgiving experience as a kid. The note

concluded, "All that I ask in return is that you take good enough care of yourself so that someday you can do the same thing for someone else." I have received more from this annual ritual than I have from any amount of money I've ever earned.

Several years ago I was in New York City with my new wife during Thanksgiving. She was sad because we were not with our family. Normally she would be home decorating the house for Christmas, but we were stuck here in a hotel room.

I said, "Honey, look, why don't we decorate some lives today instead of some old trees?" When I told her what I always do on Thanksgiving, she got excited. I said, "Let's go someplace where we can really appreciate who we are, what we are capable of and what we can really give. Let's go to Harlem!" She and several of my business partners who were with us weren't really enthusiastic about the idea. I urged them: "C'mon, let's go to Harlem and feed some people in need. We won't be the people who are giving it because that would be insulting. We'll just be the delivery people. We'll go buy enough food for six or seven families for thirty days. We've got enough. Let's just go do it! That's what Thanksgiving really is: Giving good thanks, not eating turkey. C'mon. Let's go do it!"

Because I had to do a radio interview first, I asked my partners to get us started by getting a van. When I returned from the interview, they said, "We just can't do it. There are no vans in all of New York. The rent-a-car places are all out of vans. They're just not available."

I said, "Look, the bottom line is that if we want something, we can make it happen! All we have to do is take action. There are plenty of vans here in New York City. We just don't have one. Let's go get one."

They insisted, "We've called everywhere. There aren't any."

I said, "Look down at the street. Look down there. Do you see all those vans?" They said, "Yeah, we see them."

"Let's go get one," I said. First I tried walking out in front of vans as they were driving down the street. I learned something about New York drivers that day: They don't stop; they speed up.

Then we tried waiting by the light. We'd go over and knock on the window and the driver would roll it down, looking at us kind of leery, and I'd say, "Hi. Since today is Thanksgiving, we'd like to know if you would be willing to drive us to Harlem so we can feed some people." Every time the driver would look away quickly, furiously roll up the window and pull away without saying anything.

Eventually we got better at asking. We'd knock on the window, they'd roll it down and we'd say, "Today is Thanksgiving. We'd like to help some underprivileged people, and we're curious if you'd be willing to drive us to an underprivileged area that we have in mind here in New York City." That seemed slightly more effective but still didn't work. Then we started offering people $100 to drive us. That got us even closer, but when we told them to take us to Harlem, they said no and drove off.

We had talked to about two dozen people who all said no. My partners were ready to give up on the project, but I said, "It's the law of averages: Somebody is going to say yes." Sure enough, the perfect van drove up. It was perfect because it was extra big and would accommodate all of us. We went up, knocked on the window and we asked the driver, "Could you take us to a disadvantaged area? We'll pay you a hundred dollars."

The driver said, "You don't have to pay me. I'd be happy to take you. In fact, I'll take you to some of the most difficult spots in the whole city." Then he reached over on the seat and grabbed his hat. As he put it on, I noticed that it said, "Salvation Army." The man's name was Captain John Rondon and he was the head of the Salvation Army in the South Bronx.

We climbed into the van in absolute ecstasy. He said, "I'll take you places you never even thought of going. But tell me something. Why do you people want to do this?" I told him my story and that I wanted to show gratitude for all that I had by giving something back.

Captain Rondon took us into parts of the South Bronx that make Harlem look like Beverly Hills. When we arrived, we went into a store where we bought a lot of food and some baskets. We packed enough for seven families for thirty days. Then we went out to start feeding people. We went to buildings where there were half a dozen people living in one room: "squatters" with no electricity and no heat in the dead of winter surrounded by rats, cockroaches and the smell of urine. It was both an astonishing realization that people lived this way and a truly fulfilling experience to make even a small difference.

You see, you can make anything happen if you commit to it and take action. Miracles like this happen every day—even in a city where "there are no vans."

Anthony Robbins
Chicken Soup for the Soul

"If I Were Really Important . . ."

*No one ever finds life worth living—
he has to make it worth living.*

—Author Unknown

In one of my "Dare to Connect" workshops, I instructed
all my students to participate full-out in their jobs for
one entire week. I asked them to "act as if" their actions really
made a difference to everyone around them. The key question
they were to ask themselves during the week was: "If I were
really important here, what would I be doing?" And then they
were to set about doing it.

Peggy resisted the assignment. She lamented that she
hated her job in a public relations firm and was just biding
her time until she found a new one. Each day was pure
drudgery as she watched the clock slowly move through eight
painful hours. With great skepticism, she finally agreed to try
it for just one week—to commit 100 percent to her job, "as if"
she really counted.

The following week, as I watched Peggy walk into the room,
I couldn't believe the difference in her energy level. With

excitement in her voice, she reported the events of her week.

"My first step was to brighten up the dismal office with some plants and posters. I then started to really pay attention to the people I work with. If someone seemed unhappy, I asked if there was anything wrong and if I could help. If I went out for coffee, I always asked if there was anything I could bring back for the others. I complimented people. I invited two people for lunch. I told the boss something wonderful about one of my coworkers (usually, I'm selling myself!)."

Then Peggy asked herself how she could improve things for the company itself. "First, I stopped complaining about the job—I realized I was such a nag! I became a self-starter and came up with a few very good ideas that I began implementing." Every day, she made a list of things she wanted to accomplish and set about accomplishing them. "I was really surprised by how much I could do in a day when I focused on what I was doing!" she said. "I also noticed how fast the day goes when I am involved. I put a sign on my desk that said, 'If I were really important here, what would I be doing?' And every time I started to fall back into my old patterns of boredom and complaining, the sign reminded me what I was supposed to be doing. That really helped."

What a difference a simple question made in just one short week! It made Peggy feel connected to everyone and everything around her—including the organization itself. And whether Peggy chose to stay in her current job or not, she had learned a way to transform any work experience.

Susan Jeffers, Ph.D.
Chicken Soup for the Soul at Work

The Professor and Me

I was born a writer. I understand that some writers are made, but I was quick on the uptake. I knew what I wanted to be.

My mother was quite ill during my childhood. Having two brothers and a sister all younger than myself, I entertained them by telling stories since my father refused to buy an "idiot box," i.e., television. I didn't write my stories down since this was pre-kindergarten and early learning-to-read-years, but by the time I was six, I used to grab the Sunday *Chicago Tribune* and shoot to the comics. Brenda Starr was the most intelligent woman I could imagine. Her journalism took her to foreign countries, paid her enough to afford a fabulous hairstylist and equally incredible lingerie, and her boyfriend, Basil St. John, was always stuck in some jungle leaving her free to pursue her career. How good was that?

By the time I reached college I'd had a lifetime of parents, family and teachers supporting my dream of becoming a journalist. I was bright-eyed, swallowing my education without chewing and naïve as any seventeen-year-old could be. I should have seen it coming, but I didn't.

On the recommendation of the head of the English department, I was chosen to participate in a creative-writing seminar intended for second-semester seniors headed by a travelling Harvard professor who would be on campus for six months. I was the only freshman in the group.

After a month of lectures and small assignments, we were instructed to write our first short story. The stories would be read aloud and then critiqued by the rest of the class. I had no clue I was the Christian. They were the lions.

The night before I was to read, the professor telephoned me to come to his office "for a chat."

This quintessential professor, well over six foot six, tweed jacket with leather patches on the elbows, horn-rimmed glasses and booming voice, commanded me to enter and sit down. My behind hadn't hit the chair before he slammed my folder containing my short story down on the desk with such force that it skidded across and landed in my lap.

"Frankly, Miss Lanigan, your writing stinks."

Shock kept me from bursting into tears. I saved that for later. "What's wrong with it?" I asked, my dry lips sticking to my teeth.

"You have absolutely no idea about plot structure or characterization. How you were ever recommended for this class is beyond me. You have no business being here. One thing's for sure, you'll never earn a dime as a writer."

"There's not anything redemptive?"

"I'll give you that your description is nice," he said dismissively.

Nice? I felt like Catherine in *Washington Square* at the part where her father has just paid off her lover, and she hears the carriage wheels on the cobblestones and her father says, "Don't worry, Catherine, at least your embroidery is nice."

Visions of Brenda Starr's overly stamped passport faded fast. I'd never considered other options in my life. I'd only had one dream. It was a mission. It was my life. Wringing my hands, I fought tears (badly) and asked, "What will I do?"

"I don't know. But," he said, raising his forefinger triumphantly in the air, "you are a fortunate young woman, because I have caught you at the crossroads of your life. Your parents are spending a lot of money on your education. You wouldn't want to waste that money and your time on something to which you're not suited."

"No."

"I suggest you change your major. Get out of journalism."

"And do what?" I was aghast at the thought.

"You could be a nurse."

Comebacks have always eluded me. I didn't even know I was doing it at the time, but I looked him in the eye and said, "Jeez, I could be a teacher."

It went over his head.

"Miss Lanigan, I'm mindful of the fact that you have declared your bid for summa cum laude. To do that you can't take anything less than a B in this class. [And I'd have had to have straight A's throughout the rest of my courses.] You can't even do that without a great deal of assistance . . . from me. So, I'll make a bargain with you. I'll be your crutches. I will get you through my class and give you a B if you promise never to write anything ever again."

In my mind's eye, Brenda Starr was gone. All I saw was a gaping black tunnel as my future. I felt dead inside. Being a devoted Catholic, I was taught to revere authority under any and all circumstances. Including logic.

I didn't know I was looking into the face of the devil, but I was. I knew he was asking for my soul, but I was very inexperienced in devil-deals. I wanted my writing. I wanted that summa cum laude.

"Okay," I said weakly.

I took my short story with me and went back to my dorm, grabbed a metal trash can, matches and went to the roof. It was night. I burned my story and as the ashes spiraled up, I promised God that I would never believe in childish dreams again. I would be smart. I would use logic. If I couldn't see it, taste it, chew it and spit it out, I wouldn't believe in anything again.

For fourteen years I didn't write. Instead, I read everything I could get my hands on. If I couldn't write it myself, I'd read what others had the talent and courage to do.

The summer of 1979, I was in San Antonio with my family the weekend after Judge Woods had been assassinated by the Hell's Angels. Every journalist, television producer and film crew was in town. Sitting under an umbrella table around the pool was a group of writers, and I did something I'd never had the assertiveness to do. I went up to them and said, "I just want you to know that I think what you do is the most important work in the world. Searching for truth. I always wanted to be a writer," I gushed.

One of the writers, cigar in his mouth, looked at me and said, "If you wanted to be a writer, you'd be writing."

"Oh, that's okay. I have it on good authority that I have no talent as a writer."

"Who told you that?" he asked.

I related my tale about the professor. Finally, he said, "Why,

I'm ashamed of you. You haven't even tried. Here's my card. If you ever write anything, give me a call."

I'm ashamed of you.

Of all my mother's key guilt-layering phrases, that was the one that spurred me into action. When I went home, I bought a stack of looseleaf lined paper, a pack of pens and started writing a novel about World War I. Since I didn't own a typewriter, I borrowed one from a friend, typed up the four hundred pages I had and sent them to the writer. He called me a month later and said, "I read your manuscript and it was good. I sent it to my agent, and she's going to call you in half an hour."

Thirty minutes later, Kathy Robbins called me from New York and said, "Catherine, you are startlingly talented."

Shock prevailed for the second time in my life. She asked me questions of whether I saw the book as a "soft-cover" or "hard-cover." Maybe we should go "trade." Industry terms came rattling at me like gunfire. Finally, I stopped her and asked, "Does this mean you liked it?"

"Yes! I want to sign you with my agency today. I'll send the contracts out. I think I can sell this by Christmas."

She did. In fact, she had two publishing companies bidding for that book. September 1999, marked twenty years and twenty novels I've published, including *Romancing the Stone, Jewel of the Nile* and *Wings of Destiny.*

I met a psychologist one time at the place where I worked days while getting my writing career to more financially stable ground, who explained to me about the professor. "Don't you see what happened? His response was violent and angry. To coerce you into a bargain like that means that he was jealous. He saw something he didn't have. He saw talent."

I don't know about that, but I learned that writers make something out of nothing. We make dreams into reality. That's our nature, our mission. We were born to it.

I will never give up my dream again. Never.

Catherine Lanigan
Chicken Soup for the Writer's Soul

The Interview

*Dreams are powerful reflections of
your actual growth potential.*
—Denis Waitley and Reni L. Witt

The job of a lifetime, that's what it was, secretary for
the district attorney. I couldn't wait for my interview.
This was the kind of position I'd dreamed of, what all those
years of college and entry-level positions were for.

The night before my interview, I spent two hours going
through my closet to pick out just the right outfit. *What would
I say to him?* I curled up into my pillowy bed and stared at the
ceiling, unable to sleep. *How should I act?* Nervous, I shut my
eyes and tried to get some rest, but I kept tossing and turning.

Finally, the alarm clock woke me. I tried to open my eyes,
but something was wrong. My face felt stiff, strange. My
hands flew to my cheeks.

"No!" My lips were unable to open all the way.

I ran to the bathroom and looked at myself in the bathroom
mirror, horrified. My face was contorted like a stroke victim's.
My eyes were misaligned. I couldn't move the right side of my

face. I could barely recognize myself. *What was happening to me? What nightmare did I wake up into?*

My mother came into the room, "What's wrong?" Her eyes bulged as she withdrew in terror.

"What's happening to me?" I slurred to her.

"I'll take you to the emergency room," she finally gasped.

We were rushed in. The nurse took one look at me and called in a specialist. There, under the blazing white lights, my mother and I waited.

After several hours of tests, the doctor finally explained, "You have Bell's palsy. It is a condition in which your face muscles tighten because of stress. You need to get plenty of sleep, and in a few days your face will return to normal."

"But I have a job interview this afternoon," I sadly remembered.

"I'm sorry," the doctor said, concerned. "You should reschedule, maybe for later in the week."

During the long car ride home, all I could think about was how bad it would look to reschedule. Certainly, that would dampen my chances. Nobody reschedules with the district attorney. All the other applicants would have the advantage then, I concluded.

I looked at my watch and made the decision, "Mom, drop me off on Jacob Street. I'm going to the interview."

"Honey, I don't think you should. You look . . . strange." She said ever so gently.

I knew she was right. He probably would take one look at me and judge me by my appearance rather than by my experience and talent. I probably shouldn't go. But if I didn't, I'd always wonder if I could have gotten my dream job.

"No, Mom, take me there."

Reluctantly, she took me where I wanted to go. I walked right into the formidable office with the mahogany furniture and pillars of white marble, not letting my own self-consciousness or any disease stop me. Not now, not when I had worked so hard for so long to be given this opportunity.

I went to the woman sitting behind the front desk and said, as well as I could, "Nicole Jenkins to see Mr. Robertson."

She stared at my face. "He's expecting you. Go right in."

I entered the room to her right and saw a gray-haired man sitting behind the large desk reading a file.

Suddenly my nerves got the best of me, and I had to sit. I took the chair in front of him.

"Hello," he said. "Miss Jenkins?"

"Yes. Please excuse me. I'm having a Bell's palsy attack. My doctor explained to me that it would last a few days. I came right from the hospital."

"You're very dedicated to come when you're not feeling up to speed," he responded, after a pause.

"Yes, Sir."

He spent a few minutes looking over my application. "Is everything on here correct?" He held it out to me.

I glanced over the paper, "Yes, but I failed to mention I type seventy-five words per minute."

"Wonderful," he smiled. "Out of one hundred points, you had our highest score on the application test. You scored well above average on grammar and computer programs."

"It comes easily for me," I honestly replied.

"Well, you are certainly qualified. You have an impressive background with related experience. I see here you worked for the navy."

"Directly with legal affairs," I reiterated.

"When are you available?"

"Two weeks."

He gazed down onto his desk calendar. "The 27th then, be here at 9:00 A.M."

I gasped, "You're hiring me?"

"Yes, you're perfect for the position."

I stood. "Thank you for believing in me. I won't let you down."

"I know," he smiled, rising from his desk to shake my hand. "Not only have you got the skills I'm looking for, you also have the character."

Nicole Jenkins
as told to Michele "Screech" Campanelli
Chicken Soup for the Working Woman's Soul

CHANGING THE WORLD
ONE STORY AT A TIME

Dear Jack and Mark,

One morning this summer I woke up to find half of my face paralyzed. Aside from my eyes being dry the night before, I had been perfectly fine when I had gone to bed. I have never been so terrified. The only thing I could think of was a brain tumor.

I rushed out of my room that morning, searching desperately for my mom. My fear deepened when I found the garage empty. I went back to my room and got back in bed, sobbing and feeling incredibly helpless and alone. Images of me without hair laying in a hospital bed flashed through my head.

When mom returned home, she called the doctor at once. We flew to the doctor's office where he diagnosed me with Bell's palsy. He assured me that the condition was probably completely benign, but then he explained the potential consequences. He also informed me that the normal duration for Bell's palsy is around three months, although the shortest case was three weeks and many cases lasted six months, or longer.

Feeling much better after learning the condition was probably benign and had been assigned a name, I became determined to have the shortest case of Bell's palsy in history. I was sure that it would only take me a week or two to get rid of the virus.

My positive attitude faded after three weeks when I would no longer be the shortest case in history. I became extremely depressed after four weeks. Half of my face was still paralyzed. I had made no progress whatsoever. I felt like I should have joined the circus and toured with the bearded lady and the elephant man. It was difficult to go out with my friends and to go out in public because people stared. My smile had always been my most recognized feature. Everyone commented on how often I smiled. It became difficult to smile knowing it was so different from the smile that everyone loved. I tried to be brave, but I felt like a freak.

I began to spend more time at home, devastated at the lack of improvements. Bored, I remembered that my mom's friend had brought me a copy of *2nd Helping Chicken Soup for the Soul*. I opened the cover and skimmed a review that reported that the book could warm "folks who are happy, troubled, disheartened (or) sick." "Yeah right," I thought, as I opened the book.

I became engrossed in the book and all of its heart-warming stories. Many of the stories reminded me that my likeness was not as bad as many other problems in the world. As I got further in the book, my dilemma seemed less and less severe.

I became addicted to the book, taking it with me everywhere, staying up late to read "just one more story" that turned into nine or ten. Amazingly, halfway through the book, my face began to regain motion. As the functions of my face came back, so did my positive attitude. I finished the book in record time, and with that same speed my face was quickly regaining all motion. Only a couple of days after I finished the book, I was the only one who noticed my smile was still a little crooked and my eye didn't close all the way when I slept.

Chicken Soup for the Soul will not go down in history with amazing literary accomplishments like *A Tale of Two Cities, Jane Eyre* or *Les Miserables.* Although I have enjoyed reading these classics, I got the most out of *Chicken Soup for the Soul.* I got my smile back. When I got voted "Best Smile in Senior Class," I could not help but think of this book and the profound impact it had on my life.

Kyle Christensen

Tommy's Bumper Sticker

I am only one, but I am one.
I cannot do everything
but I can do something.
And I will not let what I cannot do
interfere with what I can do.

—Edward Everett Hale

A little kid down at our church in Huntington Beach came up to me after he heard me talk about the Children's Bank. He shook my hand and said, "My name is Tommy Tighe, I'm six years old and I want to borrow money from your Children's Bank."

I said, "Tommy, that's one of my goals, to loan money to kids. And so far all the kids have paid it back. What do you want to do?"

He said, "Ever since I was four I had a vision that I could cause peace in the world. I want to make a bumper sticker that says, 'PEACE, PLEASE! DO IT FOR US KIDS,' signed 'Tommy'."

"I can get behind that," I said. He needed $454 to produce

1,000 bumper stickers. The Mark Victor Hansen Children's Free Enterprise Fund wrote a check to the printer who was printing the bumper stickers.

Tommy's dad whispered in my ear, "If he doesn't pay the loan back, are you going to foreclose on his bicycle?"

I said, "No, knock on wood, every kid is born with honesty, morality and ethics. They have to be taught something else. I believe he'll pay us back." If you have a child who is over nine, let them w-o-r-k for m-o-n-e-y for someone honest, moral and ethical so they learn the principle early.

We gave Tommy a copy of all of my tapes and he listened to them twenty-one times each and took ownership of the material. It says, "Always start selling at the top." Tommy convinced his dad to drive him up to Ronald Reagan's home. Tommy rang the bell and the gatekeeper came out. Tommy gave a two-minute, irresistible sales presentation on his bumper sticker. The gatekeeper reached in his pocket, gave Tommy $1.50 and said, "Here, I want one of those. Hold on and I'll get the former President."

I asked, "Why did you ask him to buy?" He said, "You said in the tapes to ask everyone to buy." I said, "I did. I did. I'm guilty."

He sent a bumper sticker to Mikhail Gorbachev with a bill for $1.50 in U.S. funds. Gorbachev sent him back $1.50 and a picture that said, "Go for peace, Tommy," and signed it, "Mikhail Gorbachev, President."

Since I collect autographs, I told Tommy, "I'll give you $500.00 for Gorbachev's autograph."

He said, "No thanks, Mark."

I said, "Tommy, I own several companies. When you get older, I'd like to hire you."

"Are you kidding?" he answered. "When I get older, I'm going to hire you."

The Sunday edition of the *Orange County Register* did a feature section on Tommy's story, the Children's Free Enterprise Bank and me. Marty Shaw, the journalist, interviewed Tommy for six hours and wrote a phenomenal interview. Marty asked Tommy what he thought his impact would be on world peace. Tommy said, "I don't think I am old enough yet; I think you have to be eight or nine to stop all the wars in the world."

Marty asked, "Who are your heroes?"

He said, "My dad, George Burns, Wally Joiner and Mark Victor Hansen." Tommy has good taste in role models.

Three days later, I got a call from the Hallmark Greeting Card Company. A Hallmark franchisee had faxed a copy of the *Register* article. They were having a convention in San Francisco and wanted Tommy to speak. After all, they saw that Tommy had nine goals for himself:

1. Call about cost (baseball card collateral).
2. Have bumper sticker printed.
3. Make a plan for a loan.
4. Find out how to tell people.
5. Get address of leaders.
6. Write a letter to all of the presidents and leaders of other countries and send them all a free bumper sticker.
7. Talk to everyone about peace.
8. Call the newspaper stand and talk about my business.
9. Have a talk with school.

Hallmark wanted my company, Look Who's Talking, to book Tommy to speak. While the talk did not happen because the two-week lead time was too short, the negotiation between Hallmark, myself and Tommy was fun, uplifting and powerful.

Joan Rivers called Tommy Tighe to be on her syndicated television show. Someone had also faxed her a copy of the *Register* interview on Tommy.

"Tommy," Joan said, "this is Joan Rivers and I want you on my TV show which is viewed by millions."

"Great!" said Tommy. He didn't know her from a bottle of Vicks.

"I'll pay you $300," said Joan.

"Great!" said Tommy. Having listened repeatedly to and mastered my *Sell Yourself Rich* tapes, Tommy continued selling Joan by saying: "I am only eight years old, so I can't come alone. You can afford to pay for my mom, too, can't you, Joan?"

"Yes!" Joan replied.

"By the way, I just watched a *Lifestyles of the Rich and Famous* show and it said to stay at the Trump Plaza when you're in New York. You can make that happen, can't you, Joan?"

"Yes," she answered.

"The show also said when in New York, you ought to visit the Empire State Building and the Statue of Liberty. You can get us tickets, can't you?"

"Yes . . ."

"Great. Did I tell you my mom doesn't drive? So we can use your limo, can't we?"

"Sure," said Joan.

Tommy went on *The Joan Rivers Show* and wowed Joan, the camera crew, the live and television audiences. He was so handsome, interesting, authentic and such a great self-starter. He told such captivating and persuasive stories that the audience was found pulling money out of their wallets to buy a bumper sticker on the spot.

At the end of the show, Joan leaned in and asked, "Tommy, do you really think your bumper sticker will cause peace in the world?"

Tommy, enthusiastically and with a radiant smile, said, "So far I've had it out two years and got the Berlin Wall down. I'm doing pretty good, don't you think?"

Mark Victor Hansen
Chicken Soup for the Soul

[EDITORS' NOTE:

To date, Tommy has sold more than 10,000 bumper stickers and has graduated from the University of California, Santa Barbara. He is going to start work toward a master's degree in psychology. He continues to sell bumper stickers to this day.]

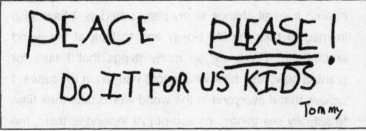

CHANGING THE WORLD
ONE STORY AT A TIME

Dear Sirs,

I am a 13-year-old female that lives with my parents and my brother and sister in Pennsylvania. I received this book and the sequel as a gift this past Christmas.

I enjoyed this book tremendously and just wanted to let someone know it. I haven't done much in my life because of my age, but in reading this book, I learned things that would have taken me years in the future to find out. I have learned that I can make a difference in the world just by making a small change in my daily schedule. I have also learned to take my life slowly and to look at the world around me. There are so many things that I take for granted now, just think what might happen in the future. I believe that if everyone in the world would take their time to actually see things, instead of just looking at them, the world would have almost no problems at all. It's human instinct to feel compassion, and if more people would see that the world needs them, they would show it. Maybe if more people could be like little Tommy Tighe, then we wouldn't be so blind to see these things.

In conclusion, I would like to say that I was deeply moved by this book and I would like to congratulate everyone who had something to do with the making and publishing of this book. You all have done a wonderful job and thank you.

Thank you again for your time.

Sincerely,
Stephanie Pieper

"This drawing is for my mom. If I'm ever famous, her fridge will be worth a bundle!"

Reprinted by permission of Stephanie Piro.

Trash Bags Are for Trash

I walked through the den on my way to get ready for bed and looked once again at the amazing mountain of duffel bags. Each bag had a stuffed animal, a luggage tag and a note from me inside of it. The pile of bags went from floor to ceiling, more than five thousand bags, enough for each and every foster-care kid in three states. My dream was coming true—big time.

After I went to bed, right before I went to sleep, I closed my eyes and thought back to when it all started . . . when I got the idea for my dream. . . .

I had been in second grade when I went with my two brothers and my parents to Paris, France. My brothers, Brock and Cory, and I had entered an essay contest about what we were going to do to change the world to make it a better place to live. We won and were chosen as three of ten kids who would represent the United States at the Children's World Summit. Nine hundred kids from around the world were chosen to meet with each other and talk about world issues. We exchanged ideas on solving the problems in our world today and had lots of fun during the days we were together.

While I was there, I met two foster-care kids. They were two boys, and after getting to know them, I learned a lot about what foster-care kids go through. They told me that when kids go into the foster-care system, they don't just lose their parents and their home, sometimes they are also separated from their brothers and sisters. Not every foster-care home wants to care for an entire family of kids. Foster-care kids also lose most of their toys and clothes. They told me that when the kids are picked up from their home by a social worker, they are given only a trash bag to put their few belongings into. This trash bag is what foster-care kids carry with them when they are moved from home to home.

I felt really sad when I heard this. I couldn't even imagine what life would be like without my family and home—much less what it would be like to have to live out of a trash bag. Trash bags are for trash, not for kids to carry their belongings in.

After I came home from France, I saw an after-school movie that was about a girl living in foster care. It was just like what the boys had described to me at the Children's World Summit, and it made me cry. Right then I decided that I wanted to help foster-care kids. These kids needed my help, because they were not being respected like they should be.

My whole family is into volunteering. Brock and Cory had started a project after they saw a show on television about some kids who died in a fire. The kids had died because the fire department didn't have this special camera that can see through smoke to find people in a burning house. My brothers began Project Rescue Vision in 1996 to raise needed money for our town's fire department. Of course, I helped, too. I was only four years old, and I was the "President of the Art Department." My job was to hand-color all of the information envelopes that were given out. I helped them until I was seven. Then I began my own project for foster-care kids.

I started by asking my mom to stop at garage sales when I saw suitcases or duffel bags for sale. I would tell the person who was having the garage sale what I wanted to do with the bags, and most of the time they gave me the bags for free. I tried to put myself into the mind of a foster-care kid, and I decided that the kids should have a stuffed animal in the bag, too. I figured that if I was in that situation I would want a cuddly friend to hug when I was sad and felt lonely for my parents. People often gave those to me for free, too.

In October 1998, I helped organize a luggage drive during our local "Make a Difference Day." Some congresspeople and senators showed up to give their support, and I came up with this idea for everyone to get their hand painted and then put their handprint on a big banner to show that they had made a difference that day. I got all these kids to help paint people's hands. It was really funny to watch these important people have their hands painted.

The senators and congresspeople went back to Washington and told other people about my project, and then a company named Freddie Mac set up a grant for me and donated fifteen thousand dollars. I am the youngest person they have ever granted money to. Because of this grant, I had a story about my project and me on the cover of the *Washington Post*. Then the most amazing thing happened. President and Mrs. Clinton read about me and wanted to meet me. I was really excited! They were so nice, and I gave the president one of my bags with a Beanie Baby in it to give to any foster kid that he may meet. A few days later, he sent some bags to me from his own collection to give to foster-care kids, so I did.

My project really started growing because of all the media attention. Radio stations called me for interviews about what I was doing and some TV shows had me on. More people then heard about me from the TV and radio interviews and from word-of-mouth, and they called me to offer help.

Every week I called my friends and family to see if they wanted to come and put bags together. I always had help from many people. My class even helped, too. My teacher announced to my class what I was doing, and everybody started bringing stuffed animals and duffel bags to school. One of my friends brought in ten big bags full of stuffed animals!

On each bag, I put a luggage tag designed by me. On the front of each luggage tag is a picture of a girl and a suitcase with wheels on it. In each bag, I put a cuddly stuffed animal and a special note I wrote, letting them know that I love and care about them. My mom helped me type this note:

> Dear Friend,
> Hi, my name is Makenzie Snyder. I am nine years old, and I'm in the third grade. I collect suitcases and duffel bags as an act of kindness for those who are in need of them. God told me you could use a duffel bag and a cuddly friend so I sent this with love to you. I want you to always know that you are loved, especially by me. And, always remember to be positive, polite and never give up.
>
> Love, your friend,
> Makenzie Snyder

After the bags are stuffed, I call social workers to tell them they can come and pick up the bags to hand out to the foster-care kids. I have had a lot of support from several big companies, schools, churches, organizations and individuals who have donated money, or sent me bags and stuffed animals. I've even been on the *Rosie O'Donnell Show!* Several thousand bags have been sent out so far, and right now I have five thousand more ready to go, sitting in my den. Those bags will go to kids in Maryland, Washington, D.C., and Virginia.

I have had a lot of help from a lot of people, but most importantly from my parents and my brothers. My brother Brock came up with the name for my project. He said I should call it "Children to Children" since it was all about kids knowing what other kids want and helping them get it. My brothers have also given me good advice about always sending thank-you notes to the people who help me. They told me I had to work hard, call tons of people and to never give up . . . and I haven't.

I know that this is just the beginning. There are 530,000 foster-care kids in the United States. My dream is for all the foster-care kids in the entire United States to receive a duffel bag and a cuddly friend. I know it can be done if everyone helps out. It is a lot of work but I never get tired of it. I remember the girl in the movie that I saw. If she had been given one of my duffel bags, she would have known that someone out there cared about what happened to her. I don't want any kid, anywhere, to go through what she or the two boys did. Kid to kid, children to children—that's what it's all about.

Makenzie Snyder, nine years old
Chicken Soup for the Preteen Soul

CHANGING THE WORLD
ONE STORY AT A TIME

Dear Chicken Soup,

Since Makenzie's story came out in your book she has had over 120,000 visitors come to her Web site, all wanting to help because they were so touched and inspired. It is amazing the response she has received. Everyone old and young loves her story.

After the story came out her project took off. Makenzie now has helped over 28,000 foster care kids, and has had her own office built on our property donated by Home Depot. She has a warehouse where she keeps the bags and animals before shipping them out. It has become a national effort and international effort.

Makenzie receives bags and animals everyday. Makenzie has also set up a way that kids can help even if they don't have the money to send things to her. She now has kids who want to help set up their own drives in their school or town and tells them to collect equal amounts of bags and animals. After they have their drive they then e-mail her and let her know how many they collected. She then sends them that amount of luggage tags. The kids then download her note that goes in every bag. They then look in their phone book and contact the nearest Social Service office and set up delivery. This has been great! These kids love taking charge. They love it!

Since her story was published in your book she has met the following people who have been touched by her efforts: Former President Clinton, Secretary of State Colin Powell, Rosie O'Donnell, Oprah Winfrey, Charlotte Church, Martin Sheen, Bob Dole and many others.

Her story and your book has inspired countless Americans to become involved with serving their communities.

Sincerely,

Margie and Makenzie Snyder (now age 12)

Children To Children

A Makenzie supporter writes:

Dear Makenzie

Hello I'm Jessica Burnham from Reading Michigan.
The other day my mother Got me the book Chicken Soup for the Preteen Soul. I just read you story 30 min. ago after I read it I told my mom and she read it then I got on the Internet and checked out your web site..... I really went to help but I can't give much I'm only 12 and my dads layed of of work. So here is 2 dollars it wount do much I know.
It would be very nice if I could here from you thanx.

Your friend
Jessica.

It's Never Too Late

*What becomes fragile when we age is
not our bodies as much as our egos.
The best time to take some daring
steps is when we get older.*

—Helen Hayes

Never Too Old to Live Your Dream

Age is something that doesn't matter
unless you are a cheese.

—Billie Burke

The first day of school our professor introduced himself to our chemistry class and challenged us to get to know someone we didn't already know. I stood up to look around when a gentle hand touched my shoulder. I turned around to find a wrinkled, little old lady beaming up at me with a smile that lit up her entire being.

She said, "Hi, handsome. My name is Rose. I'm eighty-seven years old. Can I give you a hug?"

I laughed and enthusiastically responded, "Of course you may!" and she gave me a giant squeeze.

"Why are you in college at such a young, innocent age?" I asked.

She jokingly replied, "I'm here to meet a rich husband, get married, have a couple children, and then retire and travel."

"No seriously," I asked. I was curious about what may have motivated her to be taking on this challenge at her age.

"I always dreamed of having a college education and now I'm getting one!" she told me.

After class we walked to the student union building and shared a chocolate milkshake. We became instant friends. Every day for the next three months we would leave class together and talk nonstop. I was always mesmerized listening to this "time machine" as she shared her wisdom and experience with me.

Over the course of the school year, Rose became a campus icon and easily made friends wherever she went. She loved to dress up and she reveled in the attention bestowed upon her from the other students. She was living it up.

At the end of the semester we invited Rose to speak at our football banquet and I'll never forget what she taught us. She was introduced and stepped up to the podium. As she began to deliver her prepared speech, she dropped her three-by-five cards on the floor. Frustrated and a bit embarrassed, she leaned into the microphone and simply said, "I'm sorry I'm so jittery. I gave up beer for Lent and this whiskey is killing me! I'll never get my speech back in order so let me just tell you what I know." As we laughed, she cleared her throat and began:

"We do not stop playing because we are old; we grow old because we stop playing. There are only four secrets to staying young, being happy and achieving success.

"You have to laugh and find humor each and every day.

"You've got to have a dream. When you lose your dreams, you die. We have so many people walking around who are dead and they don't even know it!

"There is a giant difference between growing older and

growing up. If you are nineteen years old and lie in bed for one full year and don't do one productive thing, you will turn twenty years old. If I am eight-seven years old and stay in bed for a year and never do anything I will turn eighty-eight. Anybody can grow older. That doesn't take any talent or ability. The idea is to grow up by always finding the opportunity in change.

"Have no regrets. The elderly usually don't have regrets for what we did, but rather for things we did not do. The only people who fear death are those with regrets."

She concluded her speech by courageously singing "The Rose." She challenged each of us to study the lyrics and live them out in our daily lives.

At year's end, Rose finished the college degree she had begun all those years ago. One week after graduation Rose died peacefully in her sleep. Over two thousand college students attended her funeral in tribute to the wonderful woman who taught by example that it's never too late to be all you can possibly be.

Dan Clark
Chicken Soup for the College Soul

Teacher at Last

*We don't have eternity to realize our
dreams, only the time we are here.*

—Susan Taylor

That January afternoon, I pulled on my black overcoat, stepped outside and paused. *Well, Atlas Plumbing Company, I've spent thirty years of my life turning you into a successful business. Now I must follow my heart.* I shut the door for the last time and hung the sign: "Gone Out of Business."

Climbing into my 1991 burgundy Explorer, at age fifty, I turned all thoughts toward my lifelong dream of being a schoolteacher. *Lord, you've brought me this far,* I pleaded, *please don't leave me now.*

While driving home, I wished Mr. Roy was still alive so we could discuss it. Mr. Roy was my mentor, my role model. Mr. Roy talked with me, asked me questions. Just like I was somebody instead of a scrawny little black kid.

I was about six when we found each other in Mayfield, South Carolina, where I was born. There was a little family-run store in our neighborhood. Out front, the American flag waved right next to the Coca-Cola sign above the screen door. Mr. Roy and some other old-timers usually were there, propped on upside-down nail kegs next to the pot-bellied stove, playing a round of checkers and swapping yarns.

Every day after school I sidled up by the checkerboard to "help out" Mr. Roy with his game. And it was there, at Mr. Roy's elbow, that many of my values were born. Not that my parents didn't teach me things. They did. But as there were seventeen of us children at home, individual attention was hard to come by.

"Eugene," Mr. Roy said one day, "whatta you want to be when you grow up?"

"A teacher," I fairly blurted out.

In a tone that left no room for doubt, Mr. Roy responded, "Then be one!"

Mr. Roy could see the pitfalls ahead. "Eugene," he said, dead serious as he wrapped one bony arm around my equally thin shoulders, "there will be times when folks will say, 'You can't do that.' Just take that in stride. Then set out to prove 'em wrong."

During my junior year of high school, Mom passed away and Dad needed me to help care for the younger children. As college now was out of the question, I put aside my teacher dream and took up a trade instead—plumbing.

I recalled another of Mr. Roy's admonitions. "One more thing, Eugene," he'd said. "Whatever you become, whether you're a ditch-digger or a schoolteacher, you be the best you can be. That's all the good Lord asks of us."

So I told myself, *If I can't be a teacher, I'll be the best plumber in the business.* I learned all I could about the trade.

I practiced what I believed—do it right the first time, and you don't have to go back. Eventually I had my own business.

Meanwhile, Annette and I married and reared two fine children. Now Michael was completing his Ph.D., and Monique was a college senior, while Annette had gone back to school several years earlier and made a fine teacher.

Now that day had come when my dream no longer would be denied. Four days after I closed my shop, I started work at Hendrix Drive Elementary School. Not as a teacher, mind you, but as a custodian. I traded my wrenches and pipe fittings for brooms and paint brushes. And a 40 percent reduction in pay. I figured the job would be a good way to test the waters—to see if I could even relate to the youngsters of today.

I hit it off with the students. In the hallways while running the floor polisher, I'd throw them a big high five and each responded with wide grin and a "five back-at-you."

Often, I found a youngster propped up against the wall outside his classroom, having been banished there for misbehavior. "What'za matter, son?" I'd ask him, truly concerned. After he had related his current infraction of rules and I had emphasized his need to comply, I'd go in and talk with his teacher, smoothing the way for a return to the classroom.

Surprisingly, I made a very fine mediator. Maybe because I could put myself in the mind-set of these youngsters. So many—like my young friend Jeffrey—came from broken homes, being raised by their single moms or by a grandmother. They were hungry for a positive male role model, someone who would show genuine interest in them, show them they are loved. They desperately needed a Mr. Roy in their lives. I wanted to be that one.

Sometimes, too, that meant being strict. More than once I pulled a young man over to the side of the hallway and reprimanded him about his baggy pants with no belt, the waist dragging down around his knees and underwear showing. In fact, that's how I met Jeffrey.

"Wait right here," I told him. From my supply closet I brought a length of venetian-blind cord to run through his belt loops. The next day, Jeffrey came to school wearing a belt. So did the other boys when it came their turn for correction. Unorthodox behavior for a custodian? Maybe. But the kids respected my opinion because they knew I cared.

I did a lot of thinking and praying while I polished those floors. *I have a ministry right here as a custodian, I rationalized. Maybe I don't need to put myself through the rigors of college courses in order to help students.*

All the while, I could hear Mr. Roy saying, "Never settle for second best, Eugene. Whatever you become, you be the best you can be."

One night I ventured to the family, "Looks like I'm gonna have to go to college after all."

They said, "Go for it!"

So I did. In the fall, I registered for night and weekend courses at the Norcross branch of Brenau University. I plain had the jitters when I approached those first classes. Would I be the oldest student there? Was I too old, too tired to learn those tough subjects?

On top of those worries, working all day then studying until 2:00 A.M. only to get up at 5:30 was rough. While cleaning those floors, I carried on a running dialogue with God. *Lord, I'm bone weary. Remind me again that this is something you want me to do. 'Cause I tell you the truth, if it's just my want-ing it, I'm about ready to quit.*

In answer, I believe God sent Jeffrey back to me. Jeffrey had graduated our school the year before; now he came to visit and found me about to replace a fluorescent bulb in a hallway. "Jeffrey, I am so glad to see you!" I said, while giving him a big bear hug. "How're you doing, Son?"

"Fine, Sir," he responded, his good manners impressing me beyond measure. "Mr. Edwards," he went on, "I want to thank you for the time you spent with me here, for caring about me. I never would have made it through sixth grade if it had not been for you."

"Jeffrey, I am so proud of you," I responded. "And you're going to finish high school, aren't you?"

"Yes, Sir," he said, his face breaking into a huge smile. "I'm even going to college, Mr. Edwards! Like you!"

I almost cried. I determined to stick it out with my studies. Jeffrey was counting on me.

Now it is early morning—May 3, 1997—a day that will go down in history. Today is graduation day!

At Gainesville's Georgia Mountain Center, I am almost overcome with emotion. Standing outside in my black robe, mortarboard with tassel atop my head, I glance at the blue-stoned college class ring on my fifty-five-year-old plumber's work-worn hand. Tears threaten to run down my cheeks.

As the music swells, the processional begins with Brenau University's president and faculty in full academic regalia looking impressive indeed, along with trustees and guest speaker: the Honorable Edward E. Elson, United States ambassador to the kingdom of Denmark.

All those dignitaries remain standing to honor us as we file in—350 evening and weekend college undergraduates, candidates for degrees. When I hear my name echoing throughout the huge hall—EUGENE EDWARDS—somehow I get on the stage, never feeling my feet touch the floor!

I float back to my seat, beaming like a lit-up Christmas tree, clutching the tangible evidence of a long-cherished dream come true: a square of parchment with those all-important words, "Bachelor of Science Degree in Middle Grades Education."

Yessiree, my inner self is thinking, *Just goes to show you. If you dream long enough—and work hard enough—the good Lord will help make your dream come true.*

A teacher at last!

Mr. Roy would be proud.

Eugene Edwards
As told to Gloria Cassity Stargel
Chicken Soup for the Teacher's Soul

Is Fire Goddess Spelled with Two Ds?

Happiness depends upon ourselves.

—Aristotle

When I was eight years old, I saw a movie about a mysterious island that had an erupting volcano and lush jungles filled with wild animals and cannibals. The island was ruled by a beautiful woman called "Tandaleah, the Fire Goddess of the Volcano." It was a terrible, low-budget movie, but to me it represented the perfect life. Being chased by molten lava, bloodthirsty animals and savages was a small price to pay for freedom. I desperately wanted to be the Fire Goddess. I wrote it on my list of "Things to Be When I Grow Up," and asked my girlfriend if "Fire Goddess" was spelled with two Ds.

Through the years, the school system did its best to mold me into a responsible, respectable citizen, and Tandaleah was forgotten. My parents approved of my suitable marriage, and I spent the next twenty-five years being a good wife, eventually the mother of four and a very respectable, responsible member of society. My life was as bland and boring as a bowl of oatmeal. I knew exactly what to expect in the future: The children would grow up and leave home, my husband and I would grow old together and we'd baby-sit the grandchildren.

The week I turned fifty my marriage came to a sudden end. My house, furniture and everything I'd owned was auctioned off to pay debts I didn't even know existed. In a week I'd lost my husband, my home and my parents, who refused to accept a divorce in the family. I'd lost everything except my four teenaged children.

I had enough money to rent a cheap apartment while I looked for a job. Or I could use every penny I had to buy five plane tickets from Missouri to the most remote island in the world, the Big Island of Hawaii. Everyone said I was crazy to think I could just run off to an island and survive. They predicted I'd come crawling back in a month. Part of me was afraid they were right.

The next day, my four children and I landed on the Big Island of Hawaii with less than two thousand dollars, knowing no one in the world was going to help us. I rented an unfurnished apartment where we slept on the floor and lived on cereal. I worked three jobs scrubbing floors on my hands and knees, selling macadamia nuts to tourists and gathering coconuts. I worked eighteen hours a day and lost thirty pounds because I lived on one meal a day. I had panic attacks that left me curled into a knot on the bathroom floor, shaking like a shell-shocked soldier.

One night, as I walked alone on the beach, I saw the red-orange glow of the lava pouring out of the Kilauea volcano in the distance. I was wading in the Pacific Ocean, watching the world's most active volcano and wasting that incredible moment because I was haunted by the past, exhausted by the present and terrified of the future. I'd almost achieved my childhood dream—but hadn't realized it because I was focused on my burdens instead of my blessings. It was time to live my imagination—not my history.

Tandaleah, the Fire Goddess of the Volcano, had finally arrived!

The next day I quit my jobs and invested my last paycheck in art supplies and began doing what I loved. I hadn't painted a picture in fifteen years because we'd barely scratched out a living on the farm in Missouri and there hadn't been money for the tubes of paint and canvas and frames. I wondered if I could still paint or if I'd forgotten how. My hands trembled the first time I picked up a brush, but before an hour had passed I was lost in the colors spreading across the canvas in front of me. I painted pictures of old sailing ships, and as soon as I started believing in myself, other people started believing in me, too. My first painting sold for fifteen hundred dollars before I even had time to frame it.

The past six years have been filled with adventures: My children and I have gone swimming with dolphins, watched whales and hiked around the crater rim of the volcano. We wake up every morning with the ocean in front of us and the volcano behind us.

The dream I'd had more than forty years ago is now reality. I live on an island with a continuously erupting volcano. The only animals in the jungle are wild boars and mongooses and there aren't any cannibals, but often in the evening, I can hear the drums from native dancers on the beach.

Well-meaning friends have tried countless times to introduce me to their uncles, neighbors, fathers and even grandfathers, hoping I'd find a mate to save me from a lonely old age. They use phrases like, "A woman of your age . . ." and "You aren't getting any younger . . ." to push me into blind dates.

I gently point out that "a woman my age" has paid her dues. I enjoyed being a wife and mother and believe in my heart that I was a good one. I did that job for over a quarter of a century. And now at my age, I have grown into the woman I wish I could have been when I was in my twenties. No, I'm not getting any younger, but neither is anyone else, and honestly, I wouldn't want to be young again. I'm happier than I've ever been. I can paint all night and sleep all day without feeling guilty. I can cook or not cook. I can live on cream puffs and Pepsi for a week at a time and no one will lecture me on the importance of a balanced diet.

It took a long time to find myself, and I had to live alone to do it. But I am not lonely. I am free for the first time in my life. I am Tandaleah, the Fire Goddess of the Volcano, spelled with two Ds . . . and I'm living happily ever after.

Linda Stafford
Chicken Soup for the Single's Soul

Never Too Late

*One of the most courageous things you can
do is identify yourself, know who you are, what
you believe in, and where you want to go.*

—Sheila Murray Bethel

It was an unusually busy day for the hospital staff on
the sixth floor. Ten new patients were admitted and
Nurse Susan spent the morning and afternoon checking them
in. Her friend Sharron, an aide, prepared ten rooms for the
patients and made sure they were comfortable. After they
were finished she grabbed Sharron and said, "We deserve a
break. Let's go eat."

Sitting across from each other in the noisy cafeteria, Susan
noticed Sharron absently wiping the moisture off the outside
of her glass with her thumbs. Her face reflected a weariness
that came from more than just a busy day.

"You're pretty quiet. Are you tired, or is something wrong?"
Susan asked.

Sharron hesitated. However, seeing the sincere concern in
her friend's face, she confessed, "I can't do this the rest of my

life, Susan. I have to find a higher-paying job to provide for my family. We barely get by. If it weren't for my parents keeping my kids, well, we wouldn't make it."

Susan noticed the bruises on Sharron's wrists peeking out from under her jacket.

"What about your husband?"

"We can't count on him. He can't seem to hold a job. He's got . . . problems."

"Sharron, you're so good with patients, and you love working here. Why don't you go to school and become a nurse. There's financial help available, and I'm sure your parents would agree to keep the kids while you are in class."

"It's too late for me, Susan; I'm too old for school. I've always wanted to be a nurse, that's why I took this job as an aide; at least I get to care for patients."

"How old are you?" Susan asked.

"Let's just say I'm thirty-something."

Susan pointed at the bruises on Sharron's wrists. "I'm familiar with 'problems' like these. Honey, it's never too late to become what you've dreamed of. Let me tell you how I know."

Susan began sharing a part of her life few knew about. It was something she normally didn't talk about, except when it helped someone else.

"I first married when I was thirteen years old and in the eighth grade."

Sharron gasped.

"My husband was twenty-two. I had no idea he was violently abusive. We were married six years and I had three sons. One night my husband beat me so savagely he knocked out all my front teeth. I grabbed the boys and left.

"At the divorce settlement, the judge gave our sons to my husband because I was only nineteen and he felt I couldn't provide for them. The shock of him taking my babies left me gasping for air. To make things worse, my ex took the boys and moved, cutting all contact I had with them.

"Just like the judge predicted, I struggled to make ends meet. I found work as a waitress, working for tips only. Many days my meals consisted of milk and crackers. The most difficult thing was the emptiness in my soul. I lived in a tiny one-room apartment and the loneliness would overwhelm me. I longed to play with my babies and hear them laugh."

She paused. Even after four decades, the memory was still painful. Sharron's eyes filled with tears as she reached out to comfort Susan. Now it didn't matter if the bruises showed.

Susan continued, "I soon discovered that waitresses with grim faces didn't get tips, so I hid behind a smiling mask and pressed on. I remarried and had a daughter. She became my reason for living, until she went to college. Then I was back where I started, not knowing what to do with myself—until the day my mother had surgery. I watched the nurses care for her and thought: I can do that. The problem was, I only had an eighth-grade education. Going back to high school seemed like a huge mountain to conquer. I decided to take small steps toward my goal. The first step was to get my GED. My daughter used to laugh at how our roles reversed. Now I was burning the midnight oil and asking *her* questions."

Susan paused and looked directly in Sharron's eyes. "I received my diploma when I was forty-six-years-old."

Tears streamed down Sharron's cheeks. Here was someone offering the key that might unlock the door in her dark life.

"The next step was to enroll in nursing school. For two long years I studied, cried and tried to quit. But my family wouldn't let me. I remember calling my daughter and yelling, 'Do you realize how many bones are in the human body, and I have to know them all! I can't do this, I'm forty-six years old!' But I did. Sharron, I can't tell you how wonderful it felt when I received my cap and pin."

Sharron's lunch was cold, and the ice had melted in her tea by the time Susan finished talking. Reaching across the table and taking Sharron's hands, Susan said, "You don't have to put up with abuse. Don't be a victim—take charge. You will be an excellent nurse. We will climb this mountain together."

Sharron wiped her mascara-stained face with her napkin. "I had no idea you suffered so much pain. You seem like someone who has always had it together."

"I guess I've developed an appreciation for the hardships of my life," Susan answered. "If I use them to help others, then I really haven't lost a thing. Sharron, promise me that you will go to school and become a nurse. Then help others by sharing your experiences."

Sharron promised. In a few years she became a registered nurse and worked alongside her friend until Susan retired. Sharron never forgot her colleague or the rest of her promise.

Now Sharron sits across the table taking the hands of those who are bruised in body and soul, telling them, "It's never too late. We will climb this mountain together."

Linda Apple
Chicken Soup for the Working Woman's Soul

How I Got into the Movies

When I was eighteen years old, I came to America from Tel Aviv to break into the movies. It was a secret I kept from my parents, whom I had sold on the idea that I was leaving home to study journalism.

Forty-five years later, I finally lived my fantasy—a gift from my eldest son.

He is Peter David, *New York Times* bestselling author of science-fiction novels, (*Star Trek: The Next Generation, Deep Space Nine, The Hulk*), comic books, television scripts (*Babylon 5, Space Cases*) and movies.

His script, *Backlash: Oblivion II*, was being filmed in Romania. Peter wrote a cameo for me. I would have words to speak and even a close-up.

I gave up my dreams of Hollywood while in my early twenties, for a career in journalism for major city newspapers and radio stations. As a youngster, Peter was my faithful companion in the newsroom, pounding away on the typewriter with his little fingers, just like Dad. "Are you cloning this kid?" an editor asked one day. I thought I was.

Yet the invitation to join Peter in Romania was totally

unexpected. My son and I had grown apart emotionally by geographic distance and the demands of his busy career and family life. He was a husband and father of three. My wife Dalia and I saw Peter perhaps three times a year, since we live in different states. We briefly talked on the phone now and then. I knew little about his life, nor did he know much about mine. I had feelings of loss, an awareness of my own mortality, and the sense that time was running out for my firstborn and me. But I could never express any of it to Peter. He is not one for sentimentality.

Our trip to Romania began on a clear, crisp fall day at Kennedy Airport in New York. "We're going to spend so much time together, you'll be sick of me," Peter said. I assured him this would never happen. Of course, I didn't know how he would come to feel about me.

But then, above the clouds, a few hours into the trip, Peter began to open up to me. My son, outwardly so self-confident, said he felt that nothing he was writing was ever good enough. He always thought he could have done better. He also said that he had a great need for the approval of others. And sometimes he feared that his flow of ideas would suddenly dry up.

I felt badly for him, and yet I was joyous. My son was sharing himself with me as he used to when he was at home, growing up. I never shared myself with my own father. As my son and I became distant, I knew how shut out my father must have felt. Now I was exhilarated; my son was coming back to me.

The morning after arriving in Bucharest we drove to the set. In the heart of plowed Romanian fields and small farm houses, there emerged a town from another time and place—the old

American West: The General Store, Miss Kitty's saloon, the town bank, horses at the post.

Since Peter's films were a blend of westerns and science fiction, a space ship was parked at the train station. The Wild West bank was equipped with an automated teller machine.

"Incredible," I exclaimed. "This is wonderful, Peter. You have such great imagination."

He smiled. "You know how when children play, they want their parents to see them?" he said. "They want to say to their parents, 'Look at me, Mom, look at me, Dad.'"

I put my hands on his shoulders. "And you brought me here, all the way to Romania, to say, 'Look at me Dad, look at what I've accomplished'?"

Peter nodded.

At that moment, layer upon layer of emotional distance, of defenses built against disappointment and hurt, began to peel off. I felt a wonderful sense of relief, as if a physical burden had been lifted off my chest. I realized how much he loved me, as I loved him, and how he needed my acknowledgment and approval. I told him then how impressed I was with all he had accomplished, and how proud I was of him.

In the days that followed, Peter and I talked a great deal, about his life, his hopes and dreams. And I told him about mine. There, in Romania, it was as if we were back home again and he was my kid once more.

My big day came about halfway through our eleven-day stay. Peter gave me tips on how to act in front of the camera. Clad in western garb, complete with a cowboy hat, leather gloves and boots, I was installed in the General Store to do some shopping.

"Action!" yelled the director. It was a magic word.

A seven-foot actor dressed in black, wearing a tall black hat, entered. He played a funeral director with psychic powers, and his appearance often meant death would soon follow.

Upon seeing him, I stammered to the shopkeeper, "I . . . I think I'll come back later." With a great deal of noise, I dropped the canned goods I had selected on the wooden floor as I dashed out, slamming the door shut behind me.

Next came the close-up. "That's a take," the director shouted. Then he, cast and crew applauded. Leading the applause was my son.

Peter thoughtfully obtained the Western hat and gloves of my costume as mementos for me. On our last evening, as cast members were writing kind words on the title page of my script, I asked Peter to do the same.

"I can't put my feelings into just a few words," he said.

But he would put some of them into the diary he kept during the trip. He was making his final entry on his laptop computer an hour before we were to land at Kennedy.

"When I started the diary, I referred to you as my father," Peter turned to me and said. "As time went on, I began referring to you as Dad. Why do you think that is?"

Tears filled my eyes. I wanted to reach over and hug him, right there, on the plane. But I was afraid to embarrass him, and perhaps myself. So instead, I took his hand in mine and squeezed it. Tight. Real tight.

My son squeezed my hand in return.

Gunter David
Chicken Soup for the Father's Soul

Grandma Moses and Me

*The sky is my ceiling and the
ground is my carpet.*

—Judy Golladay

I'm too old and it's too late, played over and over in my mind. I was discouraged and exhausted after ending my marriage and my law career at the same time. Despite my intense desire to become a writer, I doubted my ability to succeed as one. Had I wasted years pursuing the wrong goals?

I was at a low point when the voice on the radio began telling the story of Grandma Moses. Ann Mary Moses left home at thirteen, bore ten children and worked hard to raise the five who survived. Struggling to make a living on poor farms, she managed to provide a bit of beauty for herself by embroidering on canvas.

At seventy-eight, her fingers became too stiff to hold a needle. Rather than give in to debility, she went out to the barn and began to paint. On Masonite panels she created brilliantly colored, precisely detailed scenes of country life. For the first two years, these were either given away or sold for a pittance. But at the age of seventy-nine, she was "discovered" by the art world—and the rest is history. She went on to produce more than two thousand paintings, and her book illustrations for *'Twas the Night Before Christmas* were completed in her one-hundredth year!

As I listened to the radio, my mood changed. If Grandma Moses could begin a new career and succeed after eighty, my life still had hope after thirty. Before the program ended, I charged to my computer to work on the novel I'd nearly abandoned.

It was published eight months later.

Liah Kraft-Kristaine
Chicken Soup for the Woman's Soul

The Power of Support: You Can't Do It Alone

Alone we can do so little;
together we can do so much.

—Helen Keller

The Drive of a Champion

*What do we live for if not
to make life less difficult for each other?*

—George Eliot

Having already accumulated a host of trophies since starting to play competitive golf at the age of ten, Larry Alford, at sixteen, had developed into one of the best young golf prospects in the country. Already shooting in the 70s, he was elected the most valuable player of the McCullough High School team during both his sophomore and junior years. Following his junior year, Alford matched against seventy-four of the nation's best junior golfers at the Mission Hills Desert Junior Tournament in Rancho Mirage, California. He was tied for the lead going into the final round after firing a 72 and a 71, but he dipped to a 78 in the final round, which tied him for second place, five strokes behind the winner—Tiger Woods.

Alford's performance drew the interest of coaches from some of the best college golf teams in the country, including Arizona, Arizona State, Stanford and Oklahoma State.

Wanting to stay close to home, he accepted a scholarship at the University of Houston. "Just think, everything will be taken care of, and I'll be close to home, and it won't cost you anything while I'm going to college," Alford said to his mother, Missy, "and I'll be playing for one of the best college teams in the country."

Fighting back tears, Missy Alford hugged her son tightly, knowing that he had worked so hard to earn a scholarship to make it easier for her. "That's wonderful, Larry," she said. "I'm so happy for you."

That summer, Alford worked harder than ever on his golf game, hitting hundreds of balls daily while working at the golf cart barn at The Woodlands Country Club. At night, he and one of his best friends, Brendan, waded into water hazards at nearby golf courses to retrieve golf balls. Salvaging as many as two thousand a night, they sold them for eighteen cents apiece, which enabled Larry to play more golf that summer. His paychecks from his golfing job went to his mother, an art teacher who also made and sold decorative wreaths and did wallpapering. "That's Larry," his father, Larry Alford Sr., said. "Finishing second in the biggest junior golf tournament of the year and then wading into water hazards to fish out golf balls. In no way was success going to change him."

Late that summer, a golf teammate asked if Larry could do him a favor and drive the teammate's father's Corvette to a relative's house. The teammate in turn would follow in his car and then drive Larry home. Larry said fine and off they went. Shortly after 6 P.M., while it was still broad daylight, Larry lost control of the Corvette on Interstate 45. The car flipped over three times, catapulting Alford through the open sun roof and onto the highway. Alford's friend braked his car to a halt and saw his teammate lying motionless and bleeding badly from the head, face and left arm.

In the emergency room at Hermann Hospital in Houston, a doctor emerged from behind a curtain and asked Larry's parents to come in. *Oh my God!* Mrs. Alford screamed to herself on seeing her son, who was the color of gray ice with a head as big as a basketball. Out of the corner of one eye, she saw what she perceived to be a look of horror on the face of one doctor.

"I got the feeling that they wanted us to see Larry once more, maybe for the last time," Missy recalled. Then, as she and Larry Sr. were led out, she pleaded to herself, *Dear God, please save him.*

From the moment Larry Alford arrived at Hermann Hospital, Dr. James "Red" Duke, the hospital's chief trauma surgeon, knew that his severed left arm could not be saved. Far more important was a life-threatening head injury. Then there were the lesser injuries: a fractured eye orbital bone that had jarred Larry's eye partially out of its socket, a broken jaw, ankle and shoulder blade, a collapsed lung and a badly injured right arm. "I'm sorry, but we had to amputate your son's arm below the elbow," Dr. John Burns, an orthopedic surgeon, told Larry's parents.

"Is he going to be all right?" Missy Alford asked.

"We don't know," Dr. Burns answered.

Standing alongside Missy was Jay Hall, a friend of hers who could not help but wonder about Larry's reaction to the loss of his left arm if he were indeed going to survive. *How would Larry ever get along without golf?* Hall thought to himself. But then, catching himself in mid-thought, Hall also realized there was a far more pressing matter than a golf career at stake. *They've got to save Larry's life,* he said to himself. *That's all that matters right now.*

For almost ninety days Larry Alford remained unconscious and in critical condition. Then, gradually, his condition improved and he was no longer in danger. But his parents knew that difficult days lay ahead. For one thing, he would eventually learn that he had lost his left hand.

One night Larry awakened and suddenly realized that his left hand was missing. He cried out for a nurse. One hurried into his room and said softly, "I'm sorry, Larry, but they had to amputate your hand." Meanwhile, his father, alerted, raced to the hospital.

"Dad, how am I ever going to play golf?" he asked.

"Don't worry, Larry," his father replied. "You'll play again, and you'll do fine."

Young Alford did not remain depressed for long. "Mom, I did it to myself," he said one day to his mother, "so I'm to blame. And God saved my life, so I'm lucky."

A few weeks later, while talking about golf, Larry turned to his father and asked, "Dad, do you have my clubs with you?"

"Yeah, I've got them in the trunk of the car, Larry."

"Good," Larry said excitedly. "Can you get my pitching wedge? Maybe we can chip some balls outside."

Within minutes Larry and his father were on the lawn outside the Del Oro Institute in Houston where Larry was recuperating. Although he had lost forty pounds and was weak, young Larry began to chip with his right arm. Ball after ball went soaring in beautiful arcs as both father and son looked on in delight.

"Dad, will you look at those shots," Larry said, ecstatic at swinging a golf club again.

"You're doing great, Son, just great," his father replied, heartened by Larry's joy.

A week later, at young Larry's suggestion, he and his father went out to play a round of golf at one of the four courses at The Woodlands Country Club. Understandably, Larry's father was both happy and apprehensive.

God, I hope he does all right, Mr. Alford said to himself. *Don't let him be upset.*

Larry Alford Sr. needn't have worried. Though still weak and lacking in stamina, his son hit his shots cleanly and accurately during his first outing as a one-handed golfer. His chipping and putting in particular were superb. "Boy, Dad, this is great," he said at one point as he and his father walked down a fairway.

At the end of eighteen holes, Larry had shot an 86, about ten strokes above his average before his accident, but an extraordinary score for a one-handed golfer. As they headed for the clubhouse, Larry, obviously elated at how he had played, turned to his father and said, "Dad, do you think that I can still make the PGA Tour?"

Larry Sr. was prepared for the question. "Yes, I do," he replied. "But I think we're going to have to take this one day at a time."

After that, and unbeknownst to Larry, Jay Hall began calling prosthetic manufacturers to find out if there was such a thing as an artificial golf hand on the market that would enable Larry to play competitive golf. Finding none, Hall decided that he, himself, would try to design a golf hand for

Larry on his own. "First, I had to ask myself just what does the left hand do on a golf swing for a right-handed golfer," said Hall, a professional psychologist and a good golfer himself. "And the answer is quite simple. It holds the club with three fingers and it hinges or cocks the club. Essentially, it provides those two functions, and that's about all."

Of paramount importance, Hall knew, was that the hand had to grip the club firmly enough so that the handle wouldn't be twisted by the force of the swing. To ensure that, Hall designed the palm of the hand with pumped-up air cells. For the wrist, he came up with a ball and socket mechanism, which Hall felt could perform the function of a human joint.

Hall then took his design to Ted Muilenburg, the owner of a prosthetics company in Houston. "Jay knew nothing about prosthetics, and I knew nothing about golf," Muilenburg said.

"But I must say I was impressed with his design—so much so that we went ahead and made 'The Halford Grip,'" as it came to be known, blending Larry and Jay's last names. Muilenburg used an aluminum child's knee prosthesis for the wrist and some air cells, which when inflated, fit tightly around the grip on the golfing hand like human fingers. Then a silicone suction sleeve, which slides over the elbow to hold the hand in place, was attached.

Seeing the mold the first time, Missy's eyes brimmed with tears, as she envisioned her son's reaction to the hand, which she was going to give to him on Christmas morning. "It'll work," Hall said, after looking over what Muilenburg had brought. "I know it's going to work."

Unwrapping the last Christmas gift of the day, Larry peeked inside the box and, a look of amazement on his face, cried out. "It's a hand—my golf hand."

"It was Jay's idea," Missy said to her son. "He even designed it."

Overwhelmed with emotion, Larry threw his arms around Jay. "Thanks so much."

The Halford Grip has been a rousing success, although a number of adjustments have been made over the years. Larry explained, "Some golfers, seeing how well my golf hand works, have said they'd like to trade arms with me, but I tell them, 'No way.'"

Since receiving his golf hand, Alford has shot his lowest score ever—a 69. He also recorded his first hole-in-one and played three years of varsity golf at Sam Houston University. Since his graduation in 1997, Alford has worked as an assistant golf pro at his home course, The Woodlands Country Club, and has helped raise money for a number of charities by challenging golfers to try to get closer to the pin than he has on par-3 holes. "Not many people have," said Alford, who shoots in the 70s and booms his tee-shots more than 250 yards.

"My accident has been a blessing for me," said Alford, who delivers inspirational talks to young people in schools and churches in the Houston area. "It happened for a reason. I thank God for saving my life, for giving me such a positive attitude and then giving me a second chance as a golfer. As for having to play with only one real arm, I tell people that golf is hard enough with two hands, so it can't be that much harder with one."

Jack Cavanaugh
Chicken Soup for the Golfer's Soul

Riding Tandem

In 1998, my father and I set out from Denver, Colorado, to take part in the Vietnam Challenge—a sixteen-day, twelve-hundred-mile bicycle trek from Hanoi in the north to Ho Chi Minh, a city in the south. It was my first time to Vietnam and my dad's second. He had been a fighter pilot in the Vietnam War, flying over a hundred missions, and he hadn't been back since.

Since I am blind, my father and I rode a tandem bike. I wasn't always ecstatic, however, to be connected nine hours a day to my dad.

Not only did we have to ride together, our feet spinning on the pedals at an identical pace, but we also dressed the part. We wore the same tight uniforms and helmets and, when my sunglasses broke early into our trip, my dad came to the rescue with an extra pair of his "coke-bottle" prescription sunglasses.

"We're twins," my father needled.

"Yeah, right," is all I could muster. Regularly, a teammate would pull up beside us and yell, "Weihenmayer squared, how you doing?"

"I feel like a square in these dorky glasses," I'd mutter back. And yet, for all my misgivings about my father, as we cycled forth, I learned more and more about this rather private man. While passing the former DMZ, the demilitarized zone, my dad remarked, "I know this sounds corny, but even after all these years, when I hear President Kennedy's speech, 'Ask not what your country can do for you but what you can do for your country,' I still get choked up." He spoke the words as if he were admitting a precious secret. And maybe he was. I was astonished at my dad's ability to hang on to his optimism, his faith in country, when others around him became jaded.

I come from a generation of cynics. We were taught that patriotism was for the naive, and that it had died in the battlefields of South Vietnam. Even when I was younger, and the *Star Spangled Banner* played before a football game, my father would bellow out the words with unabashed gusto, his bass, ex-Marine Corps voice drowning out the mumbled sounds of me and my brothers. I'd feel my brother's elbow in my ribs and we'd both share an embarrassed chuckle.

In college, after completing a history of war class, I would argue with him, "You can't just blindly do what your country tells you to do. You have to follow your own conscience. You have to ask whether your country's cause is also your cause."

"Patriotism isn't learned in a textbook," he shot back angrily. "What if every American put his own concerns above those of his country? Where would we be now?" While I had made the argument more out of an exercise in historical debate, I was taken aback by the ferocity of his defense.

Halfway through the Vietnam Challenge, my dad and I faced our own challenge as we pedaled our tandem toward the

Hai Van Pass. Rising 3,280 feet out of the coastal plains, this six-mile stretch of road with a ten-percent grade, separated the former North from the South. It was, by far, the most physically demanding part of our entire ride; on this hot and humid day, despite our differences, we would need to be a team.

My father had been the captain of the Princeton football team. He admitted that he wasn't the best athlete, but perhaps the most "enthusiastic." Twice, on kick-offs, he had hit his opponent so hard he had knocked himself out. My dad loved a challenge, and the Hai Van Pass was that and more.

For a while, we climbed gradually, but then the road became progressively steeper. As I pedaled, I couldn't stop thinking of our experience the day before in the dusty parking lot of the My Lai War Crimes Museum. I recalled my father's words, his reluctant tears.

I had heard him cry only twice in my life, once when his father died and again after the death of my mother. But there he was, hot tears rolling down and burning into his proud face. "I am not a war criminal," he said. "I had a friend, Gus," he continued, his words coming in concentrated bursts, "He got married to the same woman three times. They kept splitting up and then getting married again. His tour of duty was done. He was going home, but on his last day he volunteered for one more mission." Dad took a deep breath. "Gus's plane was lost somewhere over North Vietnam. How can I believe that he died for nothing? I'm not proud of any war," he said softly, "but I am proud of my service to my country."

Listening to my dad against a backdrop of the Vietnamese anthem being piped out over loudspeakers, I was beginning to understand that, for my father, the meaning of patriotism was inextricably linked to the meaning of his own life. I awkwardly reached out and touched his shoulder. It was as though I were tenuously stepping out of one role and into another.

In the past, it had always been my father putting his hand on my shoulder. Just after I went blind at thirteen, our family started going on hikes together. My father would put his hand on my shoulder and inexpertly steer me over steep rocky trails. The system was imperfect and at times, after a poorly placed foot, we would find ourselves bouncing down the side of a trail. In spite of the jarring force of our falls, I could feel my father still hanging onto my shirt—refusing to let go.

On the back of our tandem bike, facing the steepest section of the Hai Van Pass, this would be my chance to do something for him. I wanted my legs to be the force that would power our small team up the steep switchbacks to the top. "We'll go as slow as you want, but we won't stop," I commanded. But hearing my father's heaving breaths, I backed off. "We can stop if you want." He kept pedaling.

Each time we reached a switchback, the road would steepen further and I'd feel my father purposely weave our bike back and forth, creating mini-switchbacks in the road. I'd pour my muscle and mind into pedaling until I felt the grade ease again. Then I'd attempt to relax and get into a new rhythm, waiting for the next rise. I wouldn't have to wait very long. Sometimes, I'd feel my father attacking the steep sections as he would attack an opposing lineman, exhausting himself in the effort. "Relax!" I'd coach. "Slow and steady until we get there."

"Another half mile," my father groaned, and I could tell he was barely hanging on. I was tired, too, and could feel my legs losing strength like a deflating tire. I could hear cheers carrying down to us from the top. It still seemed like a long way to go.

I maintained the rhythm of our pedaling. I wouldn't let us quit. "Only a hundred yards," I heard my father gasp, and I could hear the cheers growing nearer. It was only a few seconds after that exclamation of confidence that we hit a huge rock in the middle of the road. My dad had been concentrating so hard looking up the road to the finish that he hadn't seen it.

Our bike toppled over. Both of us were too tired to react. I hit the ground, rolling through the fall and was up in time to help my father, who didn't move quite so quickly. We pushed the bike the last few yards. "I feel a little dizzy, just a little dizzy," he admitted, as we walked the bike through the flock of people who had gathered to greet our team.

Away from the crowd, I stood beside the tandem with a single, persistent thought in my head. The bullheaded optimism that had kept my father charging along through the years, even against a torrent of cynicism, had also burrowed itself into my life and had given me strength. My father and I do not have a "touchy-feely" relationship. Rather, in my family, love is expressed in subtler ways.

At the top of the pass, for only the second time on the trip, I put my hand on my father's shoulder. "Good job!" I said. "*Great* job!" I was talking to him, to myself, to the both of us. We had done it together.

At our final team dinner, Diana Nyad, the world's great long-distance swimmer, recounted some inspirational words from a conversation she once had with my father.

"I have lived through a war," my father told her. "I watched my son go blind. I saw my wife die in a car accident. Some people think I'm unfeeling. But what am I supposed to do? How am I supposed to act? Should I have given up? Should I have quit? Life is too precious, and all I can do is live it."

As I listened to Diana share my dad's words, I felt like I was emerging from a long dream. For over two weeks now, I had been connected to my father by the frame of a tandem bike, but I hadn't always been connected to his story. Like my father, I, too, had struggled with my blindness and with the crushing sadness of my mother's death; like my father, I, too, had chosen to live, and in that way, I thought, my father and I were the same. Sitting at the dinner, reflecting on our bike ride across Vietnam, I was proud of my father, proud of myself, but especially proud to be my father's son.

Erik Weihenmayer
Chicken Soup for the Traveler's Soul

Hall of Fame

"From Hall of Shame to Hall of Fame" read a recent headline when I received the honor of being one of only five teachers inducted into the National Teachers Hall of Fame. Who would ever have imagined that an overweight, rebellious high-school dropout in the late 1960s would become teacher of the year? It certainly wasn't something my parents, my teachers or even I would have thought possible.

As many teens today, I was a confused and angry sixteen-year-old with low self-esteem. Not only was I extremely over-weight, but as my grades began to plummet, I gave up trying to compete with my older sister, Donna. She was head cheer-leader, prom queen and valedictorian—much as I wanted to be but couldn't. It was much easier to get attention by being the class clown, and the only honor I received in high school was being voted "wittiest." Eventually, however, I became more pathetic than funny when I began drinking, hanging out with the wrong crowd and eventually running away from home.

My mom and dad were hard-working middle-class parents who did all they could to provide a good home. They had been at school with my teachers numerous times, had taken me to doctors, counselors and always bailed me out of trouble or jail whenever they could. The last time I ran away, they couldn't find me for weeks as I stayed any place I could find. I soon found out that the freedom for which I had longed was full of empty promises, nowhere to live, no money and much danger. Once again, as the prodigal child, I found my way home to the family that welcomed me back with open arms. This time, however, their unconditional love set much-needed boundaries and I had to agree to their rules as I reluctantly returned to school.

The first day back was as miserable as I had anticipated. I heard all the names as my peers jeered, "Hey Fatso!" or "The jailbird is back!" I probably would have run away again had it not been for a familiar voice from the end of the hall. Mrs. Alma Sitton, who let us fondly call her "Miss Alma," had been one teacher who had always treated me with respect and dignity. However, she was tough on all of us and immersed us in literature, grammar and speaking. We all knew that if we missed one day of Miss Alma's class, she had neat stacks of make-up work ready to distribute. Now that I had been gone for weeks I would never catch up!

Ignoring the taunts of my classmates, I dutifully trudged down the hall as Miss Alma called to me. As expected, she ushered me into her warm familiar classroom, near the table of missed assignments. I said nothing as I rolled my eyes, bit my tongue and waited for a lecture to accompany the piles of missed homework. But what came next was totally unexpected. Miss Alma turned toward me with her back to the table and did the most paradoxical, most unbelievable thing that a teacher had ever done to me. She quietly closed the door, put her purplish ditto-streaked hands on my shoulders, looked me straight in the eyes, down to my soul, and then put her arms around me! As she hugged me, softly in my ear Miss Alma whispered, "Debbie, God has great plans for your life if you'll let him. And I'm here for you, too." I vaguely remember the piles of papers she began explaining, but I will never forget her loving smile that elicited the same from me. That ten-second gift of hope and encouragement has lasted thirty years. I don't remember the stacks of missed assignments, but it was at that point that Miss Alma became my hero.

It may have been a surprise to my entire hometown that I of all people would become a high-school teacher of English, speech and drama—just as Miss Alma had been. But it was no surprise to me—or Miss Alma. Twenty years later, having lost one hundred pounds, married and teaching in St. Louis, I was selected as teacher of the year. I was compelled to return to my hometown and thank the one who had so inspired me. Miss Alma, retired, was serving at her church social—fish and loaves of bread! How appropriate! As I approached her, I was immediately transformed into that same insecure, anxious teenager, unable to speak. Once again I was enveloped in that warm, encouraging hug. "Oh, Debbie! Look at you! You've lost a hundred pounds! And I heard you have become a teacher— I am so proud of you." I wanted to tell her what an inspiration she had been, how much I wanted to thank her for not only saving my life but also for inspiring me to be all that I watched her model. But I was too choked up to say much of anything at the time.

Now that I have traveled throughout the United States as a member of the National Teachers Hall of Fame, speaking to thousands of schools, businesses and churches, I have always included the inspiring story of Miss Alma. But next week will be the highlight of all speaking engagements. I have been invited to speak at Miss Alma's church. I know I will sob as I tell the Miss Alma story and finally have the opportunity to publicly thank her for being such a role model, such an encourager and the very reason I became a teacher. I have learned that kids don't care how much you know until they know how much you care. Above all else, I can't wait to feel her arms around me one more time and to tell her that I have passed on that hug and encouragement to over ten thousand other "Debbies" who also needed to be reminded that "God has great plans for their lives." I am so proud that many of my former students have also become teachers. The greatest compliment I have received is hearing the words, "Mrs. Peppers, you are my Miss Alma." And so her legacy lives on.

Debra Peppers, Ph.D.
Chicken Soup for the Teacher's Soul

CHANGING THE WORLD
ONE STORY AT A TIME

Dear Chicken Soup for the Soul,

The highlight of my publication in *Chicken Soup for the Teacher's Soul* was when I was contacted by one of my former high-school classmates who was organizing a reunion for classes graduating in the fifties and sixties (We had a very small high school). She asked if I would deliver a tribute to the ninety-three-year-old "Miss Alma" as I presented her a copy of *Chicken Soup for the Teacher's Soul.* After a ten-minute standing ovation for this precious lady who had taught for fifty years, we heard story after story of the many lives she had affected just as she had mine. Had it not been for "Miss Alma," I wouldn't have gone from troubled teen to Teacher of the Year, and had it not been for my story in *Chicken Soup for the Teacher's Soul,* she may never have known what an impact her life had on so many, including me! Thank you for the endless encouragement you allow through *Chicken Soup!*

Debra D. Peppers, Ph.D.

A Hundred and One Atlantic Nights

I arrived home to a message light flashing on the answering machine. Nothing really out of the ordinary, and yet I had an uneasy sense about it. I pushed the button and listened to the devastated voice of my twenty-one-year-old son, Daniel: "I'm guttered, Mum, Jaish can't do it!"

I gasped, feeling his disappointment and my own as well. Three months before, in the fall of 1995, Daniel's old school chum Jaishan had asked Danny to team up with him and enter the Great Atlantic Rowing Race and row from Tenerife, Canary Islands, to Port St. Charles, Barbados. He had accepted with great excitement. They paid the entrance fee, and planning began immediately.

I was excited to be able to use my background in public relations to help promote them, get the specially designed rowing boat custom built and help raise the needed funds. We had two years.

Both boys were British army cadets and needed permission for the time off. Danny's request had been accepted. Now we knew Jaish's request had been turned down. I reassured

Daniel that he would easily find another partner.

"It's not that easy, Mum. I need someone who can commit the next two years to promotion, fund-raising, training and skills acquisition. But mostly it has to be someone I can spend three months alone with on a twenty-three-foot boat!"

I'm not really sure what happened next. I don't know whether he asked or I offered. All I know is that at the end of the conversation I had agreed to become his new partner and row across the Atlantic with him—we were a team!

My beloved second husband Keith had died of cancer a few years before, and my old life was gone. I was fifty years old and a widow. My life felt empty and had no direction. The prospect of spending the next two years preparing for an adventure was very exciting, and the opportunity to share this unique experience with my son was irresistible. Once I had decided, there was no going back. He was offering me a once-in-a-lifetime opportunity, and I was going to seize it.

The commitment to row the Atlantic had been made. Now came the logistics. Money was a major issue. I had a marketing job, but there was no way it would begin to finance this project. So off I went to the bank.

As the former mayor of my hometown of Chipping Norton, I was fairly well known, so I did have some hopes. But when all was said and done, my presentation still sounded like a fifty-year-old widowed woman asking for a loan so she could row the Atlantic with her son. Right! So I mortgaged my home, my two-hundred-year-old little stone cottage.

We were officially a team.

When our custom-built ocean-going rowing boat was completed, we ceremoniously named it *Carpe Diem*—Seize the

Day! We began training sessions together, mostly on the Thames. Daniel began to feel quite guilty because of the financial burden he felt he had placed on me. At one point I realized, *My God, if this doesn't work, I could lose my house!* But we didn't have time for thoughts like those. We each brought our own unique skills to the venture. I knew it was my job to get us to the starting line in the Canary Islands, and Captain Daniel would get us to the finish line in Barbados.

When I finally got up the courage to tell my own mum of our plans, to my delight she offered no guilt, fear or negativity. Instead her response was: "The years between fifty and sixty go like that!" and she snapped her fingers. "DO IT! And I'm utterly behind you."

October 12, 1997, finally arrived. After two years of hard work, we departed Los Gigantes Tenerife along with twenty-nine other teams. At fifty-three, I was the oldest participant, and we were the only mother-and-son team. Our boat was designed with two rowing seats, one behind the other. For the first six hours we rowed together. After that, we began the routine we would maintain for the next one hundred days. Two hours of solo rowing, and then two hours of sleep in the tiny cabin in the bow. For the first week out, Danny was sick with food poisoning, and I had to be captain and in charge. It proved to us both that I could in fact pull my own weight on the water.

Once Daniel was better, we fell into a comfortable routine that bonded us together into a wonderful new partnership. Sometimes he would be sleeping so soundly that I would row for another hour or so. Often Dan would do the same—row for another hour or so and let his mum sleep. Our obvious kindness toward each other was awesome, and I found my son's kindness toward me to be overwhelming. We were a rowing team, yes, but in the larger picture we were still mother and son, loving and caring for each other unconditionally. If either of us could have given the other a full eight hours' sleep, we would have done so in a flash.

The constant rolling and heaving of the boat, the constant dampness and humidity, the lack of sleep and comfort and, of course, the heavy rowing all began to take a toll on my body that deeply worried us both. My hands were red and raw and stiff like claws. I had boils on my bottom and I began to suffer from sciatica. There was swelling in my hip from a muscle I had torn prior to departure, and my shoulder was injured from being thrown across the boat in high seas. Danny was worried that his drive to achieve his goal was going to permanently damage his mum, and I was worried that the frailty of my fifty-three-year-old body was going to destroy my son's dream. I suddenly felt old and a burden on the venture. But then Daniel began to experience many of the same pains, and I knew it wasn't just me, but the extraordinary conditions we were living under.

Throughout the trip, there were many things that made us think about giving up. There were the hard days when we blamed each other. "How could you do this to your poor mum?" I would shout. "This is all YOUR fault!" And Daniel would yell back, "I didn't expect you to say 'Yes!'" But in truth, we decided that the only thing that would have *really* made us give up was if a whale had smashed our boat. Daniel laughs now and says, "And oh my God, how many times we prayed for that!"

We were astonished as to how something as small as a rainbow, or a fish leaping out of the water could instantly cheer us up when we were low. In addition, before we left, we had all our friends and relatives write poems and letters to us, and seal and date them. That way, we had mail to open on each day of our journey. The humor and love in these letters picked us up and carried us when times got really rough.

We also had on board a radar beacon that allowed us to be tracked exactly. Each night the positions of all the boats were posted on the Internet, and our friends and family were able to track us. My own sweet mum rowed the Atlantic with me every night in her dreams. My stepfather drew a map to scale on the wall, and each night friends would call and report our position to my mum. They would then plot our course on that map. In a way, it was three generations rowing the Atlantic.

Both Daniel and I took a careful selection of books and taped music along. If you think rowing the Atlantic is boring, you should try *not* rowing! After a while, for variety, we began to trade books and listen to each other's music. Daniel began to appreciate my classical choices, and I began to enjoy listening to his reggae and UB40!

Every team in this race had its own reasons for participating. Some were committed to winning. We, however, were doing it for the challenge and the opportunity to spend this unique time together. Knowing we would not win, we took two hours off each night, and sat and enjoyed dinner, and talked. We told each other the stories and anecdotes of our lives, things that might not otherwise have been shared over a lifetime. One night over dinner I said, "This is a little bit like Scheherazade, you know, the story of *A Thousand and One Arabian Nights!*" Daniel replied, "Yes, Mum! Perhaps we should call our book *A Hundred and One Atlantic Nights!*" By complete coincidence (or was it?), that's exactly how many nights it took to cross—101!

On the night of January 22, 1998, we were approaching Barbados, thinking we still had twenty miles to go. We were loafing, savoring the last night of our long adventure together. One last time, my son began to make me a cup of hot chocolate and turned on his headlamp for a few moments. Suddenly the radio began to squawk. It was an escort boat, and they were looking for us. When we identified ourselves as *Carpe Diem,* we heard a lot of screaming and shouting on board: "It's them, it's them, they're safe!" They had seen Daniel's light for those few moments and were hoping it might be us. Then they told us to our shock and delight that we actually had only six miles left to go! Daniel rowed the first four, and allowed me, his aching but ecstatic mum, to row the last two. I would be the one to take us across the line of longitude that was the official finish line.

To our amazement, an entire flotilla of waiting boats carrying family and friends began to cheer. They then set off fireworks, lighting up the night sky, accompanied by the triumphant cannons of the *1812 Overture* to welcome us and celebrate our safe arrival. The thrill of our accomplishment filled me in that moment, and I burst into tears and cried out, "We've done it!! Oh Daniel, we've done it!"

Because of the heavy headwind, and our great fatigue, we chose to board the waiting escort boat, while our own weary little *Carpe Diem,* half filled with water and listing to one side, was towed in behind us. We were almost two months behind the winning KIWI team and thought that everyone would have forgotten about us—after all, we were the last boat in. But we were surprised and truly overwhelmed at the enormous welcome we received upon our arrival! Everyone wanted to meet and congratulate "Jan and Dan," the British mother-and-son team who had successfully rowed across the Atlantic and completed the race.

Aboard the escort boat we had an emotional reunion with my daughter, Daniel's sister Becky. And there was one more lovely surprise! Waiting for us on shore with tears and hugs was my own sweet mum, who had come all the way from her home in France, to welcome her jubilant daughter and grandson.

When I try and put into words what we will remember most, my journal entry from day sixty-nine speaks most poignantly of the things only my heart would know. I wrote:

> *I don't believe it is the beauty, the dolphins, whales, dawns and sunsets, although they will be with me forever. The brilliant night sky, stars, delicate new moons, brilliant full 'bright as day' moons. The power and the glory of the ocean.*
>
> *No. It is finding out how one's body and mind learn to cope. Seeing how Daniel bears up. I have found such pride in his unfailing good temper and optimism—his intrinsic kindness and thoughtfulness. I have loved the baby, the child, the boy, I have been proud of them, but now I love and admire the man, Daniel, with all my heart.*

For the rest of our lives, no matter where they may take us, we will always have the memory of this special time together, and the pride in the spectacular accomplishment that was ours, and only ours.

We did it. Together.

Jan Meek with Daniel Byles
As told to Janet Matthews
Chicken Soup for the Parent's Soul

The Kindness of Strangers

The little things?
The little moments? They aren't little.

—Jon Kabat-Zinn

One summer I was driving from my hometown of Tahoe City, California, to New Orleans. In the middle of the desert, I came upon a young man standing by the roadside. He had his thumb out and held a gas can in his other hand.

I drove right by him.

Someone else will stop for him, I reasoned. *Besides, that gas can is just a ploy to flag down a car and rob the driver.*

Several states later, I was still thinking about the hitchhiker. Leaving him stranded in the desert didn't bother me as much as how easily I'd reached the decision. I never even lifted my foot off the accelerator. *Does anyone stop anymore?* I wondered.

There was a time in this country when you'd be considered a jerk if you passed by somebody in need. Now you're a fool for helping. With gangs, drug addicts, murderers, rapists, thieves and car jackers lurking everywhere, why risk it? "I don't want to get involved" has become a national motto.

I thought of my destination—New Orleans, the setting for Tennessee Williams's play *A Streetcar Named Desire*. I recalled Blanche Dubois's famous line: "I have always depended on the kindness of strangers."

The kindness of strangers. It sounds so quaint. Could anyone rely on the kindness of strangers these days?

One way to test this would be for a person to journey from coast to coast without any money, relying solely on the goodwill of his fellow Americans. What kind of America would he find? Who would feed him, shelter him, carry him down the road?

The idea intrigued me. But who'd be crazy enough to try such a trip? *Well,* I figured, *why not me?*

The week I turned thirty-seven, I realized I'd never taken a gamble in my life. So I decided to make a leap of faith a continent wide—to go from the Pacific to the Atlantic without a penny. If I was offered money, I'd refuse it. I'd accept only rides, food and a place to rest my head. It would be a cashless journey through the land of the almighty dollar. As my final destination I chose the region of Cape Fear in North Carolina, a symbol of all the fears I'd have to conquer to go the distance.

I rose early on September 6, 1994, hoisted a fifty-pound pack onto my back and headed from the Golden Gate Bridge. Then I took a sign from my backpack, displaying my destination to passing vehicles: "America."

Drivers mouthed the word through windshields, then smiled. Two women rode by on bicycles. "It's a bit vague," said one. A young man with a German accent wandered up and asked, "Where is this 'America'?" Indeed.

For six weeks I tried to find out. I hitched eighty-two rides and covered 4,223 miles across fourteen states. As I traveled, I discovered that others shared my fear. Folks were always warning me about someplace else. In Montana they said watch out for the cowboys in Wyoming. In Nebraska they told me people aren't as nice in Iowa.

Yet I was treated with kindness in every state I traveled. I was amazed by the stubborn capacity of Americans to help a stranger, even when it seemed to run contrary to their own best interest. One day in Nebraska a four-door sedan pulled to the road shoulder. When I reached the window, I saw two little old ladies dressed in their Sunday finest.

"I know you're not supposed to pick up hitchhikers, but it's so far between towns out here, you feel bad passing a person," said the driver, who introduced herself as Vi. She and her sister Helen were going to see an eye doctor in Ainsworth, Nebraska.

I didn't know whether to kiss them or scold them for stopping. This woman was telling me she'd rather risk her life than feel bad about passing a stranger on the side of the road. When they dropped me at a highway junction, I looked at Vi. We both spoke at the same time: "Be careful."

Once when I was hitchhiking unsuccessfully in the rain, a trucker pulled over, locking his brakes so hard he skidded on the grass shoulder. The driver told me he was once robbed at knifepoint by a hitchhiker. "But I hate to see a man stand out in the rain," he added. "People don't have no heart anymore."

I found, however, that compassion was the norm. A middle-aged Iowa couple shepherded me around for an hour, trying to help me find a campground. In South Dakota a woman whose family had given me a night's lodging handed me two stamped postcards: one to let her know how my trip turned out, the other to send the next day, telling her where I was so she wouldn't worry about me.

Hearing I had no money and would take none, people in every state bought me food or shared whatever they happened to have with them. A park ranger in Ukiah, California, gave me some carrots. A college student handed me sacks filled with organic tomatoes, zucchini and melons. A woman in Iowa gave me two bundles of graham crackers, two cans of soda, two cans of tuna, two apples and two pieces of chicken—a veritable Noah's Ark sack of lunches.

The people who had the least to give often gave the most. In Oregon, a house painter named Mike noted the chilly weather and asked if I had a coat. When I replied, "a light one," he drove me to his house, rummaged through his garage and handed me a bulky green Army-style jacket.

Elsewhere in Oregon a lumber-mill worker named Tim invited me to a simple dinner with his family in their dilapidated house. He gave me a Bible. Then he offered me his tent. I refused, knowing it was probably one of the family's most valuable possessions. But Tim was determined that I have it, and finally I agreed to take it.

I was grateful to all the people I met for their rides, their food, their shelter, their gifts. But the kindest act of all was when they merely were themselves.

One day I walked into the local Chamber of Commerce in Jamestown, Tennessee. A man inside the old stone building jumped up from his cluttered desk. "Come on in," said Baxter Wilson, fifty-nine. He was the executive director.

When I asked him about camping in the area, he handed me a brochure for a local campground. "Would you like me to call for you?" he asked.

Seeing that it cost twelve dollars, I replied, "No, that's all right. I'm not sure what I'm going to do."

Then he saw my backpack. "Most anybody around here will let you pitch a tent on their land, if that's what you want," he said.

Now we're talking, I thought. "Any particular direction?" I asked.

"Tell you what. I've got a big farm about ten miles south of here. If you're here at 5:30, you can ride with me."

I accepted, and we drove out to a magnificent country house. Suddenly I realized he'd invited me to spend the night in his home.

His wife, Carol, was cooking a pot roast when we walked into the kitchen. A seventh-grade science teacher, she was the picture of Southern charm.

Baxter explained that local folks were "mountain stay-at-home people," and he considered himself one of them. "We rarely entertain in our house," he said. "When we do, it's usually kin." The revelation made my night there all the more special.

The next morning when I came downstairs, Carol asked if I'd come to her school in Allardt and talk to her class about my trip. I told her I didn't want to encourage a bunch of seventh-graders to hitchhike across the United States (in fact, in some states it's illegal). But Carol said the kids should be exposed to what else is out there—the good and the bad. "They need to know," she said.

I agreed, and before long had been scheduled to talk to every class in the school. All the kids were well-mannered and attentive. Their questions kept coming: Where were people kindest? How many pairs of shoes did I have? Had anybody tried to run me over? Were the pigs' feet as good in other parts of the country? Had I fallen in love with anyone? What was I most afraid of?

And my favorite, from a meek little girl with glasses and freckles, "You wanna eat lunch with us?"

Afterward Carol told me that one of the kids I spoke to was ordinarily quite shy. After class he came up to her and announced, "I want to grow up to be a journalist and go to all the places he's been."

I was touched. When I left San Francisco, I was thinking only of myself. I never considered that my trip might affect a child in Tennessee. This reminded me that no matter how hard we try, nothing we do is in a vacuum.

Although I hadn't planned it this way, I discovered that a patriotic tone ran through the talks that I gave that afternoon. I told the students how my faith in America had been renewed. I told them how proud I was to live in a country where people were still willing to help out a stranger.

Then with only one more state to go and my journey almost over, a realization hit me: It took giving up money to have the richest experience of my life. I knew that wherever I might go, I would always remember my continental leap of faith and the country that caught me.

Mike McIntyre
A 6th Bowl of Chicken Soup for the Soul

Be Willing
to Pay the Price

*Start by doing what is necessary;
then do what's possible; and suddenly
you are doing the impossible.*

—Saint Francis of Assisi

Willing to Pay the Price

When my wife Maryanne and I were building our Greenspoint Mall hair salon thirteen years ago, a Vietnamese fellow would stop by each day to sell us doughnuts. He spoke hardly any English, but he was always friendly and through smiles and sign language, we got to know each other. His name was Le Van Vu.

During the day Le worked in a bakery and at night he and his wife listened to audio tapes to learn English. I later learned that they slept on sacks full of sawdust on the floor of the back room of the bakery.

In Vietnam the Van Vu family was one of the wealthiest in Southeast Asia. They owned almost one-third of North Vietnam, including huge holdings in industry and real estate. However, after his father was brutally murdered, Le moved to South Vietnam with his mother, where he went to school and eventually became a lawyer.

Like his father before him, Le prospered. He saw an opportunity to construct buildings to accommodate the ever-expanding American presence in South Vietnam and soon became one of the most successful builders in the country.

On a trip to the North, however, Le was captured by the North Vietnamese and thrown into prison for three years. He escaped by killing five soldiers and made his way back to South Vietnam where he was arrested again. The South Vietnamese government had assumed he was a "plant" from the North.

After serving time in prison, Le got out and started a fishing company, eventually becoming the largest canner in South Vietnam.

When Le learned that the U.S. troops and embassy personnel were about to pull out of his country, he made a life-changing decision.

He took all of the gold he had hoarded, loaded it aboard one of his fishing vessels and sailed with his wife out to the American ships in the harbor. He then exchanged all his riches for safe passage out of Vietnam to the Philippines, where he and his wife were taken into a refugee camp.

After gaining access to the president of the Philippines, Le convinced him to make one of his boats available for fishing and Le was back in business again. Before he left the Philippines two years later en route for America (his ultimate dream), Le had successfully developed the entire fishing industry in the Philippines.

But en route to America, Le became distraught and depressed about having to start over again with nothing. His wife tells of how she found him near the railing of the ship, about to jump overboard.

"Le," she told him, "if you do jump, whatever will become of me? We've been together for so long and through so much. We can do this together." It was all the encouragement that Le Van Vu needed.

When he and his wife arrived in Houston in 1972, they were flat broke and spoke no English. In Vietnam, family takes care of family, and Le and his wife found themselves ensconced in the back room of his cousin's bakery in the Greenspoint Mall. We were building our salon just a couple of hundred feet away.

Now, as they say, here comes the "message" part of this story:

Le's cousin offered both Le and his wife jobs in the bakery. After taxes, Le would take home $175 per week, his wife $125. Their total annual income, in other words, was $15,600. Further, his cousin offered to sell them the bakery whenever they could come up with a $30,000 down payment. The cousin would finance the remainder with a note for $90,000.

Here's what Le and his wife did:

Even with a weekly income of $300, they decided to continue to live in the back room. They kept clean by taking sponge baths for two years in the mall's restrooms. For two years their diet consisted almost entirely of bakery goods. Each year, for two years, they lived on a total, that's right, a total of $600, saving $30,000 for the down payment.

Le later explained his reasoning, "If we got ourselves an apartment, which we could afford on $300 per week, we'd have to pay the rent. Then, of course, we'd have to buy furniture. Then we'd have to have transportation to and from work, so that meant we'd have to buy a car. Then we'd have to buy gasoline for the car as well as insurance. Then we'd probably want to go places in the car, so that meant we'd need to buy clothes and toiletries. So I knew that if we got that apartment, we'd never get our $30,000 together."

Now, if you think you've heard everything about Le, let me tell you, there's more: After he and his wife had saved the $30,000 and bought the bakery, Le once again sat down with his wife for a serious chat. They still owed $90,000 to his cousin, he said, and as difficult as the past two years had been, they had to remain living in that back room for one more year.

I'm proud to tell you that in one year, my friend and mentor Le Van Vu and his wife, saving virtually every nickel of profit from the business, paid off the $90,000 note, and in just three years, owned an extremely profitable business free and clear.

Then, and only then, the Van Vus went out and got their first apartment. To this day, they continue to save on a regular basis, live on an extremely small percentage of their income, and, of course, always pay cash for any of their purchases.

Do you think that Le Van Vu is a millionaire today? I am happy to tell you, many times over.

John McCormack
Chicken Soup for the Soul

A Little Courage Goes a Long Way

*What lies behind us and
what lies before us are tiny matters
compared to what lies within us.*

—Ralph Waldo Emerson

It was 1986. I had just closed my advertising agency and was close to broke, with no idea as to what to do next. Then one day, after reading a magazine article that talked about the power of networking, a light bulb went off. These were the 1980s. Why weren't people making money networking? As I began to question, the idea came: I would create a company called POWERLUNCH! People seeking contacts would call me, and in the role of a business *yenta* (matchmaker), I would, over the computer, find the exact type of person in the industry they needed, or the exact position they were looking for. Then I'd put the right people together for a power lunch. Perfect, right?

The only problem was that I had very little money to start a business, so I used the one asset that has never failed me— my mouth. I printed 10,000 brochures at an inexpensive local print shop, got up my courage and planted myself on the corner of Connecticut and K Avenues in the middle of downtown Washington, D.C. At the top of my lungs I yelled, "POWERLUNCH! Get your POWERLUNCH!" For three days, I yelled and passed out brochures. People looked at me a little funny, but they took them.

At the end of three days, all the brochures were gone and not one person had called. Penniless, lifeless and beginning to lose hope, I dragged myself home. As I walked in the door, the telephone rang. It was a *Washington Post* reporter. He had seen one of my brochures and wondered if he could interview me to be on the front page of the *Post's* "Style" section. Now, mind you, I had no company, no business phone (he called me on my personal line), and not much of a structure for my business—but I excitedly agreed.

The next day we had a great interview, and he asked me for my business phone number. I told him I would get back to him with it that afternoon. I then scrambled down to the local phone company and called him with the number: 265-EATT. (It hadn't been hooked up yet, but at least I had a number.) Amused, the reporter agreed to print it—a rarity for the *Post*.

The next day I was awakened by a phone call—on my personal line—from a friend congratulating me on the article in the paper. I sat bolt upright in bed. But my new phone number hadn't been hooked up yet! Just then, there was a knock on the door. It was the woman from the telephone company, thank goodness, who had come to hook me up. She went to the back of the house and emerged after about fifteen minutes with a piece of paper. "What's this?" I asked.

"These are the messages I took while I was on the pole," she replied with a laugh. My business was already one step ahead of me.

From there, many other media sources called, including the *New York Times*, the *Christian Science Monitor* and even *Entertainment Tonight*. I received hundreds of requests for lunches and introduced many people. I was able to fulfill my desire to have fun and do business at the same time. And it all started on the corner of Connecticut and K, with a lot of yelling . . . and a little bit of courage.

Sandra Crowe
Chicken Soup for the Soul at Work

"This, Caldwell, is the ultimate in power lunches!"

Reprinted with permission from Dave Carpenter.

The Price of a Dream

Never look where you're going.
Always look where you want to go.

—Bob Ernst

I grew up poor—living in the projects with six brothers, three sisters, a varying assortment of foster kids,
my father, and a wonderful mother, Scarlette Hunley. We had
little money and few worldly goods, but plenty of love and
attention. I was happy and energetic. I understood that no
matter how poor a person was, they could still afford a dream.

My dream was athletics. By the time I was sixteen, I could
crush a baseball, throw a ninety-mile-per-hour fastball and hit
anything that moved on the football field. I was also lucky: My
high-school coach was Ollie Jarvis, who not only believed in me,
but taught me how to believe in myself. He taught me the difference between having a dream and showing conviction. One
particular incident with Coach Jarvis changed my life forever.

It was the summer between my junior and senior years,
and a friend recommended me for a summer job. This meant
a chance for money in my pocket—cash for dates with girls,

certainly, money for a new bike and new clothes, and the start of savings for a house for my mother. The prospect of a summer job was enticing, and I wanted to jump at the opportunity.

Then I realized I would have to give up summer baseball to handle the work schedule, and that meant I would have to tell Coach Jarvis I wouldn't be playing. I was dreading this, spurring myself with the advice my mother preached to us: "If you make your bed, you have to lie in it."

When I told Coach Jarvis, he was as mad as I expected him to be. "You have your whole life to work," he said. "Your playing days are limited. You can't afford to waste them."

I stood before him with my head hanging, trying to think of the words that would explain to him why my dream of buying my mom a house and having money in my pocket was worth facing his disappointment in me.

"How much are you going to make at this job, son?" he demanded.

"Three twenty-five an hour," I replied.

"Well," he asked, "is $3.25 an hour the price of a dream?"

That question, the plainness of it, laid bare for me the difference between wanting something right now and having a goal. I dedicated myself to sports that summer, and within the year I was drafted by the Pittsburgh Pirates to play rookie-league ball, and offered a $20,000 contract. I already had a football scholarship to the University of Arizona, which led me to an education, two consensus selections as All-American linebacker and being chosen seventh overall in the first round of the NFL draft. I signed with the Denver Broncos in 1984 for $1.7 million, and bought my mother the house of my dreams.

Ricky C. Hunley
Chicken Soup for the Sports Fan's Soul

A Perfect Skate

*You've got to get up every morning with
determination if you are going to
go to bed with satisfaction.*

—George Horace Lorimer

She staggered off the practice ice supported by some of her skating-team friends. I hurried over to give Heidi her jacket and to brace her until we could find a seat. At fifteen, she had been living with cancer for a year. We'd learned the news just after returning from Chicago, where she'd won her first gold medal in an international competition.

Then came the tests, the invasive procedures and the surgery. Through it all, what mattered to her most was that she retain her ability to skate. Fortunately, her doctor agreed to let her skate as much as she was able.

Heidi's friend Greg helped me take off her skates. All of the children were initially frightened by Heidi's plight, but gradually pitched in to help keep her safe.

"Is she all right?" Greg asked.

"Yes, she just needs a nice nap before we can get her to the car," I explained.

Happy children swirled around me as Heidi slept away. They all tried to be quiet, but their exuberance for the upcoming Keystone State Games was evident. How I wished those days would return for Heidi.

Heidi had been working hard on her programs and was determined to compete, but now the deadline had passed. I woke her up and we began our journey to the car. "Mom, Coach Barb says I am skating my program well. I want to go to the State Games."

Pain shot through my heart. When I told her the registration deadline had passed, she said her coach could probably still get her in. "Mom," she pleaded, "I don't expect a medal. I just want to go there and be normal for a couple of days. Is that so bad?" A sob escaped her.

"Let's ask the doctor," I said, uncertain.

The next day at her checkup she filled the doctor in on all the details of the State Games.

"I'll tell you what," he responded. "It's okay with me if it is okay with your mom, but you'll have to get permission to miss your radiation treatments."

I added something else to the list: "You have to eat right, sleep right and take good care of yourself."

"I will, I promise!" she responded.

After getting permission from the oncologist and sending in a last-minute registration form, Heidi was set to go to the State Games. Now it was the big night and Heidi was about to alight on the ice for her freestyle routine. I prayed.

The speakers announced her name and I steadied my

hand on the camera as she flowed across the ice gracefully, like her old self. Proudly, she took up her stance. *Steel Magnolias'* theme song filled the arena, and she took off for a full performance.

She picked her toe into the ice and lifted up into a jump. She was so high that a momentary look of fear crossed her face. I cringed, whispering, "Please God, don't let her break anything on the landing."

She landed perfectly, leg out behind her just like the pros. Her face bore a huge smile as if to say, "I did it!" She tore into her next move as the audience went wild. "Go Heidi!" echoed around the arena. She leaned into her ultimate move, the inside-outside eagle, perfectly done.

The stands erupted with joyful noise. None of us could believe it. Another huge jump! She was garnering points for the team. She glided into a lovely spiral, heavy boot held high like a flag of victory. Her cheeks were pink with effort and she was beaming with pride. Heidi had outskated her best!

She exited victoriously into her coach's arms. Barb grabbed her in a huge hug, crying as they savored this incredible moment. Then her joy turned to shock. Heidi lay lifeless in her arms.

The arena quieted. I ran.

I caught them as Heidi's weight began to overpower Barb. I backed to the bleachers and rested against them. Arms reached to help. I laid her carefully down and felt her neck for a pulse. She had one.

Everyone waited in shock as I checked her over.

The quiet was suddenly shattered by a snore! Bedlam erupted. Applause ripped through the rafters of the frigid arena. Parents of her rivals shared their blankets as Heidi took a well-deserved nap. She was still sound asleep when her teammates ran over to congratulate her. She had earned the gold medal in the freestyle division!

Nancy E. Myer
Chicken Soup for the Sports Fan's Soul

Dreams Have a Price

Each writer's career begins with a dream, a fantasy, a goal that looms on the distant horizon. "I want to write a novel." "I'd love to publish poetry." "I want to see my name on the screen as the author of a movie."

My career began with a dream. I wanted to make people laugh. I wanted to write comedy.

But each writer must realize, too, that every goal has a price tag. Admission to a fantasy is never free. There's research to be done, studying to do, and practice, practice, practice. The cheapest, and usually the quickest, way to attain any desire is to pay the full price. Do the work.

When I decided to become a comedy writer, I wanted to study the profession. Bob Hope, I thought, had the most readable and useful material for analytical purposes. His comedy material was funny on paper, pure humor. Of course, Bob Hope's expert timing and delivery enhanced any joke he was telling, but it was still a joke that could be read and analyzed. Other comics, like Jerry Lewis could be funny, but it was more their antics that created the hilarity. On paper, the material was not as useful to a student as Hope's.

So, I studied Bob Hope. I would audio tape his television monologues and then type out a transcript. I'd analyze the joke forms, wording, rhythm, the arrangement of gags in a routine, and so on. Then I'd put that monologue away for awhile.

In a few weeks, I'd select new topics from the newspaper and try to write new jokes using the techniques I'd learned from Hope's latest monologue. With this technique, Bob Hope and his writers became my mentors.

It worked. I began writing for local comics, then national comics, then landed a spot on a television variety show staff.

Then it worked even better. Bob Hope called me.

"I've heard about your writing and wonder if you'd like to do some gags for me for the Academy Awards. I'm the host this year, you know, and I'd like to see if some of your jokes would work for me."

This was a part of my dream that I didn't dare dream, but here it was happening nonetheless. I took a pad and pen out to my backyard and wrote a few hundred gags about current movies, celebrities, anything that would apply to the Oscars. Naturally, I used the tricks that I had learned from years of studying Bob Hope's comedy style.

Mr. Hope did ten of my jokes on the telecast and I was thrilled. The following day he called me again and said, "I loved your material. It looks like you've been writing for me all your life."

"I have, Mr. Hope," I said. "Only you didn't know about it."

I've been writing for Bob Hope ever since.

There were two valuable lessons in this experience that all people can learn and draw inspiration from:

The first is that there is effort involved in making any dream come true. Dreams are powerful, but only when they're reinforced by research, study and effort.

The second is that if you do the work, you'll reach your goals.

Gene Perret
Chicken Soup for the Writer's Soul

Take Action

Action conquers fear.
—Peter Nivio Zarlenga

One at a Time

*A journey of a thousand miles
begins and ends with one step.*
—Lao-Tsu

It was a bleak, rainy day, and I had no desire to make the drive from the beach to the cold mountain at Lake Arrowhead where my daughter Carolyn lived.

A week earlier, she had called and insisted that I come see the daffodils some woman had planted at the top of the mountain. So, here I was, reluctantly making the two-hour journey.

By the time I saw how thick the fog was on the winding road toward the summit, it was too far to go back, so I inched my way up the perilous Rim of the World Highway to my daughter's house.

"I am not driving another inch!" I announced. "I'll stay and have lunch, but as soon as the fog lifts, I'm heading back down."

"But I need you to drive me to the garage to pick up my car," Carolyn said. "Can't we at least do that?"

"How far is it?" I asked cautiously.

"About three minutes," she answered. "I'll drive. I'm used to it."

After about ten minutes of driving, I looked at her anxiously. "I thought you said it was three minutes away."

She grinned. "This is a detour."

We were back on the mountain road, in fog like thick
veils. *Nothing could be worth this,* I thought. But it was too
late to turn back. We turned down a narrow track into a parking lot beside a little stone church. The fog was beginning to
lift a little, and gray, watery sunshine was trying to peek
through.

Carolyn got out of the car and I reluctantly followed. The
path we followed was thick with old pine needles. Dark ever-
greens towered over us, and the mountain sloped sharply
away to the right.

Gradually, the peace and silence of the place began to relax
my mind. Just then, we turned a corner, and I gasped in
amazement. From the top of the mountain, sloping down for
several acres across folds and valleys, between the trees and
bushes, following the terrain, were rivers of daffodils in radiant bloom. Every hue of the color yellow—from the palest
ivory to the deepest lemon to the most vivid salmon-orange—
blazed like a carpet before us.

It looked as though the sun had tipped over and spilled gold
in rivulets down the mountainside. At the center of this wild
color cascaded a waterfall of purple hyacinth. Throughout the
garden were little meditation platforms graced with barrels of
coral-colored tulips. And, as if this bonanza of color were not
enough, over the heads of the daffodils Western bluebirds
darted and frolicked, their magenta breasts and sapphire
wings like a flutter of jewels.

A riot of questions filled my mind: *Who created such*

beauty—such a magnificent garden? Why? Why here, in this out-of-the-way place? How?

As we approached the mountain home that stood in the center of the property, we saw a sign: *Answers to the Questions I Know You Are Asking.*

The first answer was *One Woman—Two Hands, Two Feet, and Very Little Brain.* The second was *One at a Time.* The third, *Started in 1958.*

As we drove back home, I was silent. I was so moved by what we had seen I could scarcely speak. "She changed the world," I finally said, "one bulb at a time. Just think. She started almost forty years ago. And the world is forever different and better because she did a little bit with consistent effort."

The wonder of it would not let me go. "Imagine—if I had had a vision and had worked at it, just a little bit every day for all those lost years, what might I have accomplished by now?"

Carolyn looked at me sideways, smiling. "Start tomorrow," she said. "Better yet, start today."

Jaroldeen Edwards
Chicken Soup for the Gardener's Soul

ZiGGY

©1974, Ziggy and Friends, Inc./Dist. by Universal Press Syndicate

Tom Wilson

6/12

When Dreams Won't Die

Always bear in mind that your own resolution to succeed is more important than any other one thing.

—Abraham Lincoln

Ever since I can remember, I've been fascinated by beauty. As a young girl surrounded by the numbing sameness of all those cornfields around Indianapolis, the glamorous worlds of fashion and cosmetics were a magnificent escape for me. Every time I looked at the advertisements in women's magazines—all those gorgeous models with flawless skin and expertly applied makeup, their statuesque bodies adorned with incredible designer outfits—I was whisked away to exotic places I could only revisit in dreams.

The Revlon ads were especially wonderful. But there was only one problem—not one ad in those days featured a woman of color like me. Still, there was a "whisper of wisdom" inside me, telling me that someday my dream would come true and I would have a career in the cosmetics industry.

Very few companies bothered to market cosmetics to

women of color in those days, but my inspiration came from C. J. Walker, the first African-American woman to become a millionaire. She started out with two dollars and a dream, right in my own hometown. She earned the fortune at the turn of the century, with her own line of hair-care products just for women like herself.

I graduated from college with a degree in public health education. Before long I got a job with a leader in the pharmaceuticals industry—and became the first African-American woman to sell pharmaceuticals in Indiana. People were shocked that I took the job because a woman of color selling encyclopedias in my territory had just been killed. In fact, when I started, the physicians I dealt with looked at me as if I had two heads.

But eventually my uniqueness worked to my advantage. The doctors and nurses remembered me. And I reversed the negative halo effect by doing the job better than other people. Along with pharmaceuticals, I sold them Girl Scout cookies and helped the nurses with their makeup. They began to look forward to my coming, not just for the novelty, but because we enjoyed such heartwarming visits.

Within two years, I'd broken numerous sales records and was recognized as a Distinguished Sales Representative, formerly an all-white male club. I was looking forward to some hard-earned commission checks when suddenly, the company decided to subdivide the region and hired a handsome blond man to take my place. He would enjoy the fruits of my labor, while I was reassigned to another area that needed a lot of work. At this point, my dream of that cosmetics career with Revlon seemed a million miles away.

Discouraged and disenchanted, I picked up and moved to Los Angeles. Then one Sunday, as I searched longingly through the ads in the *Los Angeles Times,* there it was: a classified ad for a regional manager job with Revlon. I lit up completely and dove for the phone first thing Monday morning. The voice at the other end said that due to overwhelming response, Revlon was taking no more résumés.

I was devastated. But then a dear friend said to me, "Marilyn, I know you aren't going to let this job slip through your fingers. Go on down there anyway." Suddenly inspired and determined to turn the challenge into an adventure, I drove down to the Marriott where they were conducting interviews. When I arrived, a desk clerk curtly informed me that there was no way I could get an interview, nor would Mr. Rick English take my résumé. I walked away, smiling. At least I now had the name of the man I needed to see.

I decided to have lunch to listen for the whisper of wisdom that would provide me with a new strategy. Sure enough, the idea came to me to explain my situation to the cashier as I was about to leave the restaurant. She immediately picked up the phone to find out what room Mr. English was in. "Room 515," she said turning to me. My heart began to pound.

I stood outside room 515, said a prayer, and knocked on the door. The minute he opened the door I said, "You haven't met the best person for the job because you haven't talked to me yet."

He looked stunned and said, "Wait a minute until I finish this interview and I'll speak to you." When I entered the room, I was clear and firm that this job was for me, and I got the job.

My first day at Revlon was like a dream come true. They

hired me to market a new line of hair-care products designed especially for people of color. And by the time I'd worked there three years, the public was beginning to demand natural, cruelty-free products.

With public sentiment on my side, here was my chance! Once again listening to the whisper of wisdom inside me, I opened my own cosmetics company, which to this day continues to give me a sense of fulfillment impossible to describe.

I truly believe we should never give up on our hopes and dreams. The path may be rocky and twisted, but the world is waiting for that special contribution each of us was born to make. What it takes is the courage to follow those whispers of wisdom that guide us from inside. When I listen to that, I expect nothing less than a miracle.

Marilyn Johnson Kondwani
Chicken Soup for the Soul at Work

Look Out, Baby,
I'm Your Love Man!

*It is better to be prepared for an opportunity
and not have one than to have
an opportunity and not be prepared.*

—Whitney Young Jr.

Les Brown and his twin brother were adopted by
Mamie Brown, a kitchen worker and maid, shortly
after their birth in a poverty-stricken Miami neighborhood.

Because of his hyperactivity and nonstop jabber, Les was
placed in special education classes for the learning disabled in
grade school and throughout high school. Upon graduation, he
became a city sanitation worker in Miami Beach. But he had
a dream of being a disc jockey.

At night he would take a transistor radio to bed where he
listened to the local jive-talking deejays. He created an imaginary radio station in his tiny room with its torn vinyl floor-
ing. A hairbrush served as his microphone as he practiced his
patter, introducing records to his ghost listeners.

His mother and brother could hear him through the thin

walls and would shout at him to quit flapping his jaws and go to sleep. But Les didn't listen to them. He was wrapped up in his own world, living a dream.

One day Les boldly went to the local radio station during his lunch break from mowing grass for the city. He got into the station manager's office and told him he wanted to be a disc jockey.

The manager eyed this disheveled young man in overalls and a straw hat and inquired, "Do you have any background in broadcasting?"

Les replied, "No, sir, I don't."

"Well, son, I'm afraid we don't have a job for you then."

Les thanked him politely and left. The station manager assumed that he had seen the last of this young man. But he underestimated the depth of Les Brown's commitment to his goal. You see, Les had a higher purpose than simply wanting to be a disc jockey. He wanted to buy a nicer house for his adoptive mother, whom he loved deeply. The disc jockey job was merely a step toward his goal.

Mamie Brown had taught Les to pursue his dreams, so he felt sure that he would get a job at that radio station in spite of what the station manager had said.

And so Les returned to the station every day for a week, asking if there were any job openings. Finally the station manager gave in and took him on as an errand boy—at no pay. At first, he fetched coffee or picked up lunches and dinner for the deejays who could not leave the studio. Eventually his enthusiasm for their work won him the confidence of the disc jockeys who would send him in their Cadillacs to pick up visiting celebrities such as the Temptations and Diana Ross and the Supremes. Little did any of them know that young Les did not have a driver's license.

Les did whatever was asked of him at the station—and more. While hanging out with the deejays, he taught himself their hand movements on the control panel. He stayed in the control rooms and soaked up whatever he could until they asked him to leave. Then, back in his bedroom at night, he practiced and prepared himself for the opportunity that he knew would present itself.

One Saturday afternoon while Les was at the station, a deejay named Rock was drinking while on the air. Les was the only other person in the building, and he realized that Rock was drinking himself toward trouble. Les stayed close. He walked back and forth in front of the window in Rock's booth. As he prowled, he said to himself, "Drink, Rock, drink!"

Les was hungry, and he was ready. He would have run down the street for more booze if Rock had asked. When the phone rang, Les pounced on it. It was that station manager, as he knew it would be.

"Les, this is Mr. Klein."

"Yes," said Les. "I know."

"Les, I don't think Rock can finish his program."

"Yes sir, I know."

"Would you call one of the other deejays to come in and take over?"

"Yes, sir. I sure will."

But when Les hung up the telephone, he said to himself, "Now, he must think I'm crazy."

Les did dial the telephone, but it wasn't to call in another deejay. He called his mother first, and then his girlfriend. "You all go out on the front porch and turn up the radio because I'm about to come on the air!" he said.

He waited about fifteen minutes before he called the general manager. "Mr. Klein, I can't find nobody," Les said.

Mr. Klein then asked, "Young man, do you know how to work the controls in the studio?"

"Yes sir," replied Les.

Les darted into the booth, gently moved Rock aside and sat down at the turntable. He was ready. And he was hungry. He flipped on the microphone switch and said, "Look out! This is me, LB, triple P—Les Brown, Your Platter Playing Poppa. There were none before me and there will be none after me. Therefore, that makes me the one and only. Young and single and love to mingle. Certified, bona fide, indubitably qualified to bring you satisfaction, a whole lot of action. Look out, baby, I'm your lo-o-ove man!"

Because of his preparation, Les was ready. He wowed the audience and his general manager. From that fateful beginning, Les went on to a successful career in broadcasting, politics, public speaking and television.

Jack Canfield
Chicken Soup for the Soul

Ask, Affirm, Take Action

*Many things are lost for
want of asking.*

—English Proverb

When my daughter, Janna, was a junior in high school, she was accepted as a foreign exchange student to Germany. We were delighted that she had been chosen for such a special experience. Then the exchange organization informed us that we had to pay $4,000 in costs—and the money was due on June 5; two months away.

At the time I was divorced with three teenage children. The idea of raising $4,000 was completely overwhelming to me. Financially, I was barely making ends meet as it was. I had no savings, no credit for a loan and no relatives who could lend me the money. At first it felt as hopeless as if I had to raise $4 million!

Luckily, I had recently attended one of Jack Canfield's Self-Esteem Seminars in Los Angeles. Three of the things I learned at the seminar were to ask for what you want, affirm for what you want and take action for what you want.

I decided to put these new-found principles to work. First, I wrote an affirmation that stated, "I am joyfully receiving $4,000 by June 1 for Janna's trip to Germany." I put the affirmation on my bathroom mirror and carried a copy in my purse so I could look at it every day. Then I wrote out an actual check for $4,000 and put it on the dashboard of my car. I spent a lot of time driving each day and this was a visible reminder. I took a picture of a hundred-dollar bill, enlarged it and put it on the ceiling over Janna's bed so it was the first thing she saw in the morning and the last thing at night.

Janna was a typical fifteen-year-old Southern California teenager and wasn't too thrilled with these rather "weird" ideas. I explained them all to her and suggested that she write her own affirmation.

Now that I was affirming what I wanted, I needed to take some action and to ask for what I wanted. I have always been a very self-sufficient and independent person who didn't need anyone else's help. It was very difficult for me to ask for money from family and friends that I knew, and even more so from strangers. But I decided to go for it anyway. What did I have to lose?

I made up a flier with Janna's photo and her statement of why she wanted to go to Germany. At the bottom was a coupon for people to tear off and mail back with their check to us by June 1. Then I asked for a $5, $20, $50 or $100 contribution. I even left a blank space for them to fill in their own amount. Then I mailed this flier to every single friend, family member and person that I knew or even slightly knew. I distributed fliers at the corporate office where I worked, and sent them to the local newspapers and radio station. I researched the addresses of thirty of the service organizations in our valley and mailed them fliers. I even wrote the airlines asking for free travel to Germany.

The newspaper didn't run an article, the radio station didn't do a story, the airline said no to my request, but I kept on asking and continued to mail out fliers. Janna began having dreams of strangers giving her money. In the weeks that followed, the money began to come in. The first gift was for $5. The largest single gift was for $800 from family and friends. But most of the gifts were $20 or $50—some from people we knew, some from strangers.

Janna became enthused about the whole idea and began to believe that this could actually become a reality. One day she asked me, "Do you think this will work for getting my driver's permit?" I assured her that an affirmation would work. She tried it and she got her permit. By June 1 we joyfully received $3,750! We were thrilled! However, while this was wonderful, I still had no idea where I was going to get the last $250. I still had until June 5th to somehow raise the remaining money. On June 3rd the phone rang. It was a woman from one of the service organizations in our town. "I know I'm past the deadline; is it too late?" she asked.

"No," I replied.

"Well, we would really like to help Janna, but we can only give her $250."

In all, Janna had two organizations and twenty-three people who sponsored her and made her dream a reality. She wrote to each one of those twenty-five sponsors several times throughout the year, telling them about her experiences. When she returned, she gave a speech at two organizations.

Janna was a foreign exchange student in Viersen, Germany, from September to May, and it was a wonderful experience for her. It broadened her perspective and gave her a new appreciation for the world and its people. She was able to see beyond the narrow Southern California life that she grew up in. Since then she has traveled throughout Europe, worked one summer in Spain and another in Germany. She graduated from college with honors, worked two years with VISTA at an AIDS Project in Vermont and is presently pursuing her master's degree in public health administration.

The year after Janna's Germany trip, I found the love of my life, again by using affirmations. We met at a Self-Esteem Seminar, married, and attended a Couples Seminar. At that seminar we created affirmations together, one of which was to travel. In the past seven years we have lived in several different states, including Alaska, spent three years in Saudi Arabia and are presently living in the Orient.

Like Janna, my horizons have broadened and my life is so much more exciting and wonderful because I learned to ask, affirm and take action for the things I want.

Claudette Hunter
A 3rd Serving of Chicken Soup for the Soul

234 ♥ Take Action

Ask, Ask, Ask

The greatest saleswoman in the world today doesn't mind if you call her a girl. That's because Markita Andrews has generated more than eighty thousand dollars selling Girl Scout cookies since she was seven years old.

Going door-to-door after school, the painfully shy Markita transformed herself into a cookie-selling dynamo when she discovered, at age thirteen, the secret of selling.

It starts with desire. Burning, white-hot desire.

For Markita and her mother, who worked as a waitress in New York after her husband left them when Markita was eight years old, their dream was to travel the globe. "I'll work hard to make enough money to send you to college," her mother said one day. "You'll go to college and when you graduate, you'll make enough money to take you and me around the world. Okay?"

So at age thirteen when Markita read in her *Girl Scout* magazine that the Scout who sold the most cookies would win an all-expenses-paid trip for two around the world, she decided to sell all the Girl Scout cookies she could—more Girl Scout cookies than anyone in the world, ever.

But desire alone is not enough. To make her dream come true, Markita knew she needed a plan.

"Always wear your right outfit, your professional garb," her aunt advised. "When you are doing business, dress like you are doing business. Wear your Girl Scout uniform. When you go up to people in their tenement buildings at 4:30 or 6:30 and especially on Friday night, ask for a big order. Always smile, whether they buy or not, always be nice. And don't ask them to buy your cookies; ask them to invest."

Lots of other Scouts may have wanted that trip around the world. Lots of other Scouts may have had a plan. But only Markita went off in her uniform each day after school, ready to ask—and keep asking —folks to invest in her dream. "Hi. I have a dream. I'm earning a trip around the world for me and my mom by merchandising Girl Scout cookies," she'd say at the door. "Would you like to invest in one dozen or two dozen boxes of cookies?"

Markita sold 3,526 boxes of Girl Scout cookies that year and won her trip around the world. Since then, she has sold more than 42,000 boxes of Girl Scout cookies, spoken at sales conventions across the country, starred in a Disney movie about her adventure and has coauthored the bestseller, *How to Sell More Cookies, Condos, Cadillacs, Computers . . . And Everything Else.*

Markita is no smarter and no more extroverted than thousands of other people, young and old, with dreams of their own. The difference is Markita has discovered the secret of selling: Ask, ask, ask! Many people fail before they even begin because they fail to *ask* for what they want. The fear of rejection leads many of us to reject ourselves and our dreams long before anyone else ever has the chance—no matter what we're selling.

And everyone is selling something. "You're selling yourself everyday—in school, to your boss, to new people you meet," said Markita at fourteen. "My mother is a waitress: She sells the daily special. Mayors and presidents trying to get votes are selling. . . . One of my favorite teachers was Mrs. Chapin. She made geography interesting, and that's really selling. . . . I see selling everywhere I look. Selling is part of the whole world."

It takes courage to ask for what you want. Courage is not the absence of fear. It's doing what it takes despite one's fear. And, as Markita has discovered, the more you ask, the easier (and more fun) it gets.

Once, on live TV, the producer decided to give Markita her toughest selling challenge. Markita was asked to sell Girl Scout cookies to another guest on the show. "Would you like to invest in one dozen or two dozen boxes of Girl Scout cookies?" she asked.

"Girl Scout cookies?! I don't buy any Girl Scout cookies!" he replied. "I'm a federal penitentiary warden. I put 2,000 rapists, robbers, criminals, muggers and child abusers to bed every night."

Unruffled, Markita quickly countered, "Mister, if you take some of these cookies, maybe you won't be so mean and angry and evil. And, Mister, I think it would be a good idea for you to take some of these cookies back for every one of your 2,000 prisoners, too."

Markita asked.

The warden wrote a check.

Jack Canfield and Mark Victor Hansen
Chicken Soup for the Soul

LEGWORK EQUALS BIG COOKIE SALES

By Abraham Estimada
News Staff Writer

Hard work and moxie help Katlyn Pickett stack up big regional cookie numbers.

The secret to nine-year-old Katlyn Pickett's success comes straight from the bestselling book, *Chicken Soup for the Soul.*

"The key to selling is you need to have a desire, you need to have a plan, and you need to ask, ask, ask," she said.

Katlyn put the advice into action and engaged, charmed and asked, asked, asked enough folks to sell 752 boxes of Girl Scout cookies.

That was an individual high among the Western Rivers Girl Scout Council, which represents troops from Bend to Coos Bay and Roseburg to Eugene.

"She's a hard worker," said Patti Luse, the council's sales director. "She was eager to earn some extra money. She had some goals, and she achieved those goals."

Katlyn, a home-schooled student, spent two weeks collecting pre-orders. After finishing her schoolwork, she went door-to-door looking for buyers. Not satisfied with her sales volume, she changed her strategy.

"Let me put it to you this way," Katlyn said, looking an interviewer in the eye, "the business community helped out a lot. The houses just took longer and or people weren't home."

Overcoming her initial shyness, Katlyn walked straight into shops and the Gateway Mall to sell her merchandise, explaining that she was selling the cookies so she and her troop could go to Disneyland. Usually, it worked.

"In the middle of it all, I was just hot on wheels," she said. "I just burned rubber."

One order form became two order forms and two forms, became four, until Katlyn had a dozen sheets filled with 565 orders from people wanting to buy cookies.

And when Katlyn delivered the cookies to her customers, other people would approach her asking to order more boxes.

Every day for at least four hours, Katlyn, with her mom or dad watching from a distance, would hit as many businesses as they could.

She would finish her homework, play soccer and practice her piano on top of selling cookies, said her mother, Tracey.

"She was the one that cracked the whip. It was her goal," she said. "When we were tired, she'd come up and say, 'All right, put on your shoes. Let's go.'"

Katlyn says she wants to come back next year and sell one thousand boxes of cookies, her original goal. But she's not about to say how she conducts business.

"I still want to keep the secrets of selling," she said. "If everyone knows the secrets, then I won't be able to sell a thousand."

238 ♥ Take Action

How Prayer Made Me a Father Again

I can't begin to count the number of times that prayer has played an important part in my life. As often as God has answered my prayers, I realize it's important to pray for others, too. So when our church started a Tuesday night prayer service, I became a regular participant. The pastor sometimes would begin with a short devotion, and then we'd sing a couple of praise choruses before getting down to serious conversations with God. From the beginning we knew we were there to pray.

During the first few months, attendance was sparse. Those who came gave their prayer requests and there'd still be plenty of time to bring them to the Lord. However, as prayers were answered, more people joined and the number of requests multiplied. It took most of the service to hear all the requests.

The pastor solved the problem. Now when we arrive for the service, we write down our prayer requests on a sign-in sheet in the foyer. During our praise time, the pastor makes a copy of these requests for each person. With list in hand, we find a quiet place to pray individually.

One Tuesday evening our prayer list was short. I prayed for

each need listed. I prayed for the church, our community, our state and our country. Then I prayed over the list again.

I looked at my watch thinking the hour ought to be up. *I still have fifteen minutes left! There has to be something more I can pray about,* I thought.

Then my son came to mind. I had not seen Teddy in twenty-seven years. When he was less than a year old, his mother and I divorced, and she moved with Teddy out of state. I smiled to myself as I thought back to those months with my firstborn son. I would get off the bus from work and could hear him crying half a block away. As soon as I walked into his room, his cries turned into laughter.

After the divorce, I made an effort to keep in touch, but my first letters were returned unopened. Later they were marked, "Addressee moved, left no forwarding address." I had no idea where either Teddy or his mother lived.

When Teddy was about five, I learned through an attorney that my ex-wife had remarried and her new husband wanted to adopt my son. I agonized over my decision.

The attorney wouldn't disclose Teddy's whereabouts unless I chose to seek custodial rights. But a custody battle might forfeit any chance for Teddy to enjoy a stable life. I reasoned: *Teddy doesn't know me. Would it really be fair to deny him a father to satisfy my own need to see him? Would my selfishness cause more emotional damage?*

I loved Teddy and missed him terribly, but I decided I couldn't interfere with a chance for happiness in his life. I waived my rights, hoping it was the best thing to do for my son.

Now years later, I simply asked prayerfully, "Lord, my son

is a grown man now. I love him and miss him. Please just let me know what kind of a man Teddy has turned out to be. Anything more than that I leave in your hands. In fact, Lord, I don't even know where to start looking for him, so I am truly leaving it all up to you. Please, let me know my son. Amen."

As I left that prayer service, the Lord gave me peace from the words of Malachi 4:6—"He will turn the hearts of fathers to their children, and the hearts of the children to their fathers."

The rest of the week I went about my normal routine and forgot about my prayer. But God hadn't forgotten.

The Saturday after the prayer meeting, I ran into our pastor at the post office. After I collected the mail from my box, we started to chat. As I scanned through my mail, a letter caught my eye.

I couldn't place the name or the return address. As the pastor commented on Sunday's church activities, I started reading the mysterious letter.

"Are you okay?" he asked me. Tears were rolling down my face. I couldn't speak; I handed him the letter I had just read—from Teddy.

Teddy explained that he had decided to search the Internet for me. This letter was one of forty-seven letters that my son had written to Richard Whetstones all over the country. Then I noticed the postmark: It was dated Wednesday, the day after my Tuesday night prayer. This wasn't a coincidence. This was a direct answer to my prayer.

When I told my wife, Rose, she was excited because she had encouraged me to try to find Teddy. Since I hadn't mentioned my Tuesday night prayer to her, she was even more thrilled when she learned the whole story.

I decided to call Teddy that day, but I was nervous as I dialed the phone number in Amarillo, Texas. When he answered the phone, I said I had received the letter and I was his father. We agreed to pursue the relationship further.

So I sat down and wrote him back, enclosing a photo I had of him—a color snapshot taken by a family friend at Teddy's christening. In the photo, Teddy was in his mother's arms while my dad and I stood proudly beside him.

In Teddy's return letter, he enclosed the exact same photo— the only family photo he had! That was the confirmation we both needed. I had found my son—or rather, he had found me.

When I told my sister Donna about Teddy, she began corresponding with him, secretly arranging a person-to-person reunion for the two of us at her wedding in May. Teddy and I had time to slip away for breakfast, then walked on the Clearwater beach, talking the whole time.

Teddy had a lot of questions. He had had suspicions about being adopted early on, but didn't learn the truth until he was fifteen years old. His mother hadn't mentioned me at all; I was thankful she hadn't painted me as a terrible person. Having heard all kinds of horror stories about reunions that turned bad, I was reminded once again that God remained faithful.

In October 1997, Teddy and his family—wife Dana, and their children Hayden and Jorden—visited Rose and me in Florida. Teddy's wife couldn't get over how similar Teddy and I were—in looks, mannerisms, speech and ideals—even though we lived completely separate lives.

My Tuesday night prayer wasn't the first or the last prayer that God has answered in my life. But it is one of the most wonderful and satisfying blessings he has ever given me. All I did was simply ask, trusting for his answer.

Richard Whetstone
Chicken Soup for the Christian Family Soul

"That was fast."

Why Wait? . . . Just Do It!

*The big question is whether
you are going to be able
to say a hearty yes to your adventure.*

—Joseph Campbell

My father told me that God must surely have a reason for me being the way I am today. I'm beginning to believe it.

I was the kind of kid that things always worked out for. I grew up in Laguna Beach, California, and I loved surfing and sports. But at a time when most kids my age thought only of TV and the beach, I started thinking of ways I could become more independent, see the country and plan my future.

I began working at the age of ten. By the time I was fifteen, I worked between one to three jobs after school. I made enough money to buy a new motorcycle. I didn't even know how to ride it . But after paying cash for the bike and one year's worth of full insurance coverage, I went to parking lots and learned to ride it. After fifteen minutes of figure eights, I rode home. I was fifteen and a half, had just received my driver's permit and had bought a new motorcycle. It changed my life.

I wasn't one of those just-for-fun-weekend riders. I loved to ride. Every spare minute of every day, every chance I got, I averaged 100 miles a day on top of that bike. Sunsets and sunrises looked prettier when I enjoyed them from a winding mountain road. Even now, I can close my eyes and still feel the bike naturally beneath me, so naturally that it was a more familiar feeling than walking. As I rode, the cool wind gave me a feeling of total relaxation. While I explored the open road outside, inside I was dreaming about what I wanted my life to be.

Two years and five new motorcycles later, I ran out of roads in California. I read motorcycle magazines every night and one night, a BMW motorcycle ad caught my eye. It showed a muddy motorcycle with a duffel bag on the back parked on the side of a dirt road in front of a large "Welcome to Alaska" sign. One year later, I took a photograph of an even muddier motorcycle in front of that exact same sign. Yes, it was me! At seventeen years old I made it to Alaska alone with my bike, conquering over 1,000 miles of dirt highway.

Prior to departing for my seven-week, 17,000-mile camping adventure, my friends said that I was crazy. My parents said that I should wait. *Crazy? Wait? For what?* Since I was a kid, I had dreamed about going across America on a motorcycle. Something strong inside of me told me that if I didn't go on this trip now, I never would. Besides, when would I have the time? I would be starting college on a scholarship very soon, then a career, perhaps even a family some day. I didn't know if it was just to satisfy me or if in my mind I felt it would somehow transform me from a boy to a man. But what I did know was that for that summer, I was going on the adventure of a lifetime.

I quit all of my jobs, and because I was only seventeen, I had my mother write a letter stating that I had her permission to go on this trip. With $1,400 in my pocket, two duffel bags, a shoe box full of maps strapped to the back of my motorcycle, a pen flashlight for protection and a lot of enthusiasm, I left for Alaska and the East Coast.

I met a lot of people, enjoyed the rugged beauty and lifestyle, ate off the open fire and thanked God every day for giving me this opportunity. Sometimes, I didn't see or hear anyone for two or three days and just rode my motorcycle in endless silence with only the wind racing around my helmet. I didn't cut my hair, I took cold showers at campgrounds when I could, and I even had several unscheduled confrontations with bears during that trip. It was the greatest adventure!

Even though I took several more trips, none can ever compare to that summer. It has always held a special place in my life. I can never go back again and explore the roads and mountains, the forests and glacial waters the same way I did back then on that trip, alone with my motorcycle. I can never make the same trip in the exact same way because at the age of twenty-three, I was in a motorcycle accident on a street in Laguna Beach where I was hit by a drunk driver/drug dealer who left me paralyzed from the ribs down.

At the time of my accident, I was in great shape, both physically and mentally. I was a full-time police officer, still riding my motorcycle on my days off. I was married and financially secure. I had it made. But in the space of less than a second, my whole life changed. I spent eight months in the hospital, got divorced, saw that I could not return to work in the way that I had known it and, along with learning how to deal with chronic pain and a wheelchair, I saw all the dreams I had for my future leaving my reach. Luckily for me, help and support helped new dreams to develop and be fulfilled.

When I think back to all of those trips I took, all of those roads that I traveled, I think of how lucky I was to have been able to do that. Every time I rode, I always said to myself, "Do it now. Enjoy your surroundings, even if you're at a smoggy city intersection; enjoy life because you cannot depend on getting a second chance to be in the same place or do the same things."

After my accident, my father said that God had a reason for me being a paraplegic. I believe it. It has made me a stronger person. I returned to work as a desk officer, bought a home and married again. I also have my own consulting business and am a professional speaker. Every now and again, when things get rough, I remind myself of all the things that I have accomplished, all the things I have yet to accomplish, and my father's words.

Yes, he was right. God sure did have a reason. Most importantly, I remind myself to enjoy every moment of every day. And if you can do something, do it. Do it now!

Glenn McIntyre
A 2nd Helping of Chicken Soup for the Soul

The First Step

To take the first step
Is a frightening thing.
To face the unknown
The uncertainty it brings.
But like the child
Who is tired of the crawl,
The first step is
The most important of all.

It expands your horizons,
You can see a new light.
The joy of discovery
Is like taking flight.
The first step you take
Will open all doors,
To see yourself as
You've seen you before.

And, like the child
Who gives it his all,
Sometimes he falters,

He will teeter and fall.
But strong arms are there
To catch him and then,
They stand him back up
To start walking again.

The longest journey,
Takes one step at a time,
But once you get going
You'll do just fine.
Take my hand, friend
I'll help you along
I'll be right beside you . . .
As two we'll be strong.

Yes, that first step's a big one,
The most important of all.
But I'll be there to catch you
Should you teeter and fall.
We'll set our sights forward
Grit our teeth and walk on . . .
When we see that road ending,
We'll break into a run.

I love you, I'll help you
All the way through.
But to take that first step,
Well . . . that's up to you.

Rabona Turner Gordon
A 6th Bowl of Chicken Soup for the Soul

Dear Jack and Mark,

Thank you so much for helping me achieve one of the most awesome experiences in my life. And to think I'm in one of the most widely read books in the nation!

This morning I got an e-mail from a nineteen-year-old girl who was in the hospital for attempted suicide. She wrote to thank me for my poem and is going to take "The First Step" and go back to school. I have no words for what this has meant to me.

You and the whole *Chicken Soup* crew have been so kind and attentive. No wonder you are such a success. Thank you so very much for being the people you are and for sharing such a wonderful thing with others and for providing some of us the opportunity to do so as well. I hope to stay in touch.

Sincerely,
Rabona Turner Gordon

The Power of Determination

*You must back up your ambition by
your whole nature, by unbounded
enthusiasm and a determination to
win that knows no failure.*

—Orison Swett Marden

Ryan's Well of Life

Feel the flame forever burn,
Teaching lessons we must learn,
To bring us closer to the power of the dream.

—David Foster

When my son Ryan was six years old and in first grade, his teacher, Nancy, talked to his class about developing countries and how they could help people, particularly children, in other parts of the world. She explained that besides not having toys or enough food, some of them didn't even have clean water. For these children sitting in their comfortable classroom in Kemptville, Ontario, the idea of children not having any toys, or enough food or water, had an enormous impact.

The principal had distributed a list that showed the costs of buying supplies in developing countries. A penny would buy a pencil, a dollar a hot meal, two dollars a blanket. Seventy dollars would buy a well. When Ryan heard people died because they didn't have clean water, he was deeply affected. He came home that day and insisted he needed seventy dollars for class the next morning.

We thought it was very nice that he wanted to do something important, but we didn't take it seriously. My husband Mark and I both do volunteer work, but Ryan was only six years old—and we just brushed it off.

The next day, Ryan came home very upset because he hadn't been able to take the seventy dollars to school. People were dying, and he insisted he needed that money.

Mark and I discussed it, then explained to Ryan that seventy dollars was a lot of money. If he was really interested in doing something, however, he could earn it.

I drew a little thermometer on a sheet of paper and said, "This is how many dollars it takes to get to seventy, and if you're prepared to earn it, we'll give you extra chores." He happily agreed, so we put an old cookie tin on top of the refrigerator and started giving him chores.

Well, Ryan worked and worked and worked. With every two dollars he earned, he got to fill in another line on the thermometer, then throw his money into the cookie tin. He never stopped working. Ryan vacuumed, washed windows and much more.

He did chores for the neighbors and his grandparents, picked up brush after an ice storm—and it all went right into the cookie tin! When we realized he was really serious, we thought, *Okay, what will we do with the money once he's raised it?* We had no clue. After four months, Ryan was nearing his goal.

I called a girlfriend at CUSO (a Canadian International Development Agency) and asked her for suggestions.

"We can take it here at CUSO," she replied. "But let me look around for a more appropriate organization that might specifically build wells."

Brenda contacted WaterCan in Ottawa and set up a meeting for us. WaterCan is a Canadian nonprofit organization providing clean water and sanitation to people in developing countries.

In April 1998 we went for our meeting, and Ryan brought his cookie tin full of money. Nicole, the executive director, and Helen, her assistant, were very gracious, thanked him and told him how important his donation was. Then they told us it would cost a lot more than $70 to build a well—in fact, it would cost $2,000.

Ryan wasn't concerned and replied simply, "That's okay. I'll just do more chores!"

News about what Ryan was doing got out, and soon we were getting calls from the media. When the *Ottawa Citizen* did a story on Ryan's well, we began to receive donations at least once a week. People from all over were catching Ryan's dream and were inspired to give.

A high school in Cornwall, Ontario, sold bottled water and presented WaterCan with a check for Ryan's well for $228. Central Children's Choir from Ottawa donated $1,000 for a Singing Well. The Ground Water Association of Eastern Ontario donated $2,700. And for every dollar Ryan raised, the Canadian International Development Agency (CIDA) matched it two for one. It wasn't long before Ryan had raised more than enough money for his well.

Ryan was invited to a board meeting to discuss details of the well. Gizaw, the engineer from Uganda who would design and build the well, was visiting from Africa. Ryan asked him:

How long would it take to build the well? Where would it be built? And would he get a picture? When Gizaw asked Ryan where he would like the well to be built, Ryan decided that it would be best near a school.

Ryan's well was built beside Angolo Primary School in Uganda, Africa, and was dedicated in April of 1999!

But Ryan's efforts had only begun. Ryan's entire school embraced his dream. First, a fund-raising project raised about $1,400. Then the school organized a pen pal letter-writing campaign between Ryan's class and the students at Angolo Primary School.

CTV and several big newspapers did lead stories on the project and interviewed Ryan. I was concerned about all the attention going to his head. When I asked Ryan's teacher, Lynn, about it she said, "I don't think so. Ryan never talks about it unless someone asks." She then told me the class had been raising funds throughout the year, and a water can had been placed on her desk. One day she'd walked into her classroom and found Ryan was at the water can, picking his picture off the side. "I already have enough money for my well," he explained. "This well will be for my class."

One day Ryan said, "I'm going to keep working until everyone in Africa has clean water." I thought, *Oh, boy! I'd heard about encouraging your children to be confident and dream big dreams.* I didn't want to say, like I almost had when he asked for the seventy dollars, that he couldn't make a difference. The truth was, he already had!

One night Ryan shared with us that one day, he would love to actually see his well. I replied, "Ryan, you will see your well. You might be twelve by the time we save enough money to visit Africa, but I promise you, will see your well."

One day, when Ryan was over visiting our neighbors, he announced, "When I'm twelve, I'm going to go over to Uganda and see my well." He wrote his pen pal Jimmy Akana in Uganda saying, "When I'm twelve, I'm coming to see you." This news spread like wildfire through the school in Uganda, and all the children wrote back to their pen pals in Ryan's class asking, "Are you coming with Ryan? Did you know Ryan is coming when he's twelve?"

When Jimmy wrote back, he said, "I always drink from your well, and I thank you for the well. We will be so happy to see you in Uganda when you're twelve."

At New Years, our neighbors, the Paynters, presented Ryan with a very special gift—enough air miles to fly three people halfway to Uganda to visit Jimmy and his well! The *Ottawa Citizen* then posted a request for more air miles. As a result of those donations, and some help from WaterCan, my husband and I were able to join Ryan. Together, we would all see the amazing well that has allowed Ryan's friends in Uganda to have fresh, clean water everyday.

On July 27, 2000, we arrived by truck in Angolo, Uganda. As we got close, a small group of children saw us and began calling out, "Ryan! Ryan!"

Ryan was astonished that they knew his name.

"Everybody for a hundred kilometers knows your name, Ryan," our companion Gizaw Shibru announced.

As we rounded a bend, we were stunned to see a crowd of about 5,000 children from nearby schools lining the roadside, waiting for us. As our truck approached, they excitedly began clapping rhythmically in welcome!

Ryan managed to wave a shy hello. A welcoming committee then led us all to Angolo Primary School. Ryan's pen pal, Jimmy, was waiting for him, and after they said hello, Jimmy took Ryan's hand and led him to the well for the ribbon-cutting ceremony. As we approached Ryan's well, we were overcome with joy. It was adorned with flowers, and on the concrete was inscribed: "Ryan's Well: Formed by Ryan H for Comm. of Angolo."

A village elder spoke words of appreciation: "Look around at our children. You can see they're healthy. This is because of Ryan and our friends in Canada. For us, water is life."

Ryan has also raised money for drilling equipment so that all districts can experience having clean, life-giving water. To date, Ryan has raised over $100,000, which, when matched with CIDA funding, totals over $300,000!

Ryan is now eleven years old and still going strong. There is a Ryan's Well Foundation. His dream has changed the lives of so many people, most of whom we will never meet. That special day in Uganda was one of the happiest days of my life, and it will live in my heart forever. Ryan ended that special day the same as usual, with his nightly prayer: "I wish for everyone in Africa to have clean water." Ryan has shown me what the power of dreams can do.

Susan Hreljac
As told to Darlene Montgomery
Chicken Soup for the Canadian Soul

Unstoppable

My mother, Beulah Hill Wetchen, was born in rural Alabama in 1908, a time when most women could not even think about having a career. As a small child, she would rise during the early hours of dawn and work long days in the cotton fields, enduring the unrelenting Alabama heat. She told me that it was at these times that she vowed to herself to become educated and pursue a career in nursing. In that era, it would take tremendous determination and ambition to fulfill her dream and goal of becoming a registered nurse.

The eldest of eleven children, Beulah was the one that her parents relied upon to help with the rest of the family. Many days she would stay home from school to help watch after the younger children while her mother and father worked in the fields. This made the decision to leave home and attend nurses' training in Tuscaloosa even more difficult because she knew her mother and father would desperately miss her assistance. In the end, however, it was this very decision which came to be more valuable to the family than any of them could have foreseen.

After my mother finished her nursing education, she stayed in Tuscaloosa, doing private-duty nursing and living in her own apartment. She was especially skilled in bedside nursing care, which at that time was at the heart of nursing.

One evening, she received a frantic call from her father. Howel, her seventeen-year-old brother, was gravely ill. He had been having abdominal pains for two days and was becoming progressively worse with fever and chills. The doctor, who had just left the house after administering an injection to Howel for pain, had told my grandparents, "If the boy lives until morning, he will probably be all right." Beulah's mother was not about to accept this extremely chilling statement and do nothing until morning. She told her husband, "We have to reach Beulah. She will know what to do."

Having no car and no phone, Beulah's father walked to the telephone office in the nearby town of Moundville to make the call. When he reached Beulah, she told him that she would take the midnight train bound for New Orleans. She immediately left for the Tuscaloosa train depot. She knew that the train was not scheduled to stop in Moundville, but she decided she would face that obstacle when she arrived at the depot.

Sure enough, when she arrived there and told the ticket agent where she needed to go, she was told the train would not be stopping in Moundville. Undeterred, my mother boarded the train and told the conductor, "You will stop this train in Moundville. My brother is very ill and may be dying. I must get to him right away, and I will be getting off this train where I need to!"

Apparently, the look in her eyes and the tone of her voice had the necessary impact on the conductor because the train stopped briefly—ever so briefly—in Moundville. My mother told me that she hadn't even completely taken her foot from the bottom step of that train when it started to move.

When my mother arrived at the house, her brother Howel was lying on a low cot in the living room. She knelt down by his side, and smelling a very distinct odor on his breath—and noting his pale, clammy skin—was certain he had suffered a ruptured appendix. She told her parents that they needed to get him to the hospital right away.

The same neighbor who had driven my grandfather to the train depot took them to the hospital in Tuscaloosa. Upon arrival at the hospital, my mother told the night nursing supervisor what she thought Howel's problem was and a surgeon was called. Within two hours after the phone call to my mother, Howel was in surgery. Beulah was allowed to stay in the operating room during the surgery. Opening the abdomen, the surgeon turned to her and said, "Miss Hill, your diagnosis is right. Your brother's appendix has ruptured. It's like muddy water in here, but we will do what we can to save him."

One week after the surgery, my uncle was recovering and on his way to good health again.

Last year my mother celebrated her ninetieth birthday and, in her true style, the party was everything she wanted it to be, with music and dancing and friends and family around her. As I watched her mingle with the guests, I pictured how she must have looked on that night long ago when she rose to her full five-foot two-inch height, looked that train conductor in the eye and said, "You *will* stop this train because I *am* going to get off!"

My Uncle Howel lived to serve his country during two world wars, marry, raise a fine family and become a loved and respected member of his community. All thanks to my mother, a woman with sufficient spirit to set out on a difficult path, ample courage to follow her dreams and enough determination to even stop a train.

Dixie Jane Sokolik
Chicken Soup for the Mother's Soul 2

The Impossible Just Takes a Little Longer

I cannot discover that anyone knows enough to say definitely what is and what is not possible.

—Henry Ford

At the age of twenty, I was happier than I had ever been before in my life. I was active physically: I was a competitive water-skier and snow-skier, and played golf, tennis, racquetball, basketball and volleyball. I even bowled on a league. I ran nearly every day. I had just started a new tennis court construction company, so my financial future looked exciting and bright. I was engaged to the most beautiful woman in the world. Then the tragedy occurred—or at least some called it that:

I awoke with a sudden jolt to the sound of twisting metal and breaking glass. As quickly as it all started, it was quiet again. Opening my eyes, my whole world was darkness. As my senses began to return, I could feel the warmth of blood covering my face. Then the pain. It was excruciating and overwhelming. I could hear voices calling my name as I slipped away again into unconsciousness.

Leaving my family in California on a beautiful Christmas evening, I had headed for Utah with a friend of mine. I was going there to spend the rest of the holidays with my fiancée, Dallas. We were to finish our upcoming wedding plans—our marriage was to be in five short weeks. I drove for the first eight hours of the trip, then, being somewhat tired and my friend having rested during that time, I climbed from the driver's seat into the passenger seat. I fastened my seat belt, and my friend drove away into the dark. After driving for another hour and a half, he fell asleep at the wheel. The car hit a cement abutment, went up and over the top of it, and rolled down the side of the road a number of times.

When the car finally came to a stop, I was gone. I had been ejected from the vehicle and had broken my neck on the desert floor. I was paralyzed from the chest down. Once I was taken by ambulance to a hospital in Las Vegas, Nevada, the doctor announced that I was now a quadriplegic. I lost the use of my feet and legs. I lost the use of my stomach muscles and two out of my three major chest muscles. I lost the use of my right triceps. I lost most of the use and strength in my shoulders and arms. And I lost the complete use of my hands.

This is where my new life began.

The doctors said I would have to dream new dreams and think new thoughts. They said because of my new physical condition, I would never work again—I was pretty excited about that one, though, because only 93 percent of those in my condition don't work. They told me that I would never drive again; that for the rest of my life I would be completely dependent on others to eat, get dressed or even to get from place to place. They said that I should never expect to get married because . . . who would want me? They concluded that I would never again play in any kind of athletic sport or competitive activity. For the first time in my young life, I was really afraid. I was afraid that what they said might really be true.

While lying in that hospital bed in Las Vegas, I wondered where all my hopes and dreams had gone. I wondered if I would ever be made whole again. I wondered if I would work, get married, have a family and enjoy any of the activities of life that had previously brought me such joy.

During this critical time of natural doubts and fears, when my whole world seemed so dark, my mother came to my bedside and whispered in my ear, "Art, while the difficult takes time . . . the impossible just takes a little longer." Suddenly a once darkened room began to fill with the light of hope and faith that tomorrow would be better.

Since hearing those words eleven years ago, I am now president of my own company. I am a professional speaker and a published author—*Some Miracles Take Time*. I travel more than 200,000 miles a year sharing the message of The Impossible Just Takes a Little Longer to Fortune 500 companies, national associations, sales organizations and youth groups, with some audiences exceeding 10,000 people. In 1992, I was named the Young Entrepreneur of the Year by the Small Business Administration for a six-state region. In 1994, *Success* magazine honored me as one of the Great Comebacks of the Year. These are dreams that have come true for me in my life. These dreams came true not in spite of my circumstances . . . but, perhaps, because of them.

Since that day I have learned to drive. I go where I want to go and I do what I want to do. I am completely independent and I take care of myself. Since that day, I have had feeling return to my body and have gained back some of the use and function of my right triceps.

I got married to that same beautiful and wonderful girl a year and a half after that fateful day. In 1992, Dallas, my wife, was named Mrs. Utah and was third runner-up to Mrs. USA! We have two children—a three-year-old daughter named McKenzie Raeanne and a one-month-old son named Dalton Arthur—the joys of our lives.

I have also returned to the world of sports. I have learned to swim, scuba dive and parasail—as far as I know I am the first quadriplegic of record to parasail. I have learned to snow ski. I have also learned to play full-contact rugby. I figure they can't hurt me any worse! I also race wheelchairs in 10Ks and marathons. On July 10, 1993, I became the first quadriplegic in the world to race thirty-two miles in seven days between Salt Lake City and St. George, Utah—probably not one of the brightest things I have ever done, but certainly one of the most difficult.

Why have I done all of these things? Because a long time ago I chose to listen to the voice of my mother and to my heart rather than to the concourse of dissenting voices around me, which included medical professionals. I decided that my current circumstances did not mean I had to let go of my dreams. I found a reason to hope again. I learned that dreams are never destroyed by circumstances; dreams are born in the heart and mind, and only there can they ever die. Because while the difficult takes time, the impossible just takes a little longer.

Art E. Berg
A 3rd Serving of Chicken Soup for the Soul

Reprinted by permission of Aaron Bacall.

Dare to Imagine

The doctors told me I would never walk again, but my mother told me I would, so I believed my mother.

—Wilma Rudolph,
"The fastest woman on Earth,"
three-time gold medalist, 1960 Olympics

When people find out that I competed in the Olympics, they assume I've always been an accomplished athlete. But it isn't true. I was not the strongest, or the fastest, and I didn't learn the quickest. For me, becoming an Olympian was not developing a gift of natural athletic ability, but was, literally, an act of will.

At the 1972 Olympics in Munich, I was a member of the U.S. pentathlon team, but the tragedy of the Israeli athletes and an injury to my ankle combined to make the experience a deeply discouraging one. I didn't quit; instead I kept training, eventually qualifying to go with the U.S. team to Montreal for the 1976 Games. The experience was much more joyous, and I was thrilled to place thirteenth. But still, I felt I could do better.

I arranged to take a leave of absence from my college

coaching job the year before the 1980 Olympics. I figured that twelve months of "twenty-four-hour-a-day training" would give me the edge I needed to bring home a medal this time. In the summer of 1979, I started intensively training for the Olympic trials to be held in June of 1980. I felt the exhilaration that comes with single-minded focus and steady progress towards a cherished goal.

But then in November, what appeared to be an insurmountable obstacle occurred. I was in a car accident and injured my lower back. The doctors weren't sure exactly what was wrong, but I had to stop training because I couldn't move without experiencing excruciating pain. It seemed all too obvious that I would have to give up my dream of going to the Olympics if I couldn't keep training. Everyone felt so sorry for me. Everyone but me.

It was strange, but I never believed this setback would stop me. I trusted that the doctors and physical therapists would get it handled soon, and I would get back to training. I held on to the affirmation: I'm getting better every day and I will place in the top three at the Olympic trials. It went through my head constantly.

But my progress was slow, and the doctors couldn't agree on a course of treatment. Time was passing, and I was still in pain, unable to move. With only a few months remaining, I had to do something or I knew I would never make it. So I started training the only way I could—in my head.

A pentathlon consists of five track and field events: the 100-meter hurdle, the shot put, the high jump, the long jump and the 200-meter sprint. I obtained films of the world-record holders in all five of my events. Sitting in a kitchen chair, I watched the films projected on my kitchen wall over and over. Sometimes, I watched them in slow motion or frame by frame. When I got bored, I watched them backwards, just for fun. I watched for hundreds of hours, studying and absorbing. Other times, I lay on the couch and visualized the experience of competing in minute detail. I know some people thought I was crazy, but I wasn't ready to give up yet. I trained as hard as I could—without ever moving a muscle.

Finally, the doctors diagnosed my problem as a bulging disc. Now I knew *why* I was in agony when I moved, but I still couldn't train. Later, when I could walk a little, I went to the track and had them set up all five of my events. Even though I couldn't practice, I would stand on the track and envision in my mind the complete physical training routine I would have gone through that day if I had been able. For months, I repeatedly imagined myself competing and qualifying at the trials.

But was visualizing enough? Was it truly possible that I could place in the top three at the Olympic trials? I believed it with all my heart.

By the time the trials actually rolled around, I had healed just enough to compete. Being very careful to keep my muscles and tendons warm, I moved through my five events as if in a dream. Afterwards, as I walked across the field, I heard a voice on the loudspeaker announcing my name.

It took my breath away, even though I had imagined it a thousand times in my mind. I felt a wave of pure joy wash over me as the announcer said, "Second place, 1980 Olympic Pentathlon: Marilyn King."

Marilyn King
As told to Carol Kline
Chicken Soup for the Unsinkable Soul

18 Holes in His Mind

Major James Nesmeth had a dream of improving his golf game—and he developed a unique method of achieving his goal. Until he devised this method, he was just your average weekend golfer, shooting in the mid- to low-nineties. Then, for seven years, he completely quit the game. Never touched a club. Never set foot on a fairway.

Ironically, it was during this seven-year break from the game that Major Nesmeth came up with his amazingly effective technique for improving his game—a technique we can all learn from. In fact, the first time he set foot on a golf course after his hiatus from the game, he shot an astonishing 74! He had cut 20 strokes off his average without having swung a golf club in seven years! Unbelievable. Not only that, but his physical condition had actually deteriorated during those seven years.

What was Major Nesmeth's secret? Visualization.

You see, Major Nesmeth had spent those seven years as a prisoner of war in North Vietnam. During those seven years, he was imprisoned in a cage that was approximately four and one-half feet high and five feet long.

During almost the entire time he was imprisoned, he saw no one, talked to no one and experienced no physical activity. During the first few months he did virtually nothing but hope and pray for his release. Then he realized he had to find some way to occupy his mind or he would lose his sanity and probably his life. That's when he learned to visualize.

In his mind, he selected his favorite golf course and started playing golf. Every day, he played a full 18 holes at the imaginary country club of his dreams. He experienced everything to the last detail. He saw himself dressed in his golfing clothes. He smelled the fragrance of the trees and the freshly trimmed grass. He experienced different weather conditions—windy spring days, overcast winter days and sunny summer mornings. In his imagination, every detail of the tee, the individual blades of grass, the trees, the singing birds, the scampering squirrels and the lay of the course became totally real.

He felt the grip of the club in his hands. He instructed himself as he practiced smoothing out his down-swing and the follow-through on his shot. Then he watched the ball arc down the exact center of the fairway, bounce a couple of times and roll to the exact spot he had selected, all in his mind.

In the real world, he was in no hurry. He had no place to go. So in his mind he took every step on his way to the ball, just as if he were physically on the course. It took him just as long in imaginary time to play 18 holes as it would have taken in reality. Not a detail was omitted. Not once did he ever miss a shot, never a hook or a slice, never a missed putt.

Seven days a week. Four hours a day. Eighteen holes. Seven years. Twenty strokes off. Shot a 74.

Bert Decker
A 2nd Helping of Chicken Soup for the Soul

Against All Odds

As she rushed up the hill toward the brownstone building in the bitter cold of a December morning, Bonnie Bentley Cewe prayed she would not let herself down.

The long gash just above her hairline barely had healed, the puncture wounds on her hand still showed, her leg ached inside the brace. She fought to keep her concentration as she took her seat in the drafty room. She wished the chairs weren't attached to the long table. They barely swiveled on their posts, and she felt cramped.

For six years, she had immersed herself in books, college courses and term papers to prepare for the next five hours. It had taken every ounce of determination to get this far; if she failed now, she wasn't sure she had it in her to try again.

Surrounded by dozens of people sniffling, coughing and blowing their noses, Bonnie looked at the other law school hopefuls, wondering whether they all had taken the preparation class for the law school admission test.

She had meant to.

In the early 1970s, when she dropped out of her junior

year of high school, Bonnie had little doubt she would never look back.

She wanted to be an artist and had lost interest in school. She quit, and in a few years was married with two sons. For a while, she dressed windows and set up displays for department stores and modeled; later, she helped her husband with the books for his home improvement business.

After four years of a stormy marriage, Bonnie sought a divorce. She didn't want her sons to grow up thinking that kind of relationship was normal.

Three days before Christmas in 1983, she walked out of her marriage and into an apartment she could barely afford, but where she and her sons, then three and four, could start over. She used money relatives had given her for the boys for Christmas to pay the first month's rent.

Christmas morning, the three gathered in the kitchen to eat their Cream of Wheat. They ate it standing up. One of the boys asked why they were eating on their feet, and the other said, "Because there are no chairs." The simplicity of the answer threw the boys into convulsions of laughter.

It was a hard Christmas, unlike any they had ever had.

Bonnie was twenty-eight years old. A high school dropout. A single mother on welfare.

She could see herself fifteen years in the future, ringing up groceries at a supermarket, for her boys who would be teenagers with no chance for college. The thought scared her.

She would have to go back to school.

Her first stop was to go to an open house at an event with a name that fit Bonnie's state of mind: "You Can" day.

At first, Bonnie planned to take the last route to college—

prepare herself for an exam to get her high school equivalency diploma. But a teacher at the program persuaded her to attend the full-time night high school program. Night classes, homework and studying would better prepare her for what she knew she would work toward: law school.

In the divorce, she had lost her house, which had been in her in-laws' name as a safeguard in case her husband's business failed. She was worse off financially than she had expected, and she felt helpless and victimized by the legal system.

But adult high school classes were a long way from law school, and about a dozen years had passed since Bonnie was a student. Now, as she walked past the locker that she had used as a teenager, she had to fight her feelings of failure.

But when she finished the year, her grades were nearly perfect.

Her sons, Daniel and Nicholas, joined the hundreds of guests at the adult education commencement exercises in the spring of 1985. When Bonnie walked to the high school stage in cap and gown to receive her diploma, Daniel and Nicholas stood up in the middle of the seated crowd and clapped their hands together so proudly, so ecstatically, that their mother would never forget it.

Now, as the proctor handed out the LSAT exam and booklets in the drafty room, Bonnie still wondered how a thirty-four-year-old single mother could compete with the young pre-law students in the seats around her.

They probably didn't worry about money, she thought. *Their parents probably put them through college, placed credit cards in their wallets, bought them cars.* In her wallet, behind her college identification card, were her week's worth of food stamps.

Who am I kidding? she thought as she looked around the room.

When she opened the test booklet, the words on the page blurred. Her thoughts raced. She fought the old fear of failure.

Earning her high school diploma gave Bonnie a yearlong taste of how crammed her life would be and how little money she would have if she went on to college. It would be another seven years of scrambling to make ends meet, another seven years of juggling studies and child-rearing and her job as a bartender.

She plunged on.

If she went part time to Albertus Magnus College in New Haven, where she was accepted after earning her diploma, and went part time to law school after that, she was looking at fifteen years of school.

Fifteen years.

She couldn't say it with a straight face. She would have to do it full time.

She worked as many nights as she could, sometimes six or seven a week, as a bartender because her ex-husband rarely sent her child support.

Albertus Magnus accepted her on the basis of her grades in the high school program. School officials were impressed by how passionately she believed in herself.

Even in those first interviews, she spoke of law school.

The head of the business department, Sister Charles Marie Brantl and a finance professor, the Reverend Charles Shannon, raised their eyebrows as they listened. It wasn't her desire they doubted, but her ability to go far with the burdens she had to carry.

It had taken Bonnie so long to be walking across a college campus, she wouldn't cheat herself of any opportunities. A finance major, she took high-level courses, sometimes with one or two other students. She joined several business clubs. She studied theater.

But sometimes the burden of trying to do everything at once overwhelmed her. One night, before final exams, she walked through the piles of clothes and toys carpeting the floor of the boys' room to put some clean clothes away. She stepped on something and heard it break. Her calm broke with it, and she angrily fled to her room in tears, slamming the door to her bedroom in her fury.

An hour or so later, she heard a tap on her door. When she opened it, her boys were standing there. Close your eyes, they said, as they marched her to their bedroom. They had done something special for her, she knew. *Boy, they really know what I'm going through,* she thought.

She opened her eyes to a surprise, but not the one she was expecting. They had not cleared the room, but merely a passage through the mess, a tunnel just wide enough for her to pass. She looked at them cross-eyed. The three fell on the floor, laughing until tears streamed down their faces.

There were other people who helped, relatives, friends. Her parents cared for her sons often. Her sons' soccer coach took the boys to after-school sports practices and games. And Bonnie couldn't afford to be embarrassed when she asked other mothers for rides or babysitting.

For six years, her boss at the restaurant, Dan Alix, overlooked her studying between drink orders, the books lying open on the bar. More than once, he worked the bar for her so she could be part of the audience at her sons' school plays or be home when they were sick.

Sometimes friends asked her why she didn't leave the restaurant for one of the better-paying restaurant jobs in various hotels in New Haven. She shook her head—bosses such as Alix were hard to come by.

Coworkers and customers at the restaurant let her know they were floored by the years she intended to put in. In some ways they let her know they didn't think her dream was possible, in other ways they encouraged her.

For a theater class, Bonnie had to do a skit. She needed an audience, but she had had little time to make friends. The day of the skit, as she walked onto the stage for her monologue, she looked down at the theater seats. Two waitresses from work were sitting there, her small but precious audience.

Working at the restaurant was barely enough to cover the bills, let alone pay for college.

She took out student loans, trying not to be conscious of the risk totals. She would owe so much, tens of thousands of dollars.

Albertus Magnus gave her financial aid, her high class standing won her scholarships.

When Gertrude M. Moshier and members of the Wallingford Business and Professional Women's Club first heard about Bonnie, they wanted to help. As Bonnie won their respect with her perseverance, Moshier came to believe "she was the most deserving person the group had ever seen."

That group, and the Wallingford Junior Women's Club, pick a different student for their scholarships each year. After they discovered Bonnie, she became a woman they kept believing in, and awarding scholarships to, throughout her time at Albertus Magnus.

There were other groups that gave her money; $500 here, $200 there, checks that added up to thousands of dollars in tuition that Bonnie would not have to pay back.

For all of them, she became a cause celebre, a symbol of what women who took control of their lives could accomplish.

She made the honors society, keeping up a 3.8 cumulative grade-point average—the equivalent of straight As—for four years.

Until this moment, in the drafty room, Bonnie somehow always had been able to pull it off. But she could lose it all in the next few hours. She refocused on the test in front of her. An essay. She read the instructions.

The question asked her to choose between two potential athletic award candidates and make a case for selecting one young women over the other. To one of the young women, winning came easily. To the other, success was a struggle, a struggle she overcame with hard work and persistence.

In her essay, Bonnie passionately argued the merits of the second young woman, the one who wasn't naturally gifted.

She was arguing for herself.

Early one hot summer morning in 1989, three months before she was to take her LSAT exam, Bonnie was sleeping in her apartment. A silent figure pushed up an unlocked screen to her living room and made his way to her bedroom.

Her room was dark, except for the dim glow of a nightlight. The man climbed on top of her in her bed. She recognized the voice; it was her neighbors' seventeen-year-old nephew, who had recently arrived to stay with his relatives. He had befriended her boys, played basketball with them.

He whispered that if she made noise, that if she resisted, he would kill her sons. Then he raped her.

She was frightened, frozen; her mind raced. He was big, strong, violent. She wouldn't be able to protect her children. She was as quiet as she could be. She prayed her sons would not awaken.

The man dragged her from the apartment and forced her to drive her tiny red Ford Escort, a used one she had gleefully bought with a loan three weeks earlier after years of worrying that one old car or another might break down.

Twice, he made her pull the car over so that he could beat her. After the second time, he forced her into the luggage compartment of the car. As it began moving again, she lay there, trying to envision escape scenes from films she had seen.

She carefully unscrewed the pliable cover above her, a small particleboard section that raised when the hatchback was opened. To keep it from rattling, she held it in place until the car slowed down.

She was certain he would kill her the next time the car stopped. *It can't be over,* she thought. *We have so much look forward to.*

She thought about her boys. She decided then that she would fight back.

When the car slowed, she picked up the jack, and, with whatever energy she had left, shot through the compartment. She slammed the jack against the side of her attacker's head. The car skidded through a row of guardrails, knocked down a highway exit sign and somersaulted down a twenty-foot drop.

She woke up hours later, her body straddling the front and back seats. Her forehead was split open. She wasn't sure whether it happened in the accident or whether her attacker used the jack to get even. He was gone.

Blood was everywhere. It matted her hair, covered her clothes. She got up and slowly stumbled up the rocky ledge to the highway. A gasoline station was ahead. She had to get to a telephone, tell someone the boys were in danger.

Somehow she reached the station and banged on the door for help. Two attendants, frightened by her appearance, told her they wouldn't protect her. They told her to go away, to the McDonald's restaurant a little farther up in the highway rest area. She shook her head and stood there, begging.

The attendants relented, but were so frightened that her attacker might return that they made her hide under the counter of the station. Her first thoughts were of her boys: *What if the attacker went back for them?* She was frantic. The attendants called 911.

Waiting for the rescue squad, she used the station telephone to call her ex-husband and ask him to get their sons.

The boys were awakened by their father and the police banging on the apartment's windows. Before they answered the door, they went to their mother's room. They saw her bed covers in a heap at the side of the bed, and they thought she was dead.

For four days, Bonnie was in the hospital, where she was treated for her head injury, her leg injury and scores of cuts, bruises and other wounds. Crisis counselors tried to help her with the psychological wounds.

Afterward, she went to stay with her parents and the boys

went with their father. She needed the boys, wanted to be with them, but her mother couldn't care for them. She had just had major surgery herself.

Bonnie lost sleep knowing he was out there, on the run. She gave up her apartment so he couldn't find her, explaining to her landlord what had happened. But he took her to court for the lost rent, many months' worth and won. She found a new apartment, but would have to pay her old landlord $5 a week until the debt was covered.

Six days after Bonnie was attacked, her senior year began at Albertus Magnus.

Intent on finishing school, she concealed her head wounds with creative hairdressing. Her leg in a brace, her head bandaged, she drove to class.

When she pulled into the school parking lot, it was empty. Determined to return, but with her emotions reeling, she had arrived a day early.

The next day, she went back again. Her dream would be her savior. She couldn't let it slip away.

Her boys' coming home, about a month after the rape, boosted her spirits. And her boss, Dan Alix, amazed her when he sent her paychecks regularly even though she couldn't work. She was on the books as a part-time employee at the time and he didn't owe her any money. But he ignored her status. He was going to help.

Bonnie had planned to take a preparation course to get ready for the law school entrance exams. But now she was out of money and emotionally battered. She couldn't do it.

Every time she tried to study for the LSAT and her regular classes, she had flashbacks. He could have killed her, left her boys motherless, even killed them.

The night before the law school entrance exam, her parents watched her two children so she could study. She sat at her worn kitchen table. She took a sample test made up of three forty-five-minute sections and then worked on a writing exercise. Her thoughts were jumbled. She was terrified about the next day. But she scored well on the test she gave herself.

About midnight, when she finally lay down, she cried herself to sleep.

She had worked so hard, overcome so much already. The man, "that creep," could take this from her, too, if she couldn't force the images away.

Bonnie turned the page of the test and took a deep breath. The next three sections were multiple choice. The questions bounced around in her mind, rebounding off the sides of her brain and then coming back like a boomerang. Sections on logical and analytical thinking—brain teasers.

Next came lengthy reading passages, followed by a string of questions, to prove her ability to understand what she had read.

She turned to the last page of the test. She was done.

Nothing could ease the anxiety during the eight weeks it took for her score to arrive in the mail.

Some of her mail still was being sent to her parents' house, where she had stayed for a while after the rape. The envelope was delivered there one day in February.

Bonnie was in her apartment, and asked her mother to open the envelope while she waited on the telephone. Her mother searched for the score box, Bonnie waiting, impatient.

Finally her mother found it. Above average. Strong enough to get her into a law school, but not into the one she wanted.

In the spring, Bonnie graduated from Albertus Magnus College with highest honors. After the ceremony, she wished that she could have her friends over, buy a bottle of wine to celebrate. She didn't have enough money.

About the same time, she was invited back to her high school to attend the adult education graduation. When the scholarships were being announced, they called her name, again and again. This time the money was for law school. She hustled up to the podium in a cropped jacket and short skirt, frosted blond hair flying. She kept her chin down, trying to hide her emotion.

Today, Bonnie is a practicing attorney, having graduated from the Quinnipiac University School of Law in 1993. Once, she had dreamed of doing so well on the LSAT that she would get accepted at Yale Law School. That's okay, Bonnie says. She'll just teach there someday.

Amy Ash Nixon
Chicken Soup for the Working Woman's Soul

[EDITORS' NOTE: *In 1994, the perpetrator was convicted of kidnapping, assaulting and raping Bonnie, and was sentenced to twenty-five years in prison, to be served after he serves a Georgia sentence for the rape of another woman.*]

"I love being a partner, Mr. Jenkins!
There's just one problem."

The Cowboy's Story

*It never occurred to me that I couldn't
do it. I always knew that if I worked
hard enough, I could.*

—Mary Kay Ash, founder of Mary Kay Cosmetics

When I started my telecommunications company, I knew I was going to need salespeople to help me expand the business. I put the word out that I was looking for qualified salespeople and began the interviewing process. The salesperson I had in mind was experienced in the telemarketing communications industry, knew the local market, had experience with the various types of systems available, had a professional demeanor and was a self-starter. I had very little time to train a person, so it was important that the sales-person I hired could "hit the ground running."

During the tiresome process of interviewing prospective salespeople, into my office walked a cowboy. I knew he was a cowboy by the way he was dressed. He had on corduroy pants and a corduroy jacket that didn't match the pants; a short-sleeved snap-button shirt; a tie that came about halfway down his chest with a knot bigger than my fist; cowboy boots; and a baseball cap. You can imagine what I was thinking: "Not what I had in mind for my new company." He sat down in front of my desk, took off his cap and said, "Mister, I'd just shore appreciate a chance to be a success in the telephone biness." And that's just how he said it, too: *biness*.

I was trying to figure out a way to tell this fellow, without being too blunt, that he just wasn't what I had in mind at all. I asked him about his background. He said he had a degree in agriculture from Oklahoma State University and that he had been a ranch hand in Bartlesville, Oklahoma, for the past few years during the summers. He announced that was all over now, he was ready to be a success in "biness," and he would just "shore appreciate a chance."

We continued to talk. He was so focused on success and how he would "shore appreciate a chance" that I decided to give him a chance. I told him that I would spend two days with him. In those two days I would teach him everything I thought he needed to know to sell one type of very small telephone system. At the end of those two days he would be on his own. He asked me how much money I thought he could make.

I told him, "Looking like you look and knowing what you know, the best you can do is about $1,000 per month." I went on to explain that the average commission on the small telephone systems he would be selling was approximately $250 per system. I told him if he would see 100 prospects per month, that he would sell four of those prospects a telephone system. Selling four telephone systems would give him $1,000. I hired him on straight commission with no base salary.

He said that sounded great to him because the most he had

ever made was $400 per month as a ranch hand and he was ready to make some money. The next morning, I sat him down to cram as much of the telephone "biness" I could into a twenty-two-year-old cowboy with no business experience, no telephone experience and no sales experience. He looked like anything but a professional salesperson in the telecommunications business. In fact, he had none of the qualities I was looking for in an employee, except one: He had an incredible focus on being a success.

At the end of two days of training, Cowboy (that's what I called him then, and still do) went to his cubicle. He took out a sheet of paper and wrote down four things:

1. I will be a success in business.
2. I will see 100 people per month.
3. I will sell four telephone systems per month.
4. I will make $1,000 per month.

He placed this sheet of paper on the cubicle wall in front of him and started to work.

At the end of the first month, he hadn't sold four telephone systems. However, at the end of his first ten days, he had sold *seven* telephone systems.

At the end of his first year, Cowboy hadn't earned $12,000 in commissions. Instead, he had earned over $60,000 in commissions.

He was indeed amazing. One day, he walked into my office with a contract and payment on a telephone system. I asked him how he had sold this one. He said, "I just told her, 'Ma'am, if it don't do nothing but ring and you answer it, it's a heck of a lot prettier than that one you got.' She bought it."

The woman wrote him a check in full for the telephone system, but Cowboy wasn't really sure I would take a check, so he drove her to the bank and had her get cash to pay for the system. He carried thousand-dollar bills into my office and said, "Larry, did I do good?" I assured him that he did good!

After three years, he owned half of my company. At the end of another year, he owned three other companies. At that time we separated as business partners. He was driving a $32,000 black pickup truck. He was wearing $600 cowboy-cut suits, $500 cowboy boots and a three-carat horseshoe-shaped diamond ring. He had become a success in "biness."

What made Cowboy a success? Was it because he was a hard worker? That helped. Was it because he was smarter than everyone else? No. He knew nothing about the telephone business when he started. So what was it? I believe it was because he knew the **Ya Gotta's for Success:**

He was focused on success. He knew that's what he wanted and he went after it.

He took responsibility. He took responsibility for where he was, who he was and what he was (a ranch hand). Then he took *action* to make it different.

He made a decision to leave the ranch in Bartlesville, Oklahoma, and to look for opportunities to become a success.

He changed. There was no way that he could keep doing the things that he had been doing and receive different results. And he was *willing* to do what was necessary to make success happen for him.

He had vision and goals. He saw himself as a success. He also had written down specific goals. He wrote down the four items that he intended to accomplish and put them on the wall in front of him. He saw those goals every day and focused on their accomplishment.

He put action to his goals and stayed with it even when it got tough. It wasn't always easy for him. He experienced slumps like everyone does. He got more doors slammed in his face and telephones in his ear than any salesperson I have ever known. But he never let it stop him. He kept on going.

He asked. Boy, did he ask! First he asked me for a chance, then he asked nearly all the people he came across if they wanted to buy a telephone system from him. And his asking paid off. As he likes to put it, "Even a blind hog finds an acorn every once in a while." That simply means that if you ask enough, eventually someone will say yes.

He cared. He cared about me and his customers. He discovered that when he cared more about taking care of his customers than he cared about taking care of himself, it wasn't long before he didn't have to worry about taking care of himself.

Most of all, **Cowboy started every day as a winner!** He hit the front door expecting something good to happen. He believed that things were going to go his way regardless of what happened. He had no expectation of failure, only an expectation of success. And I've found that when you expect success and take action on that expectation, you almost always get success.

Cowboy has made millions of dollars. He has also lost it all, only to get it all back again. In his life as in mine, it has been that once you know and practice the principles of success, they will work for you again and again.

He can also be an inspiration to you. He is proof that it's not environment or education or technical skills and ability that make you a success. He proves that it takes more: It takes the principles we so often overlook or take for granted. These are the principles of the **Ya Gotta's for Success.**

Larry Winget
A 2nd Helping of Chicken Soup for the Soul

Baby-Lift

A mother's love perceives no impossibilities.

—Paddock

As my friend Carol Dey and I rode through the dusty streets of Saigon in a creaky VW bug on April 26, 1975, I was sure we looked exactly like what we were: a couple of Iowa homemakers. Three months earlier, when Carol and I had each agreed to escort three Vietnamese orphans to their American families, the trip seemed exciting but safe. My husband, Mark, and I had applied to adopt an orphan ourselves, in the future. We all wanted somehow to make a difference. How were Carol and I to know we would arrive just as Saigon was under siege?

Bombs were falling less than three miles from the city, and even now citizens streamed past our car, their worldly possessions tied onto pushcarts or onto their backs. But our driver, Cheri Clark, the overseas director of Friends of the Children of Vietnam (FCVN), seemed more excited than scared. From the moment we landed, she had pelted us with unexpected news.

"Did you hear President Ford okayed a giant baby-lift as a

last resort to save these children? Instead of taking out six orphans, you'll be taking home 200!" Carol and I looked at each other in amazement.

"We were able to get a planeload of children out yesterday," Cheri continued. "At the last minute, the Vietnamese government refused to let it go, but the plane was already cleared for takeoff—so it just left! That's 150 children safe in San Francisco!"

Even our years as nurses hadn't prepared us for what we found at the FCVN Center. Every inch of every floor of the stately French mansion was covered with blankets or mats—each of which was covered with babies—hundreds of crying, cooing infants, each orphaned or abandoned.

Although jet lag threatened to overwhelm us, Carol and I were determined to help prepare the children for the next day's airlift. Ours was scheduled to be the first airlift out. Each child needed clothes and diapers, a check-up and a legal name. The devoted volunteers—Vietnamese and American—worked around the clock.

The next morning we learned that, in retaliation for the earlier unauthorized takeoff, our agency would not be on the first flight out after all. We would be allowed to leave only when—and if—the Vietnamese government permitted.

"There's nothing we can do but wait and pray," Cheri said calmly. We all knew that time was running out for the Americans and orphans in Saigon.

In the meantime, Carol and I joined other volunteers hastily preparing children for another flight that had been cleared, this one going to Australia.

In scorching heat, we loaded babies into a VW van from

which the middle seat had been removed. I sat on a bench seat with twenty-one infants packed around my feet; the others did likewise.

We arrived at the airport to find traffic at a standstill. An enormous black cloud billowed into the sky in front of us. As we passed through the gate, we heard a terrible rumor: The first planeload of orphans—the plane we had begged to be on—had crashed after takeoff.

It couldn't be true. We chose not to believe it. We had no time to worry as we went about the task of loading fussing, dehydrating babies onto the flight to freedom. Carol and I stood together holding hands while the plane took off. Once they were gone, we danced on the tarmac. One planeload was free!

Our joy was short-lived. We returned to find the adults at the center in stunned grief. Cheri haltingly confirmed what we'd refused to believe. Hundreds of babies and escorts had been killed when their plane blew apart after takeoff. No one knew if it had been shot down or bombed.

Relief workers and babies! Who could do such a thing? And would they do it again? Overcome, I sank onto a rattan couch and sobbed uncontrollably. The plane we fought to be on had crashed, and so had my faith. I had the terrible feeling I'd never see my husband and daughters again.

That evening, Cheri beckoned me. Even in a world of drastic surprises, I was unprepared for her words: "In the satchel of papers you brought over were your adoption papers. Instead of waiting to be assigned a son, why don't you go and choose one?"

It seemed my worst fears and deepest desires came true on

the same day. Wouldn't our daughters be thrilled if I came home with their new brother! But . . . how could I choose a child? With a prayer on my lips, I entered the next room.

As I meandered through the sea of babies, a child crawled over to me wearing only a diaper. When I lifted him to me, he nestled his head into my shoulder and seemed to hug me back. I carried him around the room, looking at and touching each baby. Upstairs, the hall was carpeted with more infants. The little one in my arms seemed to cuddle closer as I whispered a prayer for the decision I was about to make. I felt his shallow breath as he embraced my neck and settled into my heart.

"Hello, Mitchell," I whispered to him. "I'm your mom."

The next day we got the thrilling news that our flight had been cleared to leave that afternoon. Together, all the volunteers packed up the 150 children still remaining.

Babies were placed three or four to a seat on an unused city bus for the first of several trips to the airport; Carol and I rode along. Again, a disaster. We arrived at the airport to find that Vietnamese President Thieu had canceled our flight. Trying not to panic, Carol and I helped unload the babies into filthy Quonset huts in the stifling heat. Would we never get out? Would we all die in the siege of Saigon?

Finally Ross, an FCVN worker, burst in. "President Thieu is allowing only one flight, and it's got to leave immediately. Let's get these babies loaded on—and you, too!" he said to Carol and me. Our chance to leave!

"No," I said. "I left my son back at the center for a later bus. I've got to go back and get him."

"LeAnn," Ross said, "you see how things are. Leave while

you can. I promise we'll try to get your son out to you."

Yes, I saw how things were. "I won't leave without Mitchell!"

"Hurry, then," Ross said. "I'll hold the plane as long as I can, but we can't ruin these other children's chances."

I ran to the bus. The driver screeched recklessly through the chaotic city and delivered me a mile from the center. The strap of my sandal broke and the shoe flapped wildly against my ankle. I took it off while still running. My side ached fiercely as I raced up the stairs to the center.

"The plane . . ." I gasped as Cheri eased me into a chair. "I know. I just got off the phone with the airport."

"And?"

Cheri grinned. "The plane will wait for you!"

I beamed a smile while gasping for breath.

"Not only that—we can take more babies for this flight—and a second flight has been approved, as well!"

Tears streaming down my face, I found Mitchell and held him close. I made a silent vow never to leave him again.

A few hours later, I felt my heart pound as I boarded a gutted cargo plane. Twenty cardboard boxes formed a row down the center, with two to three infants per box. Toddlers and older children sat belted on the long side benches, bewilderment on their faces.

The doors were closed; the engine's roar was deafening. I couldn't remove the image of the black cloud from the downed plane from my mind. A panic came over me and I gripped Mitchell closer. I prayed the Lord's Prayer as the plane taxied down the runway. Then . . . we were airborne. If we could only live through the next five minutes, I knew we'd make it home.

Finally the captain spoke. "We're out of artillery range.

We're safe. We're going home!" Shouts of joy filled the plane.

As I thought of the chaos of war, I prayed for those we'd left behind. And then I uttered a prayer of thanks that Carol and I had been allowed to make a difference, in a bigger way than we'd ever dreamed. We were all headed for lives filled with new hope—including the son I hadn't known I had.

LeAnn Thieman
As told to Sharon Linnéa
Chicken Soup for the Mother's Soul

A Cowboy's Last Chance

Joe Wimberly sat on a tree stump and stared at his house. It sits on a skinny road that meanders out of Cool, Texas, population 238, a flat, dusty place without so much as a drugstore or a gas station.

"It ain't exactly the Ponderosa," Joe once told his wife, Paula, as he swept his arm toward the three acres or so of scrub grass that went with the little house. "But it's our ranch."

Joe wore a cowboy hat and sported a bushy black mustache that matched his eyes, as dark as Texas oil. He was missing a tooth, right on the fifty-yard line. But his jaw was square and strong. And he stood taller than his five-foot-five-inch frame.

Earlier that day, Joe received a call from the banker, who wanted money. The charge cards were full, the payments were late, the checking account was overdrawn. Joe didn't have a nickel to his name, except for the house. And he swore he would never let that go.

Being a cowboy was all Joe Wimberly knew. He had learned to ride a horse by the time he was four. At seven, he was herding cattle with his father. At thirteen, he was climbing onto the back of a steer.

When Joe turned eighteen, he set out for a world where the Old West still lives, the last untamed range for the true American cowboy—the rodeo. Soon, anybody who knew rodeo came to know the name of Joe Wimberly. There were days when he walked around with one thousand dollars in his pocket. Other times he could not afford to eat. But there was never a day when he wanted to trade his chaps for a job with a boss looking over his shoulder.

It scared Paula to watch Joe on a bull. Still, she knew being a cowboy put the sparkle in his eyes, and she never wanted to see that fade. So whenever he headed out the door, she kissed him good-bye, crossed her fingers and said a prayer.

Joe was gone to the rodeo about two hundred days a year. He was one thousand miles away on the night Paula gave birth to a daughter, Casey. They had no insurance. "How we gonna pay for things, Joe?" Paula's voice cracked across the telephone wires.

"I'm gonna win," Joe told her. "And I'm gonna keep winning."

He was as good as his word. With the grace of a gymnast and the nerve of a bank robber, Joe dazzled crowds at little county fairs and big city stadiums throughout the West. In the 1980s he qualified five times to compete in the National Finals Rodeo. In his best year, Joe won more than eighty thousand in prize money.

However, with travel expenses and entry fees ranging from twenty-five dollars to more than three hundred dollars, times were never easy, especially after the birth of another daughter, Sami. But bills got paid, and when Paula took a job in a pharmacy, they saved enough for a down payment on their house.

Joe could already envision a place for a horse corral on

what was now the Wimberly Ranch. He poured a cement slab near the back door, then took a tree twig and carved the names of the Wimberly clan in the cement. Shortly after, Paula gave birth to a son, McKennon.

Even when he was hurt, Joe seldom missed a rodeo. Once, his wrist got caught in the rope, and he dangled on the side of the bull as it kicked him and knocked him unconscious. He was taken away on a stretcher, blood running down his face.

He came back from that injury and many others. But by now weeks had passed since he'd brought home a paycheck. *Maybe I'm just not trying hard enough,* Joe thought. The bills were all way past due.

Mesquite, on the outskirts of Dallas, is the site of one of the best-known rodeos in America. One day a Dodge Truck executive called rodeo owner Neal Gay with a promotion idea. If Gay would pick the meanest, wildest bull he could find, Dodge would put up a five-thousand-dollar prize for any cowboy who could ride it for eight seconds. The pot would grow by five hundred dollars every time the bull shucked a rider. The bull would be named after a new truck, Dodge Dakota.

Gay liked the idea. He contacted Lester Meier, a rodeo producer who owned a nightmarish black bull that weighed 1,700 pounds and had a single horn crawling ominously down the side of its white face.

"You got your Dodge Dakota," Meier told Gay.

Of the thirty bull riders who competed at Mesquite every weekend, only one, assigned randomly by a computer, got a crack at Dodge Dakota. Week after week, the beast sent cowboys hurtling, even a former world champion. But Joe Wimberly was never chosen.

Joe was carrying a fifty-pound feed sack toward the horse pen at his ranch when he heard the screen door slam. Paula hurried over. "The rodeo called, Joe," she said. "You drew Dodge Dakota for Friday night."

Joe dropped the feed sack. "You're kiddin' me."

"No, Joe, I ain't kiddin'." The pot had grown to $9,500.

Joe started riding the bull in his mind. *Stay loose,* he told himself. *This is just another bull.* But Joe knew Dakota was a vicious outlaw.

According to those who had studied Dakota, the bull started every ride the same way. It blew out of the chute, took one jump, kicked over its head, stepped backward and spun to the left, all in about two seconds. After that, it was anybody's guess.

That Friday, Joe paced behind the chutes. He looked up in the stands and saw his family. When the spotlight flashed on him, he pulled himself over the rails and settled on the broad, humped back of Dodge Dakota. He wrapped the rope around his right hand; the other end was twisted around the belly of the beast.

Lord, I'm comin' to you like a friend, Joe pleaded silently. *You know how much I need this ride.* Beads of sweat grew on his forehead.

The gate swung open. Dakota bolted, and Joe's thighs squeezed tight. The beast bucked hard, lifting Joe into the air, then slammed down. The bull bellowed and twisted to its left. Foam spewed from its snout. The cowboy thumped back on his seat, the rope burning his hand. He shot in the air, his head snapping backward, hat flying off, but he hung on. The stands thundered—six thousand fans on their feet, screaming, shrieking, stomping. The clock flashed five seconds, six seconds . . .

Dakota groaned in a voice from hell and bucked violently, four hoofs in the air. Suddenly the bull ran alone.

Crashing flat on his back, Joe looked up to see the belly of the bull and its slamming hoofs. He scrambled away as the clowns chased Dakota back to its pen. Joe searched for Paula in the stands and slowly mouthed the words, "I am sorry."

Later that summer, Joe was again paired with Dodge Dakota. In an instant this time, the bull slammed him and his dreams to dirt.

Now Joe was scrambling for money. He shod horses. He entered jackpot bull-riding contests, organized a rodeo school. But none of this put much of a dent in his debts. He was finally forced to place an ad in the house-for-sale section of the newspaper. "It's only boards and paint and siding," he told a tearful Paula. "If we stay together as a family, it doesn't matter where we are."

Joe paid another humiliating visit to the banker. "Can't I have just a little more time?" the cowboy pleaded.

"You've had time, Joe," the banker said flatly.

One Friday in September, Joe was riding at Mesquite. With all his troubles at home, Joe hadn't been thinking much about bulls. The purse for Dodge Dakota had grown to seventeen thousand dollars.

They had stopped announcing ahead of time which cowboy would ride Dakota. Now they drew the name during intermission. Suddenly a rodeo official called out, "Hey, Joe Wimberly, you got Dakota."

Neal Gay came by. "Third time's the charm," the rodeo owner said with a wink.

As Paula watched from the stands, her heart began to

pound. Twice before, she had seen Joe's hopes soar as high as the stars, and then sink to the depths.

Joe climbed up to the bucking chutes. The season was almost over. Twenty-four times a cowboy had boarded Dodge Dakota, and twenty-four times the bull had won. The pot was big enough to save his house, to pay the bills, even to have a little extra.

The cowboy pulled himself over the rails and straddled the bull that stomped inside its chute. The rope was wrapped around his hand as tight as a noose. One of his favorite phrases came to mind: "If you ain't got no choice, be brave."

The gate swung open, and the clock started counting the eight most important seconds of Joe Wimberly's life. The huge black beast bellowed. Nearly a ton of muscle and bone thundered by. Dakota's head snapped violently. Its eyes flashed fire. Dust rose from its kicking hoofs. And the clock ticked— two seconds . . . three . . . four . . .

Joe bounced on the bull's hard back, straining for balance. Then another punishing buck. He dangled at the edge, fighting gravity. Six seconds . . . seven seconds . . .

Joe crashed to the dirt as the horn sounded. A sudden hush swept over the arena. The fans stared down at the rodeo boss, who was staring at the timekeeper, who was staring at the clock.

An excited official raised his arms in the air, the sign of a touchdown. Joe had made it by two-hundredths of a second.

The cowboy dropped to his knees. "Thank you, Jesus!" Joe cried.

Paula fell sobbing into the arms of a spectator. The two girls sprinted down the stairs of the grandstands, while McKennon screamed, "Daddy did it! Daddy did it!"

From his knees, Joe looked up and met Paula's eyes as she ran toward him. The roar of the crowd swept down on the arena floor, where the Wimberly family squeezed together in a ten-armed hug, their tears spilling on the dust.

It was past 2 A.M. when they got home. Joe went to the telephone and dialed the banker. "Who's this!" came a groggy mumble.

"Why, this here is Joe Wimberly," he said, "and I was just calling to say I got a check for you."

Dirk Johnson
Chicken Soup for the Country Soul

The Day Mother Cried

Coming home from school that dark winter's day so long ago, I was filled with anticipation. I had a new issue of my favorite sports magazine tucked under my arm and the house to myself. Dad was at work, my sister was away, and Mother wouldn't be home from her new job for an hour. I bounded up the steps, burst into the living room and flipped on a light.

I was shocked into stillness by what I saw. Mother, pulled into a tight ball, with her face in her hands, sat at the far end of the couch. She was crying. I had never seen her cry.

I approached cautiously and touched her shoulder. "Mother?" I asked. "What's happened?"

She took a long breath and managed a weak smile. "It's nothing, really. Nothing important. Just that I'm going to lose this new job. I can't type fast enough."

"But you've only been there three days," I said. "You'll catch on." I repeated a line she had spoken to me a hundred times when I was having trouble learning or doing something important to me.

"No," she said sadly. "There's no time for that. I can't carry my end of the load. I'm making everyone in the office work twice as hard."

"They're just giving you too much work," I said, hoping to find injustice where she saw failure. She was too honest to accept that.

"I always said I could do anything I set my mind to," she said, "and I still think I can in most things. But I can't do this."

I felt helpless and out of place. At age sixteen I still assumed Mother could do anything. Some years before, when we sold our ranch and moved to town, Mother had decided to open a day nursery. She had no training, but that didn't stand in her way. She sent away for correspondence courses in child care, did the lessons and in six months formally qualified herself for the task. It wasn't long before she had a full enrollment and a waiting list. Parents praised her, and the children proved by their reluctance to leave in the afternoon that she had won their affection. I accepted all this as a perfectly normal instance of Mother's ability.

But neither the nursery nor the motel my parents bought later had provided enough income to send my sister and me to college. I was a high-school sophomore when we sold the motel. In two years, I would be ready for college. In three more, my sister would want to go. Time was running out, and Mother was frantic for ways to save money. It was clear that Dad could do no more than he was doing already—farming eighty acres in addition to holding a full-time job.

Looking back, I sometimes wonder how much help I deserved. Like many kids of sixteen, I wanted my parents' time and attention, but it never occurred to me that they might have needs and problems of their own. In fact, I understood nothing of their lives because I looked only at my own.

A few months after we'd sold the motel, Mother arrived home with a used typewriter. It skipped between certain letters and the keyboard was soft. At dinner that night I pronounced the machine a "piece of junk."

"That's all we can afford," Mother said. "It's good enough to learn on." And from that day on, as soon as the table was cleared and the dishes were done, Mother disappeared into her sewing room to practice. The slow tap, tap, tap went on some nights until midnight.

It was nearly Christmas when I heard her tell Dad one night that a good job was available at the radio station. "It would be such interesting work," she said. "But this typing isn't coming along very fast."

"If you want the job, go ask for it," Dad encouraged her.

I was not the least bit surprised, or impressed, when Mother got the job. But she was ecstatic.

Monday, after her first day at work, I could see that the excitement was gone. Mother looked tired and drawn. I responded by ignoring her.

Tuesday, Dad made dinner and cleaned the kitchen. Mother stayed in her sewing room, practicing. "Is Mother all right?" I asked Dad.

"She's having a little trouble with her typing," he said. "She needs to practice. I think she'd appreciate it if we all helped out a bit more."

"I already do," I said, immediately on guard.

"I know you do," Dad said evenly. "And you may have to do more. You might just remember that she is working primarily so you can go to college."

I honestly didn't care. In a pique, I called a friend and went out to get a soda. When I came home the house was dark, except for the band of light showing under Mother's door. It seemed to me that her typing had gotten even slower. I wished she would just forget the whole thing.

My shock and embarrassment at finding Mother in tears on Wednesday was a perfect index of how little I understood the pressures on her. Sitting beside her on the couch, I began very slowly to understand.

"I guess we all have to fail sometime," Mother said quietly. I could sense her pain and the tension of holding back the strong emotions that were interrupted by my arrival. Suddenly, something inside me turned. I reached out and put my arms around her.

She broke then. She put her face against my shoulder and sobbed. I held her close and didn't try to talk. I knew I was doing what I should, what I could and that it was enough. In that moment, feeling Mother's back racked with emotion, I understood for the first time her vulnerability. She was still my mother, but she was something more: a person like me, capable of fear and hurt and failure. I could feel her pain as she must have felt mine on a thousand occasions when I had sought comfort in her arms.

Then it was over. Wiping away the tears, Mother stood and faced me. "Well, Son, I may be a slow typist, but I'm not a parasite and I won't keep a job I can't do. I'm going to ask tomorrow if I can finish out the week. Then I'll resign."

And that's what she did. Her boss apologized to her, saying that he had underestimated his workload as badly as she had overestimated her typing ability. They parted with mutual respect, he offering a week's pay and she refusing it. A week later Mother took a job selling dry goods at half the salary the radio station had offered. "It's a job I can do," she said simply. But the evening practice sessions on the old green typewriter continued. I had a very different feeling now when I passed her door at night and heard her tapping away. I knew there was something more going on in there than a woman learning to type.

When I left for college two years later, Mother had an office job with better pay and more responsibility. I have to believe that in some strange way she learned as much from her moment of defeat as I did, because several years later, when I finished school and proudly accepted a job as a newspaper reporter, she had already been a reporter with our hometown paper for six months.

Mother and I never spoke again about the afternoon when she broke down. But more than once, when I failed on a first attempt and was tempted by pride or frustration to scrap something I truly wanted, I remember her selling dresses while she learned to type. In seeing her weakness, I had not only learned to appreciate her strengths, I had discovered some of my own.

Not long ago, I helped Mother celebrate her sixty-second birthday. I made dinner for my parents and cleaned up the kitchen afterward. Mother came in to visit while I worked, and I was reminded of the day years before when she had come home with that terrible old typewriter. "By the way," I said, "whatever happened to that monster typewriter?"

"Oh, I still have it," she said. "It's a memento, you know . . . of the day you realized your mother was human. Things are a lot easier when people know you're human."

I had never guessed that she saw what happened to me that day. I laughed at myself. "Someday," I said, "I wish you would give me that machine."

"I will," she said, "but on one condition."

"What's that?"

"That you never have it fixed. It is nearly impossible to type on that machine, and that's the way it served this family best."

I smiled at the thought. "And another thing," she said. "Never put off hugging someone when you feel like it. You may miss the chance forever."

I put my arms around her and hugged her and felt a deep gratitude for that moment, for all the moments of joy she had given me over the years. "Happy birthday!" I said.

The old green typewriter sits in my office now, unrepaired. It is a memento, but what it recalls for me is not quite what it recalled for Mother. When I'm having trouble with a story and think about giving up, or when I start to feel sorry for myself and think things should be easier for me, I roll a piece of paper into that cranky old machine and type, word by painful word, just the way Mother did. What I remember then is not her failure, but her courage, the courage to go ahead.

It's the best memento anyone ever gave me.

Gerald Moore
Chicken Soup for the Christian Family Soul

THE FAMILY CIRCUS.   By Bil Keane

"Grandma says if y'd want to leave footprints in the
sands of time, you should wear work boots."

The Power of Determination

*Everything can be taken from a man
but one thing: the last of human freedoms—
to choose one's own way.*

—Viktor Frankl

The little country schoolhouse was heated by an old-fashioned, potbellied coal stove. A little boy had the job of coming to school early each day to start the fire and warm the room before his teacher and his classmates arrived.

One morning they arrived to find the schoolhouse engulfed in flames. They dragged the unconscious little boy out of the flaming building more dead than alive. He had major burns over the lower half of his body and was taken to the nearby county hospital.

From his bed the dreadfully burned, semi-conscious little boy faintly heard the doctor talking to his mother. The doctor told his mother that her son would surely die—which was for the best, really—for the terrible fire had devastated the lower half of his body.

But the brave boy didn't want to die. He made up his mind that he would survive. Somehow, to the amazement of the physician, he did survive. When the mortal danger was past, he again heard the doctor and his mother speaking quietly. The mother was told that since the fire had destroyed so much flesh in the lower part of his body, it would almost be better if he had died, since he was doomed to be a lifetime cripple with no use at all of his lower limbs.

Once more the brave boy made up his mind. He would not be a cripple. He would walk. But unfortunately from the waist down, he had no motor ability. His thin legs just dangled there, all but lifeless.

Ultimately he was released from the hospital. Every day his mother would massage his little legs, but there was no feeling, no control, nothing. Yet his determination that he would walk was as strong as ever.

When he wasn't in bed, he was confined to a wheelchair. One sunny day his mother wheeled him out into the yard to get some fresh air. This day, instead of sitting there, he threw himself from the chair. He pulled himself across the grass, dragging his legs behind him.

He worked his way to the white picket fence bordering their lot. With great effort, he raised himself up on the fence. Then, stake by stake, he began dragging himself along the fence, resolved that he would walk. He started to do this every day until he wore a smooth path all around the yard beside the fence. There was nothing he wanted more than to develop life in those legs.

Ultimately through his daily massages, his iron persistence and his resolute determination, he did develop the ability to stand up, then to walk haltingly, then to walk by himself—and then—to run.

He began to walk to school, then to run to school, to run for the sheer joy of running. Later in college he made the track team.

Still later in Madison Square Garden this young man who was not expected to survive, who would surely never walk, who could never hope to run—this determined young man, Dr. Glenn Cunningham, ran the world's fastest mile!

Burt Dubin
Chicken Soup for the Soul

9

Never Give Up

Never give up.
Keep your thoughts and
your mind always on the goal.
—Tom Bradley

Consider This

*One of the secrets of success
is to refuse to let temporary setbacks defeat us.*
—Mary Kay

- Henry Ford failed and went broke five times before he finally succeeded.
- Eighteen publishers turned down Richard Bach's 10,000-word story about a "soaring" seagull, *Jonathan Livingston Seagull,* before Macmillan finally published it in 1970. By 1975 it had sold more than seven million copies in the U.S. alone.
- Richard Hooker worked for seven years on his humorous war novel, *M*A*S*H,* only to have it rejected by twenty-one publishers before Morrow decided to publish it. It became a runaway bestseller, spawning a blockbusting movie and a highly successful Television series.
- When Pablo Casals reached ninety-five, a young reporter threw him the following question. "Mr. Casals, you are ninety-five and the greatest cellist that ever lived. Why do you still practice six hours a day?" Mr. Casals

answered, "Because I think I'm making progress."

- After having lost both legs in an air crash, British fighter pilot Douglas Bader rejoined the British Royal Air Force with two artificial limbs. During World War II he was captured by the Germans three times—and three times he escaped.

- Louis L'Amour, successful author of over 100 western novels with over 200 million copies in print, received 350 rejections before he made his first sale. He later became the first American novelist to receive a special congressional gold metal in recognition of his distinguished career as an author and contributor to the nation through his historically based works.

- General Douglas MacArthur might never have gained power and fame without persistence. When he applied for admission to West Point, he was turned down, not once but twice. But he tried a third time, was accepted and marched into the history books.

- In 1952, Edmund Hillary attempted to climb Mount Everest, the highest mountain then known to humans—29,000 feet straight up. A few weeks after his failed attempt, he was asked to address a group in England. Hillary walked to the edge of the stage, made a fist and pointed at a picture of the mountain. He said in a loud voice, "Mount Everest, you beat me the first time, but I'll beat you the next time because you've grown all you are going to grow ... but I'm still growing!" On May 29, only one year later, Edmund Hillary succeeded in becoming the first man to climb Mount Everest.

- After having his cancer-ridden leg amputated, young Canadian Terry Fox vowed to run on one leg from coast to coast the entire length of Canada to raise $1 million for cancer research.
- Former U.S. Senator and former New York Knicks basketball star Bill Bradley practiced relentlessly. He had five shots on the basketball court from which he would shoot twenty-five times. If he didn't hit twenty-two baskets out of the twenty-five shots. He'd start over. He was determined to stay there and do it over and over until he could do it right almost every time.
- When NFL running back Herschel Walker was in junior high school, he wanted to play football, but the coach told him he was too small. He advised young Herschel to go out for track instead. Undaunted by the lack of encouragement and support, he ignored the coach's advice and began an intensive training program to build himself up. Only a few years later, Herschel Walker won the Heisman trophy.
- David W. Hartman went blind at the age of eight. His dream to become a medical doctor was thwarted by Temple University Medical School, when he was told that no one without eyesight had ever completed medical school. He courageously faced the challenge of "reading" medical books by having twenty-five complete medical textbooks audio-recorded for him. At twenty-seven David Hartman became the first blind student to ever complete medical school.
- Colonel Sanders had the construction of a new road put him out of business in 1967. He went to over 1,000 places

trying to sell his chicken recipe before he found a buyer interested in his eleven herbs and spices. Seven years later, at the age of seventy-five, Colonel Sanders sold his fried chicken company for a finger-lickin' $15 million!

- Young Dr. Ignatius Piazza fresh out of chiropractic school, wanted to open a practice on the beautiful Monterey Bay area of California. The local chiropractic community told him that there were not enough potential patients to support another practice. For the next four months, Piazza spent ten hours a day going door-to-door and introducing himself as a new chiropractic doctor in town. He knocked on 12,500 doors, spoke to 6,500 people and invited them to come to his future open house. As a result of his perseverance and commitment, during his first month of practice he saw 233 new patients and earned a record income for that time of $72,000 in one month!

- Dr. Seuss's first children's book, *And to Think That I Saw It on Mulberry Street,* was rejected by twenty-seven publishers. The twenty-eighth publisher, Vanguard Press, sold 6 million copies of the book.

- Alex Haley got a rejection letter once a week for four years as a budding writer. Later in his career, Alex was ready to give up on the book *Roots* and himself. After nine years on the project, he felt inadequate to the task and was ready to throw himself off a freighter in the middle of the Pacific Ocean. As he was standing at the back of the freighter, looking at the wake and preparing to throw himself into the ocean, he heard the voices of all his ancestors saying. "You go do what you got to do because they are all up there watching. Don't give up. You can do it. We're counting on you." In the subsequent weeks the final draft of *Roots* poured out of him.

- After Thomas Carlye lent the manuscript of *The French Revolution* to a friend whose servant carelessly used it to kindle fire, he calmly went to work and rewrote it.

- In 1905, the University of Bern turned down a doctoral dissertation as being irrelevant and fanciful. The young physics student who wrote the dissertation was Albert Einstein, who was disappointed but not defeated.

Jack Canfield and Mark Victor Hansen

... AND EVER SINCE i FOUND OUT THAT BABE RUTH STRUCK OUT 1,330 TIMES .... i'VE BEEN FEELING LOTS BETTER !!

Begin at the Beginning

*Anyone who stops learning is old, whether
at twenty or eighty. Anyone who keeps
learning stays young. The greatest thing
in life is to keep your mind young.*

—Henry Ford

I had always wanted to go back to school. And one day, thirty years later, I did. I don't know what gave me the guts to do it, other than a burning desire to finish something I had started years ago. When the day came to register, I was terrified and got cold feet.

"I decided that I'm not going back to school," I told my family. "I don't really want this after all. I'm going to forget about it."

My daughter, who was a freshman in college at the time, sensed my apprehension. "Mom," she pleaded, "you've wanted to do this all your life. I'll go with you to register; I'll even stand in line for you." And that she did.

I had dropped out of college in my senior year, and now it was like starting all over again. I didn't know where to start.

As chance would have it, in one of the first textbooks I opened as "an older returning student," I came across a quote by Lewis Carroll (from his books, *Alice in Wonderland* and *Through the Looking Glass*): "Begin at the beginning," the King said gravely, "and go on till you come to the end; then stop." My sentiments exactly, Mr. Carroll. Thank you.

But it had been a long time since I had "cracked a book." I studied sometimes eight hours a day, forgetting to eat lunch or feed the goldfish. My husband and I would have to make dates (only on weekends) in order to see one another, and at times I felt guilty for choosing to spend an hour in the library and then having to make dinner from a box.

When my graduation day finally arrived, I was ecstatic. Not only was I fulfilling a lifelong dream, but my daughter was also graduating—on the same day. We had a mother-daughter celebration with family and friends, proudly displaying our newly acquired bachelor of arts degrees. I have never been so proud of my daughter. And when my daughter stood next to me at picture-taking time, our black robes melding into one, I could tell that she was very proud of her mother.

Shortly after graduation, I attained teaching credentials. And because I loved to learn and found teaching to be one of the best avenues to learning, I decided to continue my studies and go for a master of arts degree in education and creative writing. It was an excellent choice. I loved teaching, and I loved writing. With a degree in interdisciplinary studies, I could combine the two.

Graduate school was exhausting and overwhelming at times. I cut my hair short and got the first permanent of my life so that I wouldn't have to bother with setting my hair. I learned to make a two-hour spaghetti sauce rather than my usual six-hour one and learned that I could live without my nightly rendezvous with Ted Danson from *Cheers*.

The next two years flew by, but it wasn't easy. At one point, I came home from school, threw my books on the kitchen counter, and announced to my family, "I'm quitting! I've had it!" After crying for a couple of hours and talking it over, I realized I had come too far to quit now. I had run the race well, and I was tired. I decided I would take one day at a time, resting along the sidelines.

I was in my final quarter of graduate school with only one class left to take when I was diagnosed with cancer. *Cancer? Was I going to die? Would I have to leave my children before I wanted to? Would I be able to finish school?*

A couple of days later, shaken and apprehensive, I appeared at my professor's door, leaving a puddle of tears and broken dreams on his shoulders. "Don't worry about it," he said. "We can work something out."

"But I have to go to Los Angeles for seven weeks of radiation therapy and won't be able to come to class." He suggested that I do my work in Los Angeles and send it to him through the mail. We could keep in touch by telephone.

"And don't give up," he said adamantly. "I have never met a student with so much determination. You are the kind of student teachers come to school for. And you have to use that same determination to fight this thing."

I promised him I would finish my schoolwork, and I would fight for my life. The kitchen table in my apartment in Los Angeles became my desk for the next seven weeks. I went for my treatment across the street then returned to my apartment and kitchen table to study and write my papers. I mailed my completed assignments from a post office nearby.

Right before Christmas, I graduated with honors and a master of arts degree in education and English. My graduation day was special for a lot of reasons. I had finished my radiation treatments and had finished my schoolwork. My husband and my children, along with my mother, sister and brother, were in the audience of the auditorium when they called my name and handed me my diploma. My eyes met theirs, and I wanted to shout, "Hey! Look at me! I did it!" After I passed my tassel to the left side of my cap from the right, I waved to them like I was royalty. Queen Elizabeth had nothing on me!

As I write this piece, I am three years clean of cancer. I take each day and live it, keeping my promise to my professor and to myself to fight for my life. I have lived to see my daughter become a teacher and my son graduate from college with a degree in psychology. Talk about pride!

And still today, I continue my own journey down the avenue of learning. I learn something new every day from my students who sit in front of me with questioning faces. They are my greatest teachers. I have taught many children in these past three years and have prayed daily that I have touched their lives as they have touched mine.

And in my quiet times, I can take a pen in my hand and write my thoughts and feelings on a clean sheet of paper, something I've loved to do since I was a child. Life doesn't get much better than this.

Lola De Julio De Maci
Chicken Soup for the Teacher's Soul

Embassy of Hope

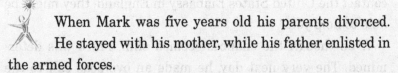

*Luck is a matter of preparation
meaning opportunity.*
—Oprah Winfrey

When Mark was five years old his parents divorced. He stayed with his mother, while his father enlisted in the armed forces.

As Mark grew up he occasionally had recollections of the brief time he shared with his father and longed to see him again one day. However, as he grew into his late teens, thoughts of his father began to subside. Mark was now more into girls, motorcycles and partying.

After he graduated from college, Mark married his high school sweetheart. A year later, she gave birth to a healthy bouncing baby boy. The years passed.

One day when Mark's son was five years old and as Mark was preparing to shave his face, his son looked up at him and laughed, "Daddy, you look like a clown with that whipped cream on your face."

Mark laughed, looked into the mirror and realized how much

his son looked like him at that age. Later, he remembered a story his mother had once told him of him telling his own father the same thing.

This event started him thinking about his own father a lot and he began quizzing his mother. It had been a long time since Mark had spoken of his father, and his mother told him that it was now over twenty years since she had spoken to him. In addition, all her knowledge of his whereabouts ceased when Mark became eighteen.

Mark looked deep into his mother's eyes and said, "I need to find my father." His mother then told him that his dad's relatives had all passed away, and she had no idea where to begin searching for him but added, "Maybe, just maybe, if you contact the United States Embassy in England, they might be able to help you."

Even though the chances seemed slim, Mark was determined. The very next day, he made an overseas call to the American Embassy and the conversation went something like this.

"U.S. Embassy, how may we help you?"

"Ahh . . . hi, my name is Mark Sullivan and I am hoping to find my father."

There was a long pause and the ruffling of some papers, and then the man said:

"Is this Mr. Mark Joseph Sullivan?"

"Yes," Mark answered anxiously.

"And were you born in Vincennes, Indiana, at the Good Samaritan Hospital on October 19, 1970?"

"Yes . . . yes," he answered again.

"Mark, please don't hang up!"

Mark then overheard the man as he made an excited announcement to his coworkers: "Everyone listen . . . I have terrific news . . . Lieutenant Ronald L. Sullivan's son is on the phone . . . he found us!"

Without a pause Mark heard in the background the roar of a crowd—obviously the entire staff of the embassy, clapping, cheering, laughing, crying and praising God.

When the man returned to the phone he said: "Mark, we are so glad you have called. Your father has been coming here in person or calling almost every single day *for the past nine years,* checking to see if we had located you."

The following day, Mark received a phone call from his overjoyed father. His father explained to him that he had been traveling to the United States every six months trying to find him. Once he was even given an address, but when he got there the landlord told him that Mark and his mother had moved out just two weeks prior, leaving no forwarding address.

Having found each other, Mark and his dad enjoyed an emotional reunion. They are now part of each other's lives, and see each other as often as possible.

David Like
Chicken Soup for the Parent's Soul

Opportunity

*If you don't hear opportunity
knocking, find another door.*

—Omar Periu

Every fiber of my small, seven-year-old body was fear-
fully shaking as we walked through Customs and
explained the purpose of our trip: "We're vacationing in
Miami," I heard my pregnant mother say as I clung to her
dress. Even though I heard those words, I knew we would
never be going home again.

Communism was quickly tightening the noose around the
free enterprise system in Cuba, and my father, a successful
entrepreneur, decided it was time to take his family and flee
to a land where freedom, promise and opportunity still
thrived. Looking back now, it was the most courageous decision I've ever seen anybody make.

Castro's regime was watching my father very carefully,
making it necessary for my mother to bring my brother and
me over first. My father met us a few weeks later. Miami
International Airport overwhelmed me. Everybody was

speaking in strange words that didn't make sense to me. We had no money, no family—nothing but the clothes on our backs.

Within a few months, we were on a church-sponsored flight to Joliet, Illinois, via Chicago's O'Hare International Airport. A burst of cold air greeted us as we walked out of the terminal into the still talked-about winter of 1961. It had snowed nearly four feet, and amidst the blowing drifts stood a young priest by a large International Suburban, waiting to take us to our new home. This was absolutely amazing for a Cuban boy who had never seen snow.

My father was an educated man and owned a chain of gas stations and a car dealership in Cuba. Unable to speak English, he adapted quickly by finding work as a mechanic; and thanks to St. Patrick's Church, we were able to find a comfortable although small apartment in a middle-class neighborhood. We didn't have a lot, but we had each other, a whole lot of love and my father's burning desire to succeed.

It was during this time that my father, with his tattered Spanish copy of Dale Carnegie's book, *How to Win Friends and Influence People,* taught me one of the greatest lessons in life. He told me over and over again: "It doesn't matter who you are, where you're from or what color you are. You can do anything you put your mind to." These words gave me comfort and inspiration as my brother and I mixed into the great Chicago melting pot.

My brother Ed and I struggled in school because we couldn't speak English. It wasn't uncommon to be called a "spic," not to be chosen to be on a team or have our hand-me-down bikes stolen, but my father's words continued to burn inside of me. We also met some truly wonderful people who helped us overcome the obstacles of adjusting to our new surroundings. Many of these people are still my best friends today.

When I was fourteen, my father was already teaching me about the great principle of free enterprise. He gave me $18 for every set of valves and engine heads I would clean and grind (what we called a valve job). Later he taught me how to hire other people to do the work for me, and I went out and found new customers and collected money—basically ran the business. Little did I know he was teaching me how to be an entrepreneur. America was truly a land of promise.

I was also fortunate to be born into a musically talented family, and I remember listening to my mother sing beautiful Spanish songs to me as I was growing up. These songs inspired me to sing in the church choir as a boy soprano, and because of this same influence, my brother Ed started a contemporary rock band. I attended every band rehearsal and at night harmonized with him and my mother. Later, through working as a laborer in a stone quarry and a scholarship, I studied opera and music at Southern Illinois University. After two years of college, I went back to work in the stone quarry and saved the money I earned for my move west to California.

My goal in moving to California was to break into the music business and cut my own records. It didn't take very long for reality to set in. I had to take a job selling health club memberships to support myself. Depression set in. I was broke and didn't know where to turn. Then I met Tom Murphy, one of the owners of the health club.

My father always told me that if you want to be wealthy, you have to do what wealthy people do, so I asked Mr.

Murphy if we could talk over coffee to find out what made him so successful. It just so happened that Mr. Murphy was the business partner of Tom Hopkins, one of the country's top sales trainers. So, of course, he recommended that I start attending sales training seminars, reading self-improvement books and listening to sales tapes. He also introduced me to many successful business men and women and their published materials. I was so hungry for success that it didn't take long before I was the top salesperson in the company. But that wasn't good enough. After saving every penny I could, I invested in my own health club. By the time I was finished, I owned nine of the most successful health clubs and sports medicine facilities in the United States, but I still hadn't achieved my goal—to cut my own record.

Recording my first demo was exciting yet discouraging, as I presented it to record company after record company. Each time I heard the word "no." Not to be defeated, I recorded the demo in Spanish and took it back to the same record companies—all with the same results. On the verge of giving up, I called my father to discuss what had happened. He said, "Omar, you're doing very well financially, aren't you?" I replied that I was. "Well, why don't you just buy a record company and record your music!"

When I went back to the record company I intended to buy, hoping to save my ego, I asked the company executives one more time to record my music. They said, "Omar, we can't help you. Go to Broadway. You'll be great there." You should have seen their faces when I told them I was going to be the new owner.

I then set out to finance, record and produce my first album in Spanish. From there I went on to be named "Best Latin

Male Vocalist" and "Entertainer of the Year" in 1986, 1987 and 1988 "CHIN de PLATA" and "OTTO."

Today I am enjoying success as a public speaker and trainer with Tom Hopkins International. It's such a thrill for me now to help others learn how to find the right opportunities to achieve their career goals. Take it from me, my father was right: You can achieve anything you want in life when you set your mind to it.

Omar Periu
A 3rd Serving of Chicken Soup for the Soul

The Magic Skates

*It's okay if you fail at something,
as long as you don't give up, as long as
you say—okay, I will try it again!*

—Marilyn Bell Di Lascio

We had one hour left before skating the program we'd worked toward for years. I tried to stay focused, but in an hour we could be the Olympic pairs champions!

I thought back to the end of 1983, and how we had finished the season on a high—taking the bronze medal at the World Championships in Helsinki. Some people, however, felt we should have taken the gold. Now, suddenly, Underhill and Martini were one of the favorites going into the 1984 season—and the Olympic year.

I was nineteen and Paul was twenty-two. Here we were, with all these extraordinary expectations for us, and the additional pressure of knowing that this would be our last year. No matter what the outcome of our competitions, we would be leaving amateur skating at the end of the season. Along with our coaches, Louis Strong and Sandra Bezic, we had made the decision to focus exclusively on preparing for the Canadian Championships in January, then the Olympics, and finally, the World Championships in Ottawa.

From the beginning of the season, however, things just started to unravel. My skates had always allowed me to fly, but now they were failing me. I struggled with my equipment for the entire season, never feeling totally on top of my game. Nothing would flow, and we were both constantly frustrated. Then, in early January, a bad fall left me with torn ligaments in my foot, so we weren't able to skate at the Canadian Championships—our only tune-up event before the Olympics.

By the time we could skate again, there were only three weeks left until the Olympics. On the plane to Sarajevo, we saw the cover of *Mcleans* magazine: "Barbara Underhill and Paul Martini—Canada's Olympic Hopefuls!" Everybody felt we could do it, but we just knew we weren't totally prepared.

Once in Sarajevo, though, we caught the excitement. Our practices weren't the best, but we still felt we could do it when it counted—in front of the judges.

When we stepped onto the ice, we knew this was our one shot at our dream. We skated well, nailing all the hard elements, and I thought to myself: *We did it!* And then it happened. As we were stepping into an easy element (a spin we could do in our sleep), my edge just slid off. I smashed right into Paul as he was coming around, sending us both crashing onto the ice. We were very lucky. His blade was just inches from my head, and the fall could have been catastrophic.

We picked ourselves up and somehow finished the program, but it was just a blur after that. We were totally shattered. We finished sixth after that short program, leaving us stunned and without hope. Then, after a sleepless night, we still had to get out on the ice for an early morning practice, which was just terrible.

When we finally stepped onto the ice to skate our long program, we were both just empty shells. We went through the motions anyway, and to add insult to injury, we dropped from sixth to seventh place. We were devastated.

When we arrived home, there was a big crowd waiting for the Canadian team at the airport. Brian Orser walked through ahead of us, and a huge cheer went up because he had brought home the silver medal. We came out next, and suddenly there was total silence. People didn't know what to say to us. They avoided us, and we felt alone and heartbroken. It felt like people had given up on us—like we didn't have their support anymore. I had never been to a funeral, but I thought this was what it must be like. It was the death of our dream.

It was only three weeks before the World Championships in Ottawa. As we began to practice, all the same frustrations continued—no matter what we tried. Everything was a struggle, and we just couldn't figure out what was wrong. Communication was difficult between us, and I had never felt so alone. We'd always had fun skating, but this was more like torture with so much tension.

About a week before the World Championships, we were at the rink for our daily practice. Paul was sitting in the coffee shop, with his feet up, and I was circling the ice—tears streaming down my face. Our coach, Louis, called us into his office and said, "Look, there's no point in embarrassing ourselves. I'm going to phone Ottawa and just call it off. There's no point in going."

He later told us he had been bluffing, but I didn't think so then. We'd never given up on anything before, and I just couldn't handle the thought of giving up now. I left his office.

It just happened that Brian Orser was at the rink that day. He came down every couple of weeks to train at the Granite Club. He and I had started together at the Junior Worlds back in 1978, and we were very, very close friends. He was still tying on his skates, so I sat down beside him, put my head on his shoulder and just started to sob. "It's over," I managed to get out. "We're not going."

He looked at me, thought for a second, and then said, "Why don't you go back to last year's boots?" He said it *so easily*.

Now I had thought those boots were totally done. But it just so happened they were in my car with all my other stuff, because I was moving. I probably wouldn't have done it if they hadn't been out there—but they were. I thought to myself, *Why not? What do I have to lose?* I retrieved them from the car, Paul switched my good blades to the old boots—and then I stepped out onto the ice.

What happened then was like magic! Within five minutes I knew. The wings were back on my feet, and I was flying again. Paul came out and joined me. He was so excited. After working so hard all season, everything was suddenly effortless, just the way it used to be! I didn't know whether Louis had made that telephone call yet or not, but I wasn't even going to talk to him. We were just out there skating, making him watch. The first time we tried a run-through, it was perfect! We hadn't done that all year. We stayed on the ice that entire day, skating right until midnight!

It was suddenly clear that everything that had happened was all a result of firmly believing that my new skates would eventually "break in" like any other pair of skates. But they hadn't, and they never were going to.

The rest of the week was unbelievable. Every day, it was all just there: the excitement, the energy, the fun! In one instant we'd gone from the most devastating low to believing that maybe this could still happen.

We went to Ottawa, and every practice was perfect. Our routines flowed and clicked just the way they used to. People couldn't believe the difference in our skating.

The day of the World Championship finals arrived. When we stepped onto the ice, we knew, right from the first moment. We were in such a zone. Everything happened so easily. We skated flawlessly, effortlessly—and I wouldn't allow myself to look at the crowd and get caught up in their reactions. However, about thirty seconds before the end of our program, as I was coming down from the top of a lift, I allowed myself a peek at the crowd for just an instant. The people were on their feet, and the building was starting to erupt—something I had never experienced in my life. It felt like the roof was about to come off!

When we finished, the feeling of relief was indescribable. To top it off, everyone who had ever played a role in our career was there in Ottawa that day. We were able to share this incredible moment with all of them. As I looked into the audience, I saw my two sisters sobbing, with their arms wrapped around each other.

It was a long two minutes while we waited for our scores. We were in the "kiss and cry" area with Louis and Sandra,

jumping up and down. Everyone was screaming. We kept looking up to Johnny Esaw—he always had the results first on his
monitor—but he was so excited that he pulled the cord out of
his computer by accident, and the screen went blank!
Everyone was wondering: *Did we do it? Did we do it?* I think
we all knew in our hearts that we had, but it wasn't until we
saw and heard the string of 5.8s and 5.9s that we really
believed it.

Our dream had come true: We were the new world champions! It was so amazing to realize that we had gone from the
lowest possible low to the highest possible high in just three
weeks. We had defeated the Russian team that had taken the
Olympic gold only three weeks earlier, and the East Germans
who had been world champions two years previously.

We stood on the podium with two sets of world champions
and the Olympic champions. The flags began to go up. We
waited, hearts beating, for the Canadian flag to rise to the top
of the pole—but it became caught on something and was low-
ered again! I thought, *No, no, no. This is such an amazing
moment. Don't ruin it.* But they unhooked the flag, sent it
back up and then the sounds of "O Canada" spread across the
arena. As we stood there listening to our national anthem, it
felt like we had ten thousand friends sharing this special
moment with us. After all we had been through, it seemed like
a miracle that we had managed to deliver two perfect programs. We both had tears running down our faces. It was
amazing going from what we were feeling a week earlier to
being part of this incredible celebration! To this day, every
time I see a Canadian flag go up, I relive that moment at the
World Championships.

All these years later, people will stop one of us in a mall or on the street—they recognize us—and say, "I was there that day. . . . I was there." And we instantly know that they mean they were there in Ottawa, when we skated that miraculous, memorable skate.

Barbara Underhill and Paul Martini
Chicken Soup for the Canadian Soul

A Little Girl's Dream

*Far away there in the sunshine are my
highest aspirations. I may not reach them
but I can look up and see their beauty,
believe in them and try to follow them.*

—Louisa May Alcott

 The promise was a long time keeping. But then, so was
the dream.

In the early 1950s in a small Southern California town, a
little girl hefted yet another load of books onto the tiny
library's counter.

The girl was a reader. Her parents had books all over their
home, but not always the ones she wanted. So she'd make her
weekly trek to the yellow library with the brown trim, the little one-room building where the children's library actually
was just a nook. Frequently, she ventured out of that nook in
search of heftier fare.

As the white-haired librarian hand-stamped the due dates
in the ten-year-old's choices, the little girl looked longingly at
"The New Book" prominently displayed on the counter. She

marveled again at the wonder of writing a book and having it honored like that, right there for the world to see.

That particular day, she confessed her goal.

"When I grow up," she said, "I'm going to be a writer. I'm going to write books."

The librarian looked up from her stamping and smiled, not with the condescension so many children receive, but with encouragement.

"When you do write that book," she replied, "bring it into our library and we'll put it on display, right here on the counter."

The little girl promised she would.

As she grew, so did her dream. She got her first job in ninth grade, writing brief personality profiles, which earned her $1.50 each from the local newspaper. The money palled in comparison with the magic of seeing her words on paper.

A book was a long way off.

She edited her high-school paper, married and started a family, but the itch to write burned deep. She got a part-time job covering school news at a weekly newspaper. It kept her brain busy as she balanced babies.

But no book.

She went to work full time for a major daily. Even tried her hand at magazines.

Still no book.

Finally, she believed she had something to say and started a book. She sent it off to two publishers and was rejected. She put it away, sadly. Several years later, the old dream increased in persistence. She got an agent and wrote another book. She pulled the other out of hiding, and soon both were sold.

But the world of book publishing moves slower than that of

daily newspapers, and she waited two long years. The day the box arrived on her doorstep with its free author's copies, she ripped it open. Then she cried. She'd waited so long to hold her dream in her hands.

Then she remembered that librarian's invitation, and her promise.

Of course, that particular librarian had died long ago, and the little library had been razed to make way for a larger incarnation.

The woman called and got the name of the head librarian. She wrote a letter, telling her how much her predecessor's words had meant to the girl. She'd be in town for her thirtieth high school reunion, she wrote, and could she please bring her two books by and give them to the library? It would mean so much to that ten-year-old girl, and seemed a way of honoring all the librarians who had ever encouraged a child.

The librarian called and said, "Come." So she did, clutching a copy of each book.

She found the big new library right across the street from her old high school; just opposite the room where she'd struggled through algebra, mourning the necessity of a subject that writers would surely never use, and nearly on top of the spot where her old house once stood, the neighborhood demolished for a civic center and this looming library.

Inside, the librarian welcomed her warmly. She introduced a reporter from the local newspaper—a descendant of the paper she'd begged a chance to write for long ago.

Then she presented her books to the librarian, who placed them on the counter with a sign of explanation. Tears rolled down the woman's cheeks.

Then she hugged the librarian and left, pausing for a picture outside, which proved that dreams can come true and promises can be kept. Even if it takes thirty-eight years.

The ten-year-old girl and the writer she'd become posed by the library sign, right next to the readerboard, which said:

WELCOME BACK,
JANN MITCHELL

Jann Mitchell
A 2nd Helping of Chicken Soup for the Soul

How to Be New and Different

*If I could wish for my life to be perfect,
it would be tempting, but I would have to
decline, for life would no longer
teach me anything.*

—Allyson Jones

The year 1993 wasn't shaping up to be the best year of my life. I was into my eighth year as a single parent, had three kids in college, my unmarried daughter had just given birth to my first grandchild and I was about to break up with a very nice man I'd dated for over two years. Faced with all this, I was spending lots of time feeling sorry for myself.

That April, I was asked to interview and write about a woman who lived in a small town in Minnesota. So during Easter vacation, Andrew, my thirteen-year-old, and I drove across two states to meet Jan Turner.

Andrew dozed most of the way during the long drive, but every once in a while I'd start a conversation.

"She's handicapped, you know."

"So what's wrong with her? Does she have a disease?"

"I don't think so. But for some reason, she had to have both arms and legs amputated."

"Wow. How does she get around?"

"I'm not sure. We'll see when we get there."

"Does she have any kids?"

"Two boys—Tyler and Cody—both adopted. She's a single parent, too. Only she's never been married."

"So what happened to her?"

"Four years ago Jan was just like me, a busy single mother. She was a full-time music teacher at a grade school and taught all sorts of musical instruments. She was also the music director at her church."

Andrew fell asleep again before I could finish telling him what little I did know about what had happened to Jan. As I drove across Minnesota, I began to wonder how the woman I was about to meet could cope with such devastating news that all four limbs had to be amputated. How did she learn to survive? Did she have live-in help?

When we arrived in Willmar, Minnesota, I called Jan from our hotel to tell her that I could come to her house and pick her and the boys up, so they could swim at our hotel while we talked.

"That's okay, Pat, I can drive. The boys and I will be there in ten minutes. Would you like to go out to eat first? There's a Ponderosa close to your hotel."

"Sure, that'll be fine," I said haltingly, wondering what it would be like to eat in a public restaurant with a woman who had no arms or legs. *And how on earth does she drive?* I wondered.

Ten minutes later, Jan pulled up in front of the hotel. She

got out of the car, walked over to me with perfect posture on legs and feet that looked every bit as real as mine, and extended her right arm with its shiny hook on the end to shake my hand. "Hello, Pat, I'm sure glad to meet you. And this must be Andrew."

I grabbed her hook, pumped it a bit and smiled sheepishly. "Uh, yes, this is Andrew." I looked in the back seat of her car and smiled at the two boys who grinned back. Cody, the younger one, was practically effervescent at the thought of going swimming in the hotel pool after dinner.

Jan bubbled as she slid back behind the driver's seat, "So hop in. Cody, move over and make room for Andrew."

We arrived at the restaurant, went through the line, paid for our food, and ate and talked amidst the chattering of our three sons. The only thing I had to do for Jan Turner that entire evening was unscrew the top on the ketchup bottle.

Later that night, as our three sons splashed in the pool, Jan and I sat on the side and she told me about life before her illness.

"We were a typical single-parent family. You know, busy all the time. Life was so good, in fact, that I was seriously thinking about adopting a third child."

My conscience stung. I had to face it—the woman next to me was better at single parenting than I ever thought about being.

Jan continued. "One Sunday in November of 1989, I was playing my trumpet at the front of my church when I suddenly felt weak, dizzy and nauseous. I struggled down the aisle, motioned for the boys to follow me and drove home. I crawled into bed, but by evening I knew I had to get help."

Jan then explained that by the time she arrived at the hospital, she was comatose. Her blood pressure had dropped so much that her body was already shutting down. She had pneumococcal pneumonia, the same bacterial infection that took the life of Muppets creator Jim Henson. One of its disastrous side effects is an activation of the body's clotting system, which causes the blood vessels to plug up. Because there was suddenly no blood flow to her hands or feet, she quickly developed gangrene in all four extremities. Two weeks after being admitted to the hospital, Jan's arms had to be amputated at mid-forearm and her legs at mid-shin.

Just before the surgery, she said she cried out, "Oh God, no! How can I live without arms and legs, feet or hands? Never walk again? Never play the trumpet, guitar, piano or any of the instruments I teach? I'll never be able to hug my sons or take care of them. Oh God, don't let me depend on others for the rest of my life!"

Six weeks after the amputations as her dangling limbs healed, a doctor talked to Jan about prosthetics. She said Jan could learn to walk, drive a car, go back to school, even go back to teaching.

Jan found that hard to believe so she picked up her Bible. It fell open to Romans, chapter twelve, verse two: "Don't copy the behavior and customs of this world, but be a new and different person with a fresh newness in all you do and think. Then you will learn from your own experience how his ways will really satisfy you."

Jan thought about that—about being a new and different person—and she decided to give the prosthetics a try. With a walker strapped onto her forearms near the elbow and a therapist on either side, she could only wobble on her new legs for two to three minutes before she collapsed in exhaustion and pain.

Take it slowly, Jan said to herself. *Be a new person in all that you do and think, but take it one step at a time.*

The next day she tried on the prosthetic arms, a crude system of cables, rubber bands and hooks operated by a harness across the shoulders. By moving her shoulder muscles she was soon able to open and close the hooks to pick up and hold objects, and dress and feed herself.

Within a few months, Jan learned she could do almost everything she used to do—only in a new and different way.

"Still, when I finally got to go home after four months of physical and occupational therapy, I was so nervous about what life would be like with my boys and me alone in the house. But when I got there, I got out of the car, walked up the steps to our house, hugged my boys with all my might, and we haven't looked back since."

As Jan and I continued to talk, Cody, who'd climbed out of the hotel pool, stood close to his mom with his arm around her shoulders. As she told me about her newly improved cooking skills, Cody grinned. "Yup," he said, "she's a better mom now than before she got sick, because now she can even flip pancakes!" Jan laughed like a woman who is blessed with tremendous happiness, contentment and unswerving faith in God.

Since our visit, Jan has completed a second college degree, this one in communications, and she is now an announcer for the local radio station. She also studied theology and has been ordained as the children's pastor at her church, the Triumphant Life Church in Willmar. Simply put, Jan says,

"I'm a new and different person, triumphant because of God's unending love and wisdom."

After meeting Jan, I was a new and different person as well. I learned to praise God for everything in my life that makes *me* new and different, whether it's struggling through one more part-time job to keep my kids in college, learning to be a grandmother for the first time or having the courage to end a relationship with a wonderful friend who just wasn't the right one for me.

Jan may not have real flesh-and-blood arms, legs, hands or feet, but that woman has more heart and soul than anyone I've ever met before or since. She taught me to grab on to every "new and different" thing that comes into my life with all the gusto I can muster . . . to live my life triumphantly.

Patricia Lorenz
Chicken Soup for the Unsinkable Soul

Who Is Jack Canfield?

Jack Canfield is one of America's leading experts in the development of human potential and personal effectiveness. He is both a dynamic, entertaining keynote speaker and a highly sought-after trainer. Jack has a wonderful ability to inform and inspire audiences toward increased levels of self-esteem and peak performance.

He is the author and narrator of several bestselling audio- and video-cassette programs, including *Self-Esteem and Peak Performance, How to Build High Self-Esteem, Self-Esteem in the Classroom* and *Chicken Soup for the Soul—Live.* He is regularly seen on television shows such as *Good Morning America, 20/20* and *NBC Nightly News.* Jack has co-authored over sixty books, including the *Chicken Soup for the Soul* series, *Dare to Win, The Aladdin Factor, 100 Ways to Build Self-Concept in the Classroom, Heart at Work* and *The Power of Focus: How to Hit Your Business, Personal and Financial Targets with Absolute Certainty.*

Jack is a regularly featured inspirational and motivational speaker for professional associations, school districts, government agencies, churches, hospitals, nonprofit organizations, sales organizations and corporations. His clients have included the American Heart Association, the Children's Miracle Network, the Boys Club of America, Reading Fun, the American Dental Association, the American Management Association, AT&T, Campbell's Soup, Clairol, Domino's Pizza, GE, ITT, Hartford Insurance, Johnson & Johnson, the Million Dollar Round Table, NCR, New England Telephone, Re/Max, Scott Paper, TRW and Virgin Records.

Jack's speaking topics include The Power of Focus, Self-Esteem and Peak Performance, The 10 Steps to Success, The Success Principles, Dare to Win, Living Your Dreams and Chicken Soup for the Soul.

For further information about Jack's books, tapes and training programs, or to schedule him for a presentation, please contact:

Self-Esteem Seminars
P.O. Box 30880
Santa Barbara, CA 93130
phone: 805-563-2935 • fax: 805-563-2945
Web site: *www.jackcanfield.com*

Who Is Mark Victor Hansen?

In the area of human potential, no one is better known and more respected than Mark Victor Hansen. For more than thirty years, Mark has focused solely on helping people from all walks of life reshape their personal vision of what's possible. His powerful messages of possibility, opportunity and action have helped create startling and powerful change in thousands of organizations and millions of individuals worldwide.

He is a sought-after keynote speaker, bestselling author and marketing maven. Mark's credentials include a lifetime of entrepreneurial success, in addition to an extensive academic background. He is a prolific writer with many bestselling books such as *The One Minute Millionaire, The Power of Focus, The Aladdin Factor* and *Dare to Win,* in addition to the *Chicken Soup for the Soul* series. Mark has also made a profound influence through his extensive library of audio programs, video programs and enriching articles in the areas of big thinking, sales achievement, wealth building, publishing success, and personal and professional development.

Mark is also the founder of MEGA Book Marketing University and Building Your MEGA Speaking Empire. Both are annual conferences where Mark coaches and teaches new and aspiring authors, speakers and experts on building lucrative publishing and speaking careers.

His energy and exuberance travel still further through mediums such as television (*Oprah*, CNN and *The Today Show*), print (*Time, U.S. News & World Report, USA Today, New York Times* and *Entrepreneur*) and countless radio and newspaper interviews as he assures our planet's people that *"you can easily create the life you deserve."*

As a passionate philanthropist and humanitarian, he's been the recipient of numerous awards that honor his entrepreneurial spirit, philanthropic heart and business acumen, including the prestigious Horatio Alger Award for his extraordinary life achievements, which stand as a powerful example that the free enterprise system still offers opportunity to all.

Mark Victor Hansen is an enthusiastic crusader of what's possible and is *driven* to make the world a better place.

Mark Victor Hansen & Associates, Inc.
P.O. Box 7665 • Newport Beach, CA 92658
phone: 949-764-2640 • fax: 949-722-6912
FREE resources online at: *www.markvictorhansen.com*

Contributors

Linda Apple lives in Springdale, Arkansas, with her husband Neal. They have five children and two grandchildren. She co-directs the women's ministry in her church, Christian Life Cathedral. She is an inspirational speaker and writer who had the honor of being published in *Chicken Soup for the Nurse's Soul*. E-mail: *psalm10218@cox-internet.com*.

Sue Augustine is currently considered Canada's leading female international motivational speaker. She is the author of *5-Minute Retreats for Women* and *5-Minute Retreats for Moms* (Harvest House), *With Wings, There Are No Barriers* (Pelican) and a contributor to *Chicken Soup for the Woman's Soul*. Contact Sue at R.R.#1, St. Catharines, ON L2R 6P7, phone (905) 687-8474, e-mail *wings@vaxxine.com* or visit *www.sueaugustine.com*.

Aaron Bacall has been cartooning for twenty-five years and his work has appeared in most major publications including *The New Yorker, Reader's Digest, Barron's, The Wall Street Journal* and others. Many corporations such as Citicorp have used his cartoons as well. He has had three cartoon collections published and is under contract for two more books. He can be reached at *abacall@msn.com*.

Jessica Lynn Burnham is a twelve-year-old student in seventh grade. She lives in Michigan and enjoys playing all sports and also likes music and movies. She hopes to graduate from University of Michigan and become a veterinarian.

Michele "Screech" Campanelli is a national bestselling author. She lives in Palm Bay, Florida, with her husband, Louis V. Campanelli III. She has written stories in more than twenty-two anthologies and penned several novels including, *Keeper of the Shroud, Jamison* and *Margarita* published by Americana Books. Her personal editor is Fontaine M. Wallace. *www.michelecampanelli.com*.

Dave Carpenter has been a full-time cartoonist since 1981. His cartoons have appeared in such publications as *Harvard Business Review, Barron's, The Wall Street Journal, Reader's Digest, Good Housekeeping, Better Homes & Gardens, The Saturday Evening Post* as well as numerous other publications, including other *Chicken Soup for the Soul* books. Dave can be reached at *davecarp@ncn.net* or through his Web site at *www.carptoons.com*.

Jack Cavanaugh writes for the *New York Times*. He also has contributed to *Sports Illustrated, Reader's Digest, Golf Digest* and a number of other national publications. Cavanaugh is also the author of the book, *Damn the Disabilities: Full Speed Ahead*. He lives in Wilton, Connecticut.

Kyle Christensen received her bachelor of arts, with honors, from the University of Arizona in 2000. She is now married and living in Phoenix, Arizona. She enjoys friends, family and volunteering.

Dan Clark, C.S.P., is the primary contributing author to the *Chicken Soup for the Soul* series and coauthor of *Chicken Soup for the College Soul*, along with ten of his own highly acclaimed books, including *Puppies for Sale and Other Inspirational Tales*. In 1982, Zig Ziglar sponsored Dan into the National Speakers Association. He has since spoken to more than two million people in all fifty states, Canada and fifteen other foreign countries. An award-winning athlete, he fought his way back from a paralyzing injury that cut short his football career. He can be reached at P.O. Box 58689, Salt Lake City, UT 84108, (800) 676-1121, or by e-mail at *SDANCLARKP@aol.com*.

Sandra Crowe, a speaker, consultant and trainer in the domain of dealing with difficult people is the author of a book on the subject called *Since Strangling Isn't an Option*. She has appeared on the *CBS Morning News*, *To Tell the Truth* and had a television show "Stress Busters." Her Web site is *www.pivpoint.com* and her e-mail address is *pivpoint@cyberrealm.net*.

Gunter David was a reporter on major city newspapers for twenty-five years and a Pulitzer-Prize nominee by the *Evening Bulletin* of Philadelphia, before obtaining a masters degree in family therapy. Retired from Johnson & Johnson, where he counseled employees and their families, he has had numerous stories and memoirs published in literary journals and anthologies, including *Chicken Soup for the College Soul* and *Chicken Soup for the Father's Soul*. He may be reached at *Dretnug@aol.com*.

Lola De Julio De Maci received her master of arts in Interdisciplinary Studies (education and English) in 1995 from California State University. In addition to being an elementary school teacher and a writer, Lola enjoys conducting creative writing workshops for children, visiting schools as a children's author, and appearing as a motivational speaker for both children and adults. The mother of Maria, Christopher and Angela, Lola considers this her greatest calling. Please contact her at *LDeMaci@aol.com*.

Burt Dubin works with people who want to be paid speakers and with speakers who want to be masters. Those who know him consider him a master of the craft of speaking for money. Click on the heading, "Glowing Testimonials," on his Web site, *www.SpeakingSuccess.com*. Reach Burt at (800) 321-1225.

Eugene Edwards received his bachelor of science from Brenzu University in Gainesville, Georgia, in 1997. Eugene enjoys traveling, reading, fishing, golfing, coaching Little League sports and working with children. Please fax him at: (404) 508-7550 Attn: Helen Hayes.

Randy Glasbergen is one of America's most widely and frequently published cartoonists. More than 25,000 of his cartoons have been published by *Funny Times, Reader's Digest, Guideposts for Teens, Campus Life, Group Magazine* and many others. His daily comic panel "The Better Half" is syndicated worldwide by King Features Syndicate. He is also the author of three cartooning instruction books and several cartoon anthologies. To read a cartoon a day, please visit Randy's Web site at: *www.glasbergen.com*.

Mike Gordon is a reporter and columnist for *The Honolulu Advertiser in Hawai'i*. His stories are diverse and include the unsolved case of missing child abuse victim, Peter Boy Kema, the fatal collision of a U.S. submarine and the Ehime Maru and several profiles of ordinary people struggling with life. He was born and raised in the islands and never plans to leave because the surf there is too good.

Rabona Turner Gordon gets her inspiration from writing poetry from her five children. She is a single mother and she and her children have endured and enjoyed many of life's challenges. She quite often does customized poems for her church, friends and coworkers. Rabona resides with her children in Marietta, Georgia. She can be reached by e-mail at *rabona.gordon@repironics.com.*

Jean Harper is a wife, mother and pilot for United Airlines, currently captain on the Boeing 757 and 767. A past contributor to the *Chicken Soup for the Soul* series, Jean enjoys cooking, sewing, writing and spending as much time as possible with her husband Victor and their two teenaged children. She can be reached at *victorjean-harper@aol.com.*

Rob and **Toni Harris** are the owners of Re/Max Results Realtors and the proud parents of Nick. Nick has been raised to be a positive thinker, with a strong belief in himself.

Susan Hreljac received her B.S.S. with honors from the Univeresity of Ottawa in 1982. Susan and Mark Hreljac run the Ryan's Well Foundation with the help of a small board and other dedicated volunteers. Visit the Ryan's Well Foundation Web site at *www.ryanswell.ca.* E-mail Susan at *susan@ryanswell.ca.*

Ricky Hunley was born November 11, 1961, in Petersburg, Virginia. He earned a bachelor's degree in business administration from The University of Arizona in 1987. In 1990, he was voted executive vice-president of the NFL Players Association, a position he held for two years. He has also served on the board of directors for the Black Coaches Association and on the Minority Issues Committee of the American Football Coaches Association, and he has represented the Big XII and the SEC on the AFCA's Assistant Coach Committee. He has returned to a Bengals team which drafted him as a player in 1994. A two-time consensus All-American linebacker at the University of Arizona, a former All-American college linebacker and a starting linebacker in two Super Bowls, Hunley will coach his old position for Cincinnati. Please e-mail him at: *Ricky.Hunley@Bengals.nfl.net.*

Claudette Hunter took her first Jack Canfield Self-Esteem Seminar eighteen years ago. She went on to teach Jack's workshop, Success Through Action and Responsibility (STAR), in Saudi Arabia, Dubai and Japan. She and husband, Jim, have lived in Japan for the past six years. Their company, STAR International, is living their dream of empowering Japanese women and corporations. Her next goals are to live in the States near her seven grandchildren and to continue her passion for altered books.

Susan Jeffers, Ph.D., is an international bestselling author and speaker. Her many books include *Feel the Fear and Do It Anyway,* (over five million copies sold), the award-winning *Embracing Uncertainty, End the Struggle and Dance with Life, Opening Our Hearts to Men, Dare to Connect* and *I Can Handle It!* Contact Susan at *www.susanjeffers.com.*

Bil Keane created "The Family Circus" in 1960 and gathered most of his ideas from his own family: his wife Thel and their five children. His cartoon is now read by an estimated 188 million people daily, and his nine grandchildren provide much of the inspiration for the award-winning feature. Web site: *www.familycircus.com.*

Marilyn King is a two-time Olympian (Munich 1972 and Montreal 1976) in the grueling pentathlon (100-meter hurdles, shot put, high jump, long jump, 800 meters).

Her twenty-year athletic career includes five national titles and a world record. Her story launched her exploration into the field of exceptional human performance. Her joint Russian-American venture called the Peace Team, prompted two invitations to speak at the United Nations. She is currently featured in numerous articles and books including *Dream Makers* by Michelle Hunt and by Lyle Nelson and Thorn Baclon, and appeared recently on the *News Hour* with Jim Lehrer.

Marilyn J. Kondwani, M.A., is a certified medical aromatherapist, journal writing instructor, herbalist, cosmetologist and founder of Treasure of Egypt Aromatherapy Scent Shops. She demonstrates how self-esteem is the ultimate healer as a consultant to complementary and alternative medicine research studies worldwide and as publisher of *The Natural Health News.* Contact her at *www.treasureofegypt.com* or *thenaturalhealthnews@hotmail.com.*

Liah Kraft-Kristaine, J.D., is an international speaker on management, achievement, well-being and spiritual development, and the author of nine books. She is CEO of LifeKraft Institute International and is currently looking for stories for the upcoming *Chicken Soup for the Victorious Woman's Soul.* For speaking, story contributions, books, videos and more, contact Liah at *www.lifekraft.com online.*

Catherine Lanigan is the bestselling author of *Romancing the Stone, Jewel of the Nile, Tender Malice* and *Wings of Destiny.* She is the creator of the "evolving woman," a new breed of heroine, who makes choices that enrich her internally, and as a result, enrich the world around her as well. Lanigan drew upon her own life experiences to create this amalgam, and she does so from a perspective that is as passionate as it is personal.

David Like resides in Orlando, Florida. The story, "Embassy of Hope," is dedicated to his grandmother, Opal Stayley Mathews; his two nieces, Jennifer and Jacqueline; his grandfather, Elzie Roy Mathews; his mother, Patty; and his friend, Chatta Denis Foster. David can be reached at *Beatleman-33@webtv.net.*

Sharon Linnéa has enjoyed a long association writing and editing for *Chicken Soup for the Soul,* and is coauthor of *Chicken Soup from the Soul of Hawai'i.* A nationally known journalist, she was the founding inspiration producer for *Beliefnet.com,* a writer for *Hallmark's New Morning Show,* the primary biographer for the *Heroes Cirriculum,* used in schools in all fifty states, and the award-winning author of biographies of *Princess Ka'iulani and Raoul Wallenberg.* Contact her through her Web site at *SharonLinnea.com.*

Patricia Lorenz is a full-time freelance writer and speaker who works out of her home in Oak Creek, Wisconsin, who has a twelve-second commute to work. She is one of the top five contributors to the *Chicken Soup for the Soul* books with stories in over a dozen of them. She's the author of four books, over four hundred articles, a contributing writer for fifteen *Daily Guideposts* books, and an award-winning columnist for two newspapers. To contact Patricia for speaking opportunities, e-mail her at *patricialorenz@juno.com.*

Dandi Daley Mackall has been writing professionally for more than twenty years. She's published over three hundred books for children and thirty for grown-ups, including 2003 releases: *Are We There Yet?,* Dutton/Penguin-Putnam; *First Day,* Harcourt; *Silent Dreams,* Eerdmans; *Winnie the Horse Gentler* series, Tyndale

House; *Off to Bethlehem!*, HarperCollins; *Degrees of Guilt: Kyra's Story*, Tyndale; *Off to Plymouth Rock & No, No Noah!*, Tommy Nelson; *Must Be Halloween & Love You, Bunny*, Simon & Schuster; *Kids' Rules for Life*, SourceBooks; *The Imagination Line*, Augsburg; *Until the Christ Child Came*, Concordia. She's the author of the *Cinnamon Lake Mysteries & Horsefeathers!* books, and has written for Hanna Barbera, Warner Brothers, Dreamworks and Disney. Dandi gives Young Author assemblies to schools across the nation. She writes from rural Ohio, with her husband, Joe, and her three children, Jen, Katy, and Dan, along with horses, dogs, cats, newts, etc.

Paul Martini skated with partner Barbara Underhill for twenty-two years. Before retiring in 1998, they were five-time Canadian Pair Champions, 1984 World Pair Champions, two-time Olympians, and won seven professional titles. In 1988, they were inducted into the Canadian Sports Hall of Fame. Paul has provided color commentary for skating events on CBC TV since 1991, including three Olympic Games. He and wife Elizabeth have two children, Robert and Kate. In addition to working with the CBC, Paul is the president of iskater, a company with a Web site dedicated to the sport of figure skating, *www.iskater.com*.

As a young police officer, **Glenn McIntyre**'s life was forever altered when a drunk driver rendered him a paraplegic. Glenn had to learn to endure, overcome and then excel at life again. Armed with his "Always there is a way!" attitude, Glenn returned to law enforcement for fifteen years and has since created a successful career as a speaker, trainer and consultant. Glenn, with wife and coauthor **Hellmi**, the driving force in Glenn's life, has captured the essence of his personal experience in the story that has been featured in *Chicken Soup for the Soul* books. Glenn has also appeared in major publications and on major television networks. Hellmi, a talented speaker, is also the author of several multicultural children's books based upon her own experience and is currently working on picture books based on the "adventures" of their young twin daughters. The McIntyres make their home in Southern California and travel the world improving lives through their inspiring keynote presentation "Always there is a Way! Contact: Glenn McIntyre, 753 Jewel Court, Camarillo, CA 93010. P: (805) 988-6533 F: (805) 988-6534. e-mail: *glenn@glennmcintyre.com*. Web site: *www.glennmcintyre.com*.

Janice Meek has packed so much into her fifty-four years, her life reads like the plot of a book from working in the film business with well-known stars; living and working in Saudi Arabia, being elected mayor of her home town; learning Chinese while backpacking around China, to her Guiness Book of World Records Atlantic Rowing record. Now a professional speaker, she's authored the book *101 Atlantic Nights*, the full version of her Atlantic crossing with her son, Daniel. She also has a daughter Becky. Jan lives in Chipping Norton, England. Contact her at *JaniceMeek@aol.com*.

Jann Mitchell-Sandström realized still another dream by taking early retirement from her newspaper to move to Stockholm, Sweden, and marry her long-lost Swedish sweetheart, whom she rediscovered through the Internet several years ago. They travel often to Tanzania, East Africa, where Jann supports a preschool named for her. Reach her at *jannmmitchell@aol.com*.

Darlene Montgomery is an internationally respected authority on dreams, spiritual perspectives and ideas. Author, speaker and clergywoman, she speaks to groups and organizations on uplifiting subjects. Her book, *Dream Yourself Awake*, chronicles her personal journey to discover her own divine mission. To learn more about Darlene Montgomery's keynotes and seminars, visit www.lifedreams.org, call (416) 696-1684 or e-mail her at *lifedreams@idirect.com*.

Gerald Moore, whose written work ranges from short stories to political speeches, is the author of numerous magazine articles. Born in Albuquerque, New Mexico, he has been a reporter and magazine editor. He worked as an environmental technical writer in New York City where he lives with his wife, Joyce Nereaux.

Nancy E. Myer is the author of *Silent Witness: The True Story of a Psychic Detective*. Her anecdotes have appeared in *Chicken Soup for the Sports Fan's Soul, More Hot Chocolate for the Mystical Soul* and *Magical Souvenirs. A Perfect Skate* was reprinted in the *Professional Skating Association Magazine*. Nancy finished her first murder mystery and is at work on the second one. Next is an autobiographical book about the two years she lived in Afghanistan. She is known internationally for her work as a psychic investigator. She appeared on *Unsolved Mysteries, Sightings, Paranormal Borderline* and is presently "commuting" to Japan to appear in a series of specials for Nippon TV. You can reach Nancy at P.O. Box 3015, Greensburg, PA 15601, phone: (724) 539-9299.

Amy Ash Nixon has been a journalist since 1985, when she graduated with a degree in print journalism from Emerson College. Since 1988, she has written for *The Hartford Courant*. Amy also has taught writing at the college level and is now a certified language arts teacher for middle school students in Connecticut.

Debra Peppers, Ph.D., a retired thirty-year English teacher, is a university instructor, and Emmy–award-winning author. Having been inducted into the national Teachers Hall of Fame, she has hosted a television program and a daily three-hour radio program, authored, *It's Your Turn Now* and *How I Lost 100 Pounds*. Now a professional speaker, Debra has traveled to all 50 states and 50 foreign countries. A member of the National Speakers Association, Dr. Peppers is available for bookings at (314) 842-7425 or through *www.pepperseed.org*.

Omar Periu is the author of one of the biggest-selling books in America, *Investigative Selling*. His more recent books, *From Management to Leadership* and *The One Minute Meeting,* are receiving rave reviews. Omar has been a public speaker for over two decades training over two million people and more than two-thirds of the Fortune 500 companies. For more information about having him speak at your next event, please contact *omar@omarperiu.com* or call (888) 777-4519.

Gene Perret is a three-time Emmy-winner for his work on *The Carol Burnett Show* writing staff. Gene has also written for Bob Hope since 1969, several of those years as his head writer. He traveled with Hope on his military shows to Beirut, the Persian Gulf, Saudi Arabia and on his final tour around the world. Presently, Gene writes a monthly humor column for *Arizona Highways*. He has written more than twenty books on humor, including the top-selling book in the field, *Comedy Writing Step by Step*.

Katlyn McKenzie Pickett is currently a home-schooled sophomore. Her studies include early-morning LDS church seminary, piano, violin, French and Advanced Placement courses. She plans to attend BYU. She's an accompanist for the Shasta school choir. She enjoys skiing, reading, music, sewing and traveling to Europe. Please reach her at: *Kpickett6@attbi.com.*

Stephanie Pieper resides in Erie, Pennsylvania, on the shores of Lake Erie and enjoys swimming, hiking, reading, writing and laying on the beach. She currently works as a waitress and has plans to become a writer.

Stephanie Piro is a cartoonist, designer and mom. She considers her fabulous daughter Nico, her greatest inspiration. She is one of King Features cartoon team, *Six Chix* (she's Saturday!) and she also self-syndicates "Fair Game," a daily cartoon panel and designs T-shirts and other items for her company, Strip T's. Contact her at: *piro@worldpath.net* or *www.stephaniepiro.com* or write to: Stephanie Piro, P.O. Box 605, Farmington, NH 03835.

Bob Proctor is an author, consultant and Fortune 500 trainer. For forty years he has focused his agenda around helping people create lush lives of prosperity, rewarding relationships and spiritual awareness. Proctor's seminars and recordings will show you how to BE more, DO more and HAVE more. Visit *www.bobproctor.com.*

Nora Profit is an investigative journalist and freelance writer whose articles have appeared in the *San Francisco Chronicle, San Jose Magazine* and PBS (Public Broadcasting Service). She is currently working on a book about the plight of the families of America's condemned—men who are incarcerated. She can be contacted at 5005 Arden Way, Paradise, CA 95969. Phone 530-877-2292. E-mail: *noraprofitross@msn.com* or *noraprofit@journalist.com.*

For over a quarter of a century, **Anthony Robbins** has served as an advisor to leaders around the world. A recognized authority on the psychology of leadership, negotiations, organizational turnaround and peak performance, he has been honored for his strategic intellect and humanitarian endeavors. He has directly impacted the lives of more than fifty million people from eighty countries with his bestselling products and live appearances.

Glenna Salsbury, CSP, CPAE, Speaker Hall of Fame, graduated from Northwestern University in Evanston, Illinois, obtained her master's degree from UCLA, and sixteen years later, earned a master's in theology from Fuller Seminary. In 1980, Glenna founded her own company, which provides keynote presentations and personal growth seminars. Glenna is past president of the National Speakers Association. In her personal life, Glenna was married to the late Jim Salsbury, a former Detroit Lion and Green Bay Packer. She has three daughters and five grandchildren. Call, e-mail or write to obtain her powerful six-pack tape album entitled *Passion, Prayer and Purpose* and/or her book, *The Art of the Fresh Start*. She can be reached at *ISpeak4U@aol.com,* 9228 N. 64th Place, Paradise Valley, AZ 85253 or call 480-483-7732.

Alan Shultz is a writer and a real estate broker. When he's not selling real estate in Chicago, he's busy composing at the keyboard on a rural family farm near the Wabash River in northern Indiana. He can be reached at *ashultz@coldwellbanker.com* or at 5852 W 1000 N, Delphi, IN 46923.

Makenzie Snyder is a twelve-year-old from Maryland who enjoys twirling baton, ballet and drawing. She would like to thank God, her parents and especially her brothers Cory and Brock, for all their support with Children to Children and in her everyday life. Makenzie can be reached at Children to Children, 3262 Superior Ln., PMB#288, Bowie, Maryland 20715, or at the Web site, *www.childrentochildren.org.*

Dixie Jane Sokolik is a retired registered nurse. She and her husband, Jim, live in Winona, Minnesota. They have four grown children and five grandchildren. She is a contributor to *Chicken Soup for the Mother's Soul 2* and writes a monthly column for the *Winona Daily News.* She and her husband enjoy music, hiking, reading, traveling and playing with their grandchildren. Her mother, who is now ninety-five years old, continues to be an inspiration for Dixie and her entire family, and encourages them to always pursue their dreams.

Linda Stafford lives in Hawaii and enjoys writing inspirational stories and painting. She teaches writing classes at the University of Hawaii at Hilo. She has four children who make life sparkle.

Gloria Cassity Stargel writes for *Guideposts, Decision, God Allows U-Turns* and others. Her award-winning book *The Healing: One Family's Victorious Struggle with Cancer Strengthens Faith, Gives Hope.* ($14.95 pp). Read portions of Gift for You at www.brightmorning.com. Order online; or (800) 888-9529; or write Applied Images, 312 Bradford St., N.W., Gainesville, GA 30501.

LeAnn Thieman is a nationally acclaimed speaker and author. A member of the National Speakers Association, she inspires audiences to balance their lives, truly live their priorities and make a difference in the world. She has written stories for several *Chicken Soup for the Soul* books and is coauthor of *Chicken Soup for the Nurse's Soul* and *Chicken Soup for the Christian Woman's Soul.* She may be reached at *www.LeAnnThieman.com* or phone: 877-THIEMAN.

Barbara Underhill skated with partner Paul Martini for twenty-one years. Before retiring in 1998, they were five-time Canadian Pair Champions, 1984 World Pair Champions, two-time Olympians, won seven Professional World titles, and in 1988, were inducted into the Canadian Sports Hall of Fame. Barbara has done color commentary for skating events with various TV networks, since 1992, including three Olympic Games. She and husband, Rick Gaetz, have three children, Samantha, Matthew and Scott. After the sudden death of their daughter in 1993, Barbara and Rick founded The Stephanie Gaetz Keepsafe Foundation. Now in demand as a motivational speaker, Barbara shares her story with audiences everywhere. Contact her at *www.keepsafefoundation.com.*

Penny and **Vicky Vilagos** learned a thing or two about teamwork while training thirty thousand hours in a swimming pool. What they learned while striving to achieve their Olympic dream is not taught, so they share their secrets as motivational speakers. Penny and Vicky are contributing authors to *Chicken Soup for the Sister's Soul, Chicken Soup for the Canadian Soul, Expert Women Who Speak: Speak Out! Vol. 2* and *Réussir n'est pas un péché.* To arrange a speaking engagement or to sign up for their free success newsletter, visit *www.VilagosInternational.com* or call (866) 426-5122. Dare to dream!

Erik Weihenmayer is the first and only blind person to climb Mount Everest and the Seven Summits. He is entered in the 2004 Eco Challenge, the most arduous adventure race in the world. His book, *Touch the Top of the World,* is published in nine countries. He has written for *Time* and *Outside,* and is a frequent speaker at major corporate events. See *www.touchthetop.com.* "Someone once told me that I needed to realize my limitations, but I've always thought it more exciting to try to realize my potential."

Richard Whetstone has tried to follow the words of Helen Keller, "Life is an adventure, or it's nothing." He has been a lawman, cowboy, nurse's assistant, salesman and whatever else it took to pay the bills. He's traveled to every state in the Union except Hawaii. Richard has been happily married for the past fourteen years. He has two children and seven grandchildren.

Permissions

Together, Achieving Our Olympic Dream. Reprinted by permission of Penny and Vicky Vilagos. ©2002 Penny Vilagos and Vicky Vilagos.

A Chicken Soup Contributor Responds. Reprinted by permission of Jean Harper. ©1996 Jean Harper.

Finding My Wings. Reprinted by permission of Sue Augustine. ©1996 Sue Augustine.

Glenna's Goal Book. Reprinted by permission of Glenna Salsbury. ©1991 Salsbury Enterprises.

The Little Girl Who Dared to Wish. Reprinted by permission of Alan D. Shultz. ©1999 Alan D. Shultz.

One Person Can Make a Difference. Reprinted by permission of Robert Proctor and Robert Templeton. ©1992 Robert Proctor.

Standing Tall on a Surfboard in Midlife. Reprinted by permission of Michael J. Gordon. ©1998 Michael J. Gordon.

You Can't Afford to Doubt Yourself. Reprinted by permission of Nora Profit. ©1984 Nora Profit.

A Salesman's First Sale. Reprinted by permission of Rob, Toni and Nick Harris. ©1984 Rob, Toni and Nick Harris.

Batgirl. Reprinted by permission of Dandi Daley Mackall. ©1998 Dandi Daley Mackall.

There Are No Vans. Reprinted by permission of Anthony Robbins.

"If I Were Really Important. . . ." Excerpted from *Dare to Connect,* (Judy Piatkus Books, Ltd., London, England), ©1992 Susan Jeffers, Ph.D. Reprinted by permission of Susan Jeffers, Ph.D.

The Professor and Me. Reprinted by permission of Catherine Lanigan. ©1999 Catherine Lanigan.

The Interview. Reprinted by permission of Nicole Jenkins and Michele "Screech" Campanelli. ©1999 Michele "Screech" Campanelli.

A Chicken Soup Reader Responds. Reprinted by permission of Kyle Christensen. ©1995 Kyle Christensen.

A Chicken Soup Reader Responds. Reprinted by permission of Stephanie K. Pieper. ©1996 Stephanie K. Pieper.

Trash Bags Are for Trash. Reprinted by permission of Makenzie Snyder and Margie Snyder. ©2000 Makenzie Snyder.

A Chicken Soup Reader Responds. Reprinted by permission of Jessica Lynn Burnham. ©2003 Jessica Burnham.

Never Too Old to Live Your Dream. Reprinted by permission of Dan Clark. ©1999 Dan Clark.

Chicken Soup for the Soul

Improving Your Life Every Day

Real people sharing real stories—for nineteen years. Now, Chicken Soup for the Soul has gone beyond the bookstore to become a world leader in life improvement. Through books, movies, DVDs, online resources and other partnerships, we bring hope, courage, inspiration and love to hundreds of millions of people around the world. Chicken Soup for the Soul's writers and readers belong to a one-of-a-kind global community, sharing advice, support, guidance, comfort, and knowledge.

Chicken Soup for the Soul stories have been translated into more than 40 languages and can be found in more than one hundred countries. Every day, millions of people experience a Chicken Soup for the Soul story in a book, magazine, newspaper or online. As we share our life experiences through these stories, we offer hope, comfort and inspiration to one another. The stories travel from person to person, and from country to country, helping to improve lives everywhere.

Chicken Soup for the Soul®

Share with Us

We all have had Chicken Soup for the Soul moments in our lives. If you would like to share your story or poem with millions of people around the world, go to chicken-soup.com and click on "Submit Your Story." You may be able to help another reader, and become a published author at the same time. Some of our past contributors have launched writing and speaking careers from the publication of their stories in our books!

Our submission volume has been increasing steadily — the quality and quantity of your submissions has been fabulous. We only accept story submissions via our website. They are no longer accepted via mail or fax.

To contact us regarding other matters, please send us an e-mail through webmaster@chickensoupforthesoul.com, or fax or write us at:

Chicken Soup for the Soul
P.O. Box 700
Cos Cob, CT 06807-0700
Fax: 203-861-7194

One more note from your friends at Chicken Soup for the Soul: Occasionally, we receive an unsolicited book manuscript from one of our readers, and we would like to respectfully inform you that we do not accept unsolicited manuscripts and we must discard the ones that appear.

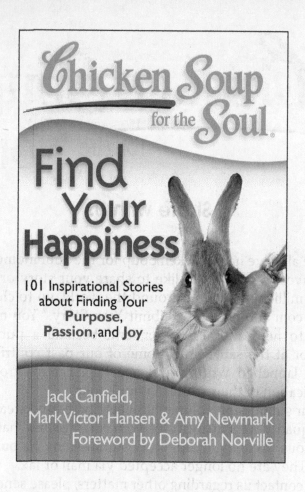

Chicken Soup for the Soul.

Find Your Happiness

101 Inspirational Stories about Finding Your Purpose, Passion, and Joy

Jack Canfield,
Mark Victor Hansen & Amy Newmark
Foreword by Deborah Norville

Others share how they found their passion, purpose, and joy in life in these 101 personal and exciting stories that are sure to encourage readers to find their own happiness. Stories in this collection will inspire readers to pursue their dreams, find their passion and seek joy in their life. This book continues Chicken Soup for the Soul's focus on inspiration and hope, reminding readers that they can find their own happiness.

978-1-935096-77-1

Chicken Soup for the Soul.

Think Positive

101 Inspirational
Stories about
Counting Your Blessings and
Having a Positive Attitude

Jack Canfield,
Mark Victor Hansen & Amy Newmark
Foreword by Deborah Norville

Every cloud has a silver lining. Readers will be inspired by these 101 real-life stories from people just like them, taking a positive attitude to the ups and downs of life, and remembering to be grateful and count their blessings. This book continues Chicken Soup for the Soul's focus on inspiration and hope, and its stories of optimism and faith will encourage readers to stay positive during challenging times and in their everyday lives.

978-1-935096-56-6

Chicken Soup for the Soul: The Power of Positive

101 Inspirational Stories about Changing Your Life through Positive Thinking

Jack Canfield,
Mark Victor Hansen,
and Amy Newmark

Attitude is everything. And this book will uplift and inspire readers with its 101 success stories about the power of positive thinking and how contributors changed their lives, solved problems, or overcame challenges through a positive attitude, counting their blessings, or other epiphanies.

978-1-61159-903-9

Chicken Soup for the Soul®

Count Your Blessings

101 Stories of Gratitude, Fortitude, and Silver Linings

Jack Canfield,
Mark Victor Hansen, Amy Newmark,
Laura Robinson & Elizabeth Bryan

This uplifting book reminds readers of the blessings in their lives, despite financial stress, natural disasters, health scares and illnesses, housing challenges and family worries. This feel-good book is a great gift for New Year's or Easter, for someone going through a difficult time, or for Christmas. These stories of optimism, faith, and strength remind us of the simple pleasures of family, home, health, and inexpensive good times.

978-1-935096-42-9